D070124-4

Treaties and Treachery:

The Northwest Indians'
Resistance to Conquest

Treaties and Treachery:

The Northwest Indians'
Resistance to Conquest

Kurt R. Nelson

To my favorite Neighbor To The North of us

Kurt

Caxton Press
Caldwell, Idaho
2011

ISBN 978-0-87004-499-1

Library of Congress Cataloging-in-Publication Data

Nelson, Kurt R.
  Treaties and treachery : the Northwest Indians' resistance to conquest / Kurt R. Nelson.
     p. cm.
  Includes bibliographical references and index.
  ISBN 978-0-87004-499-1 (trade paper)
  1. Indians of North America--Northwest, Pacific--Treaties. 2. Indians of North America--Northwest, Pacific--Government relations. 3. Indians of North America--Northwest, Pacific--History--19th century. 4. Northwest, Pacific--History--19th century. 5. Government, Resistance to--Northwest, Pacific--History--19th century. I. Title.
  E78.N77N46 2011
  323.1197--dc22
                                    2010049909

Cover
By Jim D. Nelson
www.jdnelsonportraits.com

Lithographed and bound in the United States of America

CAXTON PRESS
Caldwell, Idaho
180394

Dedication

To three men who helped me to become who I am: Harvey Rones, Stuart Gryziec, and Gary Nelson.

Table of contents

Illustrations

Treaties and Treachery

Maps

Kurt R. Nelson

Introduction

The great political conflicts of the Pacific Northwest in the 21st century have their roots in the 18th century. The constants have been land and water, and who will control them: Is there enough water for irrigation and migrating fish? Should we remove dams to allow spawning salmon to swim freely? What is the aesthetic value of the Columbia River Gorge National Scenic Area and other natural locales? Will we rob the gorge of its beauty by erecting electricity generating windmills throughout the wind-blown chasm? What of casinos? Can we allow Confederated Tribes of the Warm Springs to build a casino, malls, hotels, and parking lots in the heart of that majestic gorge? Should Indian economic self-sufficiency trump the rights to unspoiled lands?

These are just a few of the disputes daily argued in the Pacific Northwest. What many people today fail to understand is elements of these and other issues stem from the time when Oregon and Washington became territories. Migration brought white pioneers into the far northwest corner of the United States, but it did so at the expense of those who had been living here all along: the Indians.

The pressures of immigration and race continue. Newcomers still head for opportunity found in the Northwest, while race is an element of the migration, as Hispanic numbers swell with many from Spanish-speaking America. Our history provides insight into how we deal with each other as we struggle to find civility despite disputes, be it the pioneers of the 1850s, or the crisis of migration as Hispanics come into our country today.

And that is what this book is about. It tells how one people competed with another, and who ultimately gained control. It tells the story, often in the actors' own words, of how the Americans broke the Indian power in the Pacific Northwest and seized control of the region's resources.

Certainly, the conflict between the white and red peoples was old and not a fresh creation in the Northwest; the quarrel predates English settlement. However, this racial belligerency in the Pacific Northwest has distinctions not present with Indian wars in other parts of North America.

First, because of the frequency of contact, and the egos of white participants, Indian words were recorded surprisingly often. Wishing to keep an appearance of legality and justice, whites often insisted on transcriptions of their meetings with the natives. From those recorded conversations, we know what the Indians actually said. The Indians spoke with elegant expressions of their beliefs, desires, and their hope for justice.

Second, the mass movement of white Americans had a clear starting period and thus, while the Indians had had previous encounters with British and American fur traders and trappers, the period of the Oregon Trail came on abruptly. This rapid expansion of white population to critical mass ensured war. This white competition for Indian land and resources happened in such a compact period of time that it had to result in a race war between the red and white people.

Third, unlike many American struggles between Indians and whites, the combatants' numbers were close, and the weaponry more evenly matched than in any other Indian war. White victory was inevitable. While victory was an historical certainty, the wars had to be fought to the death, lest the whites suffer that fate if only on a local scale of individual settlements. Furthermore, the effect on non-combatants was total war; each side committed atrocities in an effort to achieve victory or to stave off defeat.

These factors supply the interest the wars continue to generate. However, our concern in this period is predicated on other issues as well. The Oregon Territory (which was what the entire Pacific Northwest was known as until 1853) suffered from the national politics, albeit on a local and smaller scale, that characterizes the 1850s. The death of the Whig Party, the battle for the American soul by the Know-Nothing Party, the internal struggle within the Democratic Party over racial issues, and the emergence of the Republican Party all found their stories played out in the Pacific Northwest, as well as on the national stage. Racial hatred would be codified in the Northwest through the adoption of the Oregon State Constitution (1857) which barred blacks from the state, as well by whites' actions to exterminate the Indian people. It was a time for the people of the Northwest to decide if civil protections, such as habeas corpus were worth fighting to protect. These times shaped Northwest history, and the times were shaped by immigration pressures, political machinations, and racial animosity.

So many of the troubles facing us now stem from how our ancestors dealt with their issues then. The main way our red and white ancestors dealt with each other is best viewed through the prism of the treaties themselves. If the series of Indian treaties enacted between 1853 and 1859 had not been written as they were, the issues we face today and the solutions we seek would be different. We have been driven by those treaties.

The seven years of 1853-1859 are more important to the Pacific Northwest than any other seven years of its recorded history. The 1850s started carving the Oregon Territory into the states that were ultimately created. It was the period when most Indian tribes signed treaties defining who they would become, and how they live with their white neighbors. It was when Oregon became a state.

If not the most important, then certainly these seven years were the most exciting. While other eras would have other wars, even other Indian wars, no other period would have the entire region engulfed in conflict. One in ten white citizens of the Northwest served under arms as either a member of the regular army forces or with one of the territorial units. Another two in ten whites directly felt the anguish of war, either by being attacked or by having a loved one killed or injured. Certainly, everyone read of massacres, of atrocities, and of towns being raided, placed under siege, or burned to the ground.

For almost every major tribe of the Northwest, these seven years marked the end of their way of life. Even for those tribes that were not conquered or displaced, the blows of the era determined where they could go and how they would live.

These years were patriotic years. The people on both sides believed that they were fighting with right on their side and that they were God's chosen people. With hindsight, we can see with clarity the injustices done. While one side suffered greater injustice, neither side can claim purity of action. Innocents were killed by both sides. Atrocities were not limited to one race nor was hatred solely sown by one side.

We must study our history if we are to understand how we arrived at the problems we face today. We must study our history if we are to understand how our history directs our future, for these issues are still very much alive. Perhaps the issues within the treaties are most alive to the citizens of the Pacific Northwest today, but the larger truth, how we live with each other is a question we must resolve, no matter what part of the country we reside in, or of what era we are a part. Every section of our country has treaties and treachery. This is the story of one corner of our country, and how its history shapes its course today.

Chapter One

Fever

It raced across the valleys of the Midwest with incredible swiftness. Illinois, Ohio, Tennessee, any town, settlement, or farm near the rivers that fed the Ohio River seemed susceptible. Other locales were afflicted, too, but it was most potent in the old Northwest states.

Townspeople suffered, but it was on the farms where the majority of people lived that you could see the fever's effects most tellingly. The farmsteads stood empty, doors ajar, windows without burning candles, lifeless skulls amidst the body of farm buildings: no one living there anymore after the fever came through.

Those the fever did not carry off would comment among themselves, grieving the loss of this family or that, wondering what would happen to the land now that no one lived to tend it. The sense of loss was deep as many knew that they would never see their cherished kin again. Fever caused family rifts. One brother was gone, another remained. Grandparents mourned the loss of grandchildren.

One farmer's wife, Kit Belknap, lamented in her diary, "This past winter there has been a strange fever raging here….it seems to be contagious and it is raging terribly, nothing seems to stop it…"[1] Each spring the fever grew, each year more people were gone.

The contagion had a name: Oregon Fever. And, it had a cure. Kit Belknap knew the prescription: "…nothing seems to stop it but to tear up and take a six months trip across the plains with ox teams to the Pacific Ocean."[2] The fever had started in the early 1840s, but with the Oregon Land Donation Act of 1850, the fever swelled. Each man was entitled to 320 acres and, if married, he and his wife were given 320 more acres—free, and the richest, most fertile land anywhere. At least that was what the guidebooks promised.

In four short years, starting with 1850, an estimated 56,000 people crossed the Oregon Trail. They spread throughout the Pacific Northwest, Utah, and into California. The estimated white population for the entire Oregon Territory in 1850 was fewer than 13,000 people. When Washington Territory was carved out of the Oregon Territory in 1853, the population was estimated to be about 53,000, and when Oregon became a state in 1859, its population was nearly 60,000. The cure for many fever-stricken people was to head west, and in particular, the Pacific Northwest.

But, that "six months trip across the plains" was an undertaking like none they had ever known or imagined. Still, the end goal was worth the risk. As John Biles wrote, affirming his optimism, "I am unacquainted with the land route yet I believe a man is well paid for his trouble if he arrives…in good health. No doubt the journey is a great one to surmount. Oregon is still progressing with rapture."[3]

The pioneers sold that which they could not carry (if they could find a buyer), packed up their wagons, took what livestock they could drive and started. Most went in trains, a caravan of like-minded immigrants that ranged from a few wagons to dozens, but some started the trip alone. Sometimes trains coalesced as they moved west. "Some of our friends have started for Oregon…They will meet others at the crossing of the Missouri River and make laws and join together in a large company," wrote pioneer Belknap.[4]

While there were drawbacks to large trains, such as the depletion of grazing land, there was the advantage of mutual support. The obstacles each sojourner faced were huge, and having friends and family near was useful and comforting. This meant an ill person was not a stranger, but someone dear who could die.

And die they did. Of the many diseases that struck the pioneers, cholera was one of the most common. As the trains moved west, popular campsites were overburdened with human waste. The watering holes became contaminated, festering sources for the spread of a disease caused by people-polluted water. And as the pioneers became sick, their waste just added source for the contagion's spread. In the case of cholera, patients could die in three hours after the first symptom, which was often a withering bout of uncontrolled diarrhea.

One diarist of 1852, Mary Ann Boatman, recalled,

Fever

We moved on for a time, all keeping in moderate health for a short time, oft passing new made graves by the dozen in one camp ground. On one occasion we passed a camped train that had buried six during the night and [had] six more lying dead in camp. We never knew how many died in that camp. On the south side of the Plat[te] River there was much more cholera than on the north side [therefore] some trains crossed over from the south side to the north. [One train] said they had buried a family of seven in one grave in one day and night. Another lady said that forty of their people in their train died in two nights and one day on the Plat[te] River just before....crossing to the north side.

Thousands of testimonies like these could be given and some [even] more thrilling.[5]

Many a traveler recorded how sickness stalked the trains. Margaret Frink despaired in her journal, "Saturday, June 29. Mr. Rose was now taken sick with mountain fever. Mr. Frink was still confined to his bed. The outlook for the future became, for a while, quite dark and discouraging."[6] Disease was the big killer on the Oregon Trail.

But, disease murdered those who stayed behind, too. Because medical science was crude, disease was more a daily occurrence than a new specter haunting the hopeful souls crossing the plains and mountains. Disease and accidents were common, daily life events, sad to be sure, but not unexpected, and certainly not an unknown feature of life. Since illness could claim you if you stayed where you were, why worry overly much about leaving if you had a world to gain.

The pioneers left behind a settled life, and were braving the journey to seek the promised Eden of Oregon. Their previous homes were largely "civilized," but the trip was through a wilderness of beasts and savages.

They now had unestablished lives. What they now faced was something completely different. It was exciting, it was new, and the travelers on the trail felt it. They recorded their response to each day's adventure right from the start.

Just as the sun was gladdening the clear east....throwing its golden light over the fair west, the cattle we[re] driven in from the grass growing plains to be yoked and hitched to the wagons for our first day's journey through a wild and unknown country inhabited only by savage Indians and wild beasts.[7]

The unknown is that which most frightens. Disease, accidents, even death were known. But, fierce beasts and "savage Indians" were fearful novelties. The animals were soon known, but each Indian encounter was a new terror to the sojourners.

For many pioneers the knowledge of Indians was all second or third hand. Newspapers— then as now—often resort to scare headlines to sell papers. "The most vivid press portrayal of Indians…was the bad Indian, a creature of violence and certain cruelty."[8] The Mid-West papers had reported the second Seminole Indian War (1835-1842), while reports of the Whitman massacre and the Cayuse Indian War of the Oregon Territory (1847-1850) seemed to be fillers in the papers, drowned by the news of the Mexican War, and what few tales of the Rogue Indian Wars (1850 and on-going) making it east were overwhelmed by word of California gold (!). Certainly their parents' and grandparents' tales of the Blackhawk Indian War (1832) in Illinois, Michigan, and Wisconsin were as old as the War of 1812—there were no more Sauk, Fox, or Kickapoo Indians threatening the settlements. The old tales fed their fear, and increased that they did not know what to expect from the future Indians that were said to swarm their path to the Pacific.

"Massacre" tales spread and were retold from one emigrant train to the next train. Mary Ann Boatman traveling the Oregon Trail wrote of an incident that she feared would be repeated, even though it had taken place in the Arizona Territory:

> We wer[e] now in a state of confusion as we all knew the Oatman family had been way laid…[and] part of the family taken in captivity. 9 in all. Two girls [were] taken in captivity 7 left for dead. Lorenzo, a boy of 14 revived after the heartless savages had gone. Knowing of this, we wer[e] at a loss to know what to do. It was finely decided to move on, not wishing to shear [share] the same fate, not know[ing] but the savage and murderous fiends…might return to [the] scen[e] of slaughter and treat us in the same manner.[9]

Fever

The white settlers viewed Indians as a monoculture. Traveling across the land they saw undifferentiated savages, not distinct peoples. An Indian encounter on the Platte River was the same as an Indian encounter on the Columbia River, or the Gila River where the Oatman family had been killed. And since they were the same, there was little attempt to distinguish between a friendly or a curious Indian and a truly hostile Indian. The journals frequently testify to the pioneers' fears of Indian attack.

> Not many days had passed before we began to hear frightful tales of Indian depredations....which had a tendency, at first, to shake the resolution of some members of the party.—Margaret Frink[10]

> I was very much frightened while at this camp, and lie awake all night—I expected every minite we would all be killed, however we all found our scalps on in the morning.—Amelia Stewart Knight[11]

Heading west, the trains would do what they could to minimize risk. The few forts (such as Laramie or Hall) were viewed as safe oases in the hostile land, and the rare sightings of army troops were appreciated. However, the travelers were condemned to self-reliance. The best protection was a large wagon train. Mary Ann Boatman reassured herself of the safety in numbers by recording, "From now on we got to face the savage....word had been sent back from the emigrant[s]... ahead of us that they were having trouble with the Indians and for all to move in large trains as it was unsafe for small parties to start out."[12]

Strength in numbers helped, but so did experience as Mrs. Boatman also noted, "Mr. Warner cheered us up with his narrative and adventures of crossing the plains in '46, assuring us that we would not have any trouble with the Indians, as he knew the Chinook[13] language and could talk to them and that would be in our favor."[14]

Besides experience, the chief form of self-reliance was the firearm.

> "Our men are all well-armed. William carries a brace of pistols and a bowie knife. Aint that blood-curdling?"—Lucy Cooke[15]

"The men…stand or sit with gun in hand, ready for any attack whatever that might be made by Indians…" —Mary Ann Boatman[16]

While the sojourners were ready to defend themselves, most Indian encounters were friendly. Often the Indians were merely curious, sought trade, or made accidental contact. Still, the unknown savages made quite a sight! Lucy Ann Henderson Deady wrote in her diary of the impression made by some Indians wanting to trade, "They looked so naked and wild. The men got their guns, but all the Indians wanted was to see us and to see if we would give them anything."[17]

With the whites fearing the worst and ready to defend themselves, things could easily escalate into bloodshed. As reports true and false spread from wagon train to wagon train, fear could be the spark that ignited anxiety into conflict.

For a short time all was excitement and alarm, as we had heard before leaving the Missouri river that Indians had made an attack on…emigrants that had gone before us. So all the men that were in camp rushed for their fire arms, while the women and children crouched behind tents and under wagons, saying, as they thought their last prayer, their hearts ready to burst with fear, and eyes wet with tears. [But, as soon as] the riders were in front of the camp our fears [were] all put to flight, as it was only a dozen or more friendly Indians who chanced to be passing by and stopped to beg something to eat. –Mary Ann Boatman.[18]

We were met by 15 Indians today well armed which gave us somewhat of a start. They paraded themselves across the road ahead of us and would not give the road. They wanted we should give them something but we did not. There were about 17 wagons along at the time. We turned out and went on and left them. –Martha Reed[19]

Most Indian encounters were peaceful, but hostilities did break out. First were the reports of violent encounters, which heightened sojourner fears. Lucena Parsons worried over one such account passed on to her wagon train:

> We have but 54 men & we think this a small number as we have heard that the Indians are getting very bad on this road, on acct of small companies going on late last fall. They took one company of 13 men, killed them all & carried the women off on the Yellow Stone river & tried to sell them at Fort Hall.[20]

Moreover, the whites saw evidence of attacks along the trail. Mary Ann Boatman chronicled a mass murder near the Bear River, of Idaho:

> O reader, on reaching its banks what pang of sudden fright met our gaze. There were three new graves, and on a sheet of writing paper wer[e] written these words, "We a company of emigrants of five wagons called a halt here yesterday noon finding a man about 40 years old, woman about 35, with front teeth filled with gold, a swcingle [sic] around her neck, been dragged down to waters edg[e]. A boy about 10 years old all have their throats cut from ear to ear. Advising all that coming to be on the look out for Indians."[21]

Other pioneers related similar grisly scenes. In her diary, Sarah Davis vented her fear as she recorded one pioneer found killed by the Indians. "We then went on a little ways and come to the river[.] their we found a man that had bin killed buy the Indians and his heart taken out….it appears he was alone and the Indians came upon him and he shot one an then they shot him[.] he was found with four arrows shot in his breast…"[22]

Of course, we will never know who started the fight. Was it the white out of fear, or was it an unprovoked Indian attack? Often the triggering event was theft, at least from the white point of view. Here are two events from the journal of Lucena Parsons, showing how confrontations were easily triggered. "This afternoon saw an Indian who had been killed by emigrants before because he had killed a mewl." And on a different day, "About noon a company of 7 Indians rode up & in plain sight drove off 4 head of our cattle. Our men pursued them & the Indians shot back at them."[23]

Sometimes the trouble started with the Indians seeing the cattle as an easy source of wealth and food. Of course, the whites perceived the Indians' action as theft of precious and much needed livestock to start the pioneers' new life. These clashes did lead to real incidents that terrified the wagon trains as they traveled. Three such events marked 1854 on the Oregon Trail.

The first bloodshed occurred in August, near Fort Laramie (Wyoming). A Sioux named High Forehead fired an arrow into an ox as the animal trailed behind a wagon train. The pioneer protested to the nearby Army post. Lieutenant John Grattan armed with two cannon and thirty soldiers proceeded to the Sioux demanding the arrest of High Forehead. When the criminal did not surrender, Grattan punished the whole village by opening fire with his cannon, killing and wounding many Indians, including Brave Bear, a chief of the Brule Sioux. Defending themselves, the Indian warriors swarmed over the command, killing all but one soldier.

The "Grattan Massacre" had two immediate results. First, the army sought revenge. General William S. Harney earned his Sioux Indian appellation of "The Butcher" when he led 600 soldiers against the Indians, killing eighty-five Brule warriors and taking the women and children captive.

The other shock of the Grattan annihilation was the quickly adopted fear that if even the army could be attacked so easily, then what of the hapless men, women, and children of the passing wagon trains?

A wagon train along the Snake River, about ninety-five miles east of the Oregon-Idaho border, was approached by Shoshoni Indians, on August 29. The Indians feigned friendliness as a ruse and opened fire, killing three of the whites. In a fierce, but short fight, the Indians were driven off, but not before having made a successful horse-stealing raid, a long tradition of the Shoshoni.

The third event underscored the American fear of defenseless women and children being killed, and kindled the embers of troubles that flamed across the Pacific Northwest for the next five years.

On August 30, 1854, about twenty-five miles up the Boise River from its confluence with the Snake River, the Ward wagon train stopped for the noon meal. Sixty Indians approached the twenty members of the very small train. An Indian mounted one of the Ward horses, rode it, and brought it back. This heightened pioneer fears that the Indians were going to plunder the wagon train, and when one of the pioneer men thought he saw an Indian readying his musket, the white shot first. This triggered indiscriminate fire from both sides.

Wayne Cornell photo

Ward Massacre site near Caldwell, Idaho.

As the gunfight raged, another party of whites (looking for their straying cattle) happened upon the scene. They opened fire upon the Indians, trying to shoot their way into rescuing the other whites. Instead, they fled for their lives, having one of their party killed by the Indians' return fire. Reaching the succor of the nearby Hudson's Bay post, Fort Boise, they eventually brought a relief force, but too late to save the Wards. What the party found shocked the entire Pacific Northwest.

All of the men had been killed, scalped and mutilated. Prior to killing the women, they had been raped, with one woman having had a hot metal rod inserted into her genitals. Of the children, two would survive, one wounded, who crawled twenty-five miles to Fort Boise. Another boy survived hidden in some bushes. He reported that the women and children had been burned alive.

This event became the backdrop for Northwest white-Indian relations. It also prompted a need to punish the guilty. The savagery displayed in the attack was prime newspapers fodder. On September 9 *The Oregonian* ran with the headline of, "Indian War—American Citizens Murdered." The newspaper reported the event as, "…a party of snake river Indians, numbering about 60 warriors, attacked an immigrant train…"

The territorial authorities of Oregon ordered volunteers to the scene. Captain Nathan Olney, a pioneer who had crossed the prairies to Oregon in 1846, led a volunteer company in search for the guilty, and eventually captured four. They died attempting to "escape." The U.S. Army from Fort [The] Dalles (the nearest army post), sortied under Major Granville Haller, who patrolled the Oregon Trail to prevent further attacks.

The Oregonian kept the revenge fever high in its September 23 editorial by calling for authorities, "… to strike a blow which shall either exterminate the race of Indians, or prevent further wholesale butcheries by these worthless races resembling the human form."

But what of the Indians? Who had committed the attack on the wagon trains? We cannot be certain which Indians attacked, and certainly in 1854, no effort was made to distinguish the attackers. The August 29 attack seemed to have been done by Shoshoni. The Ward massacre has been attributed to several tribes. Some have said it was the work of the Boise Shoshoni,[24] also known at the Winass or Winnestah Snake Indians.[25] Certainly some of those who would be killed in punishment for the massacre were Shoshoni. Other sources have blamed the Bannock.[26] However, the Yakima Indians got roped up in the blame, too.[27]

In the summer of 1855, the army again moved out from Fort Dalles in another expedition to hunt out the Wards' murderers. Major Haller captured four Indians, asserted his evidence was irrefutable, and hanged them on gallows built over the Wards' gravesite. The Indians he executed were Yakima and the brother of one of those who swung swore to avenge his death. The Yakima Mo-sheel would revenge Haller's hanging of his brother and uncle.

And, still the wagon trains brought whites to the Northwest. And they wanted more land, more wealth in the form of gold, and they wanted the government "…to strike a blow which shall either exterminate the race of Indians, or prevent further wholesale butcheries by these worthless races resembling the human form." A different fever raged in the west, a fever of racial hatred.

Fever

Chapter 1 notes

[1] Butruille, *Women's Voices from the Oregon Trail*, page 51.
[2] Ibid.
[3] Schlissel, Gibbens, and Hampsten, Far from Home, page 23.
[4] Butruille, page 51.
[5] Rau, in *Surviving the Oregon Trail*, 1852, page 75.
[6] Holmes, *Covered Wagon Women*, page 109.
[7] Rau, page 33.
[8] Coward, *The Newspaper Indian*, page 56.
[9] Rau, page 130.
[10] Holmes, page 76.
[11] Brutruille, page 93.
[12] Rau, page 32.
[13] The Chinook language was a dialect found mostly along the Columbia River, and was the basis of a trade language that came to be called Chinook. It was composed of words taken from the Chinook tribal language, other Indian languages, French, and English, and was limited to about 500 words. It was not used by every tribe, but in a belief that all Indians were the same, it was attempted to be used whenever encountering Indians other than in the Pacific Northwest. Further, it was most useful in conveying simple ideas, such as barter and trade. It would be impossible to use Chinook to communicate complex ideas or terms, a critical factor in latter interactions between whites and Indians.
[14] Rau, page 64.
[15] Brutruille, page 57.
[16] Rau, page 34.
[17] Brutruille, page 22.
[18] Rau, page 35.
[19] Rau, page 93.
[20] Holmes, page 277.
[21] Rau, page 129.
[22] Holmes, page 199.
[23] Holmes, page 280.
[24] Ruby and Brown, in *Indians of the Pacific Northwest*, page 186.
[25] Madsen, B., in *The Bannock*, page 77, and Carey, in *General History of Oregon*, page 566.
[26] Jackson, in *A Little War of Destiny*. Page 10.
[27] Dary, in *The Oregon Trail*, page 261.

Chapter Two

The First People

T he Great Spirit chose the People as his blessed race. They had been given the land to be born on, to live upon, and to return to when they died. The Indians were part of the grand cycle of life that was the land they lived with and on. Indian culture was based on their love of the land and their great ties to it. Yakima[1] chief Owhi spoke for many Indians when he said,

> God gave us day and night, the night to rest in and the day to see, and that as long as the earth shall last he gave us the morning with our breath. And so he takes care of us on this earth. And here we have met under his care. Is the earth before the day or the day before earth? God was before the earth. The heavens were clear and good and all things in the heaven were good. God looked one way then the other and named our lands for us to take care of. God made the other, we did not make the other. We did not make it, he made it to last forever. It is the earth that is our parent, as it is God is our elder brother.[2]

Although geographically distinct, Indian people viewed their paradise and its gifts with a similar passion and reverence. The wide differences between the tribes rested on their geographically dictated way of life, while some similarities rested on linguistic ties.

Indians are generally classified ethnologically by linguistic groups, with tribes that are within the same linguistic group often having closer cultural connection than with a nearer tribe from a different language group. Within the Oregon Country, fifteen language groups have been identified: Shastan, Takilman, Athapascan, Chinookan, Chimakuan,

Waiilatpu, site of the Whitman Mission, was in the heart of Cayuse country.

Wakashan, Yakonan, Weitspekan, Kalapuyan, Waiilatpuan, Shoshon-ian, Salishan, Lutuamin, Kitunahan, and Shahaptian.

Shastan include tribes such as the Shastas of Northern California, and the related Rogue River Indians (a catchall for a variety of tribes living in the greater Rogue River Basin) which fell under the Takilman and Athapascan language groups. These close language groups help to explain the ready alliances of the Indians who fought throughout the southwestern Oregon area.

The Cayuse are a tribe of the Waiilatpuan language group, from which the Whitman Mission, Waiilatpu, arrived at its Indian name. Three language groups are very closely identified with one tribe: Chinookan with the Chinook Indians, Kalapuyan with the Kalapooia Indians, and Shoshoian with the Shoshoni. However, each of the three had other well known tribes using a language within the language group. For example, other tribes of the Shoshoian language group included the Bannock and Paiute Indian tribes.

Shahaptian was the language group of such tribes as the Yakima, Umatilla, Nez Perce, and Walla Walla, all allies and trade partners. Many of these peoples had very limited contact with the whites prior to the influx of pioneers over the Oregon Trail.

The language group with the greatest geographic distribution was Salishan. Its range extends from the Kalispels and Flatheads in the far

14

northeast part of the region, to the Lummi and Nisqually Indians of Puget Sound. The spread of similar or related languages often added to the confusion of whites, giving them a perception of greater harmony and cooperation between tribes than might actually exist. Of course, tribes within one language group, but adjacent to another often developed cultural ties and the ability to communicate with each other. Thus, the Nisqually (of the Salish language stock) could communicate with the Yakima (of the Shahaptian group) who could interact with the Cayuse (of the Waiilatpuan group). Thus proximity allowed some cross communication between tribes of different language stock, from inter-tribal marriage, councils, and even joint military action.

This closeness of tribes, either linguistically or geographically, created common traits, religion, and folklore. Some of these beliefs intermingled with one another, crossing tribal boundaries, and came to be universal religious tenants.

One universal belief was reliance on spirits. For example, the Nisqually Indians believed in *tamanous*, or a savior spirit sent by the Great Spirit. The Duwamish Indians spoke of a *tahmanawis*, or a spirit that would cherish the land, even after the Duwamish themselves had been destroyed.

A shaman or spiritual healer of the Columbia River Indians (probably the Wasco Indians) gave a prophesy he received from his spirit:

> I am a very old man, so old that I have seen generations come and go. I have always been a great medicine man and prophet. When my tam-man-a-was (spirit) appears to me, I lie as asleep and as in a dream I see the future. There is a vision before me now of things to come. Far to the East, I see a pale-faced people pushing the red-man back to the setting sun. The red-men fight this onward march to no avail. They are driven away from the lands of their forefathers; their dead lie strewn along the trails; their bones dry on the sandhills, while the living move farther into the West, pursued by their relentless foe. You are a happy people now, but you will not always remain so. For many snows the same fate will come to you.[3]

Many tribes shared and feared this prophecy and they recalled and retold it as the whites came across the Oregon Trail. "Some of the holy men and women had foretold a time when the *suyapo* [white men] would force every Indian to a specific area."[4]

As the settlers moved on to the prime lands, such as the Willamette Valley, the Indians watched as their brethren were forced off their home land, killed, or simply disappeared as they succumbed to disease.

Most Indians had stood neutral when the Cayuse fought the whites (1847-1850). They understood the Cayuse had triggered the white ire by the murder of Marcus and Narcissa Whitman. It was common within the Indian tradition to seek revenge.

The great Walla Walla chief, Peo-peo-mox-mox may have stood aside during the Cayuse Indian War, but he came to know of the white ways as his son had traveled with John C. Fremont to fight in California in the Mexican War, only to be murdered by a white man. He understood that no punishment was ever levied against the white, because he had killed an Indian.

Contact was plentiful between the various tribes. As early as 1850, whites had used Klickitat Indians as mercenaries when warring against the Rogue Indians. The Klickitats reported that the whites had assured the Rogues peace, offered treaties, and promised goods in return for Rogue Indian land. However, even as the Rogues signed the treaty documents the agreements were violated. Many Indians signed the Willamette Valley treaties, only to have white promises never fulfilled.

Further fueling tribal fears, in 1851 Oregon Superintendent of Indian affairs Anson Dart met with the eastern tribes at The Dalles to reassure them that the whites were not their enemy. Nonetheless, the June meetings did not reassure the Indians. Dart had negotiated many treaties with displaced Willamette Valley Indians. But, the treaties were never ratified by the U.S. Senate. Many tribes said the white plan was to drive them off their homelands. "According to Father Durieu a Ricard, stories circulated that the Palouses and others would 'be banished to the Artic, i.e. to a land where the sun never shines, where eternal night reigns.'"[5]

It was into this sense of distrust that two U.S. Army parties entered Central and Eastern Washington in the summer of 1853. The first party was scouting for a northern railroad route that was being surveyed and mapped by a young army officer, Captain George McClellan. This

16

ambitious and callow officer saw a chance in aligning himself with Governor Isaac Stevens. Although destined to be the greatest failed general in the Union Army, right now he sought to further his career with this effort in the Washington Territory.

McClellan's first priority was to seek the best pass over the Cascade Mountains of Washington, and as he did so he entered the land of the Yakima. When the McClellan party advanced into the Indian homeland, they were met by Kamiakin, the great Yakima chief.

Drawing by Gustavus Sohon 1855
Yakima Chief Kamiakin

One of the supreme Indian leaders in history, Kamiakin was a chief not merely by birth, but by his ability. One historian described his influence thusly,

> Although he was careful not to act as a spokesman for any but his own followers, his wealth, ability, and powerful connections gave him an influence and authority that Te-i-as and Owhi [two other Yakima chiefs] could not match. He was a natural leader and a convincing orator, and in times of difficulty headsmen of other bands came to seek his counsel. As a result, many interior Indians regarded him as the strongest and most important leader among the Yakimas...[6]

Strength of character radiated from his personal demeanor and physical appearance. A visitor to the Yakima Valley in 1851, Theodore Winthrop, described Kamiakin:

> He was a tall, large man, very dark, with a massive square face, and grave reflective look...his manner strikingly distinguished, quiet, and dignified....He had the advantage of an imposing presence and bearing, and above all a good face....[7]

As McClellan entered the valley, he was questioned by Kamiakin about the true purpose of the Army's presence. McClellan explained that he was searching for a pass to carry a railroad. This seemed a lie to Kamiakin. He knew that the whites already used a rough road over the passes, but what he did not know, what he could not know from his experience, was the road being sought had to have as gentle a grade as possible in order for an engine and rail cars to cross the mountains. Because the Indians had no experience of railroads, it seemed as if the whites were lying. Expressing further distrust, when McClellan offered gifts, "Kamiakin replied that the English had told him that the Americans would one day come with a few presents and then say that they had bought the land."[8] Kamiakin here began his practice of refusing Americans' presents, so as never to be told he had sold his lands.

While the Army moved north (to check another pass), Kamiakin met with other Indian leaders. He spoke his fears that what the whites sought was not a road, but to drive the Indians from their homes. He recalled the prophesies of two Yakima shamans, Temteiquin and Wattilki, that white men's ("Kooyawowculth") arrival would be an event presaging Yakima ruin, as the whites would steal their lands.[9] Their leader's decision was to keep a wary eye on the McClellan party, and two bands of Indians tracked the Army survey as it moved. Accompanying the McClellan survey in a peaceful group trying to find the truth were Owhi[10] of the Yakima and Quil-ten-e-nock of the Sinkiuse tribe. What they reported back to Kamiakin seemed to confirm the deceitful intent of the McClellan party's action. The truth, as seen by the Indians, was that McClellan was en route to meet with a new Indian superintendent, Isaac Stevens, whose intent was to take the Indians' land from them by treaty, and if not successful that way, to force them off by arms. Kamiakin ordered runners to go to allied tribes, informing other chiefs of the danger.

The second Army unit left Fort Dalles in July 1853, tasked with supplying the Stevens party, while surveying a new military road. The proposed road connected Fort Dalles (Oregon Territory, or O.T.) to Fort Benton (Missouri Territory), situated on the upper Missouri River. It was from Fort Benton that Stevens traveled to the Northwest. As the party moved under the command of Lieutenant Rufus Saxton, the Indians, warned by Kamiakin, became convinced that his mission was to steal their lands. Saxton met with leaders from tribes such as the Cayuse, Walla Walla, Nez Perce, and Palouse, and reassured them that his mission was peaceful. Still, as Saxton moved through

Edward Curtis Collection, Library of Congress
Skokomish Mat Shelter

the Palouse country he found the grasslands burned. The lieutenant quickly found the reason for the scorched earth was that the Palouse "had heard that 'a large body of American soldiers were coming to cut them off, and take possession of their homes.'"[11] Clearly, Kamiakin's warning was a clarion being heeded by chiefs throughout the region.

Southern Oregon

But it was not just in central Washington that the whites were encroaching on Indian land. When gold was discovered in California, the Rogue River Valley became a conduit for men and supplies to the south, and when gold was also discovered in southwestern Oregon, whites poured into that area.

Conflicts between whites and Indians had been almost continuous from 1850, when then Territorial Governor Joseph Lane had signed the first treaty with the Indians of the Rogue River Valley (an unratified treaty, never put into effect). By 1853, another war was raging throughout the Rogue Valley, a war that had its foundation in greed and revenge.

The whites were avid for the land, for the mineral wealth within the land, and when economic times were bad (as during 1853, a period of high unemployment), for the money paid to volunteer troops who fought the Indian menace. It became politically expedient for local politicians to see Indian troubles calling for volunteer troops paid to combat the savages. The politically astute move meant constituents drew pay, always welcome but even more so in economic bad times.

Seeing some Indians with gold dust in the spring of 1853, the miners convinced themselves the only way the Indians could have gotten the gold was through the murder of white miners who had disappeared during the winter. Thus, volunteer companies grabbed the suspects and hanged them. Other volunteers tied Indians' hands behind their backs, told them to run, and then used them as moving targets, gunning them down.

Through acts of revenge and criminality (that is, theft), the Indians struck back. On August 3, whites found a miner named Edwards dead and mutilated with ax blows over his entire body. The next day, Indians stole from a cabin and ran off cattle, wounding two protesting settlers. Another miner, Rhodes Noland, was found dead at his cabin.

Fear gripped the valley. One pioneer wrote, "The Indians are becoming very hostile in this valley. They have killed one man [Edwards] and two oxen without cause or provocation at the present time they are hostile yet pretending friendship."[12] The final act that triggered open warfare occurred on the outskirts of Jacksonville. An owner of a packing company, Thomas Wills (of Wills and Kyle) was ambushed at dusk. So close to the town was the attack that the towns-people could hear the screams of the mortally wounded Wills.

With terror gripping the town, the Jacksonville populace sought "protection" through revenge. Two Indians were hanged, but the truly innocent were also killed: "…some settlers who had fled their homes…arrived in town with an Indian boy about seven years old. Upon seeing him, the miners ran through the streets shouting, 'hang him hang him…Exterminate! the whole Indian race. When he is old he will kill you.'" One packer, William Dowell, tried to reason with the mob of an estimated 800 murder-bent men, and was succeeding in saving the child's life when a miner named Martin Angel excited the crowd with, "exterminate the whole race. Knits [sic] breed lice." The boy was strung up next to the Indians already swaying from their nooses.[13]

More volunteers swarmed through the valley. On the same day as the hangings, an Indian village was attacked by a surprise raid. Indiscriminate musket fire killed six, regardless whether the victims were men, women, or children.

The attack prompted more Indian reprisals and that, in turn, provoked more white attacks. One company's battle flag consisted of a single word, in bright yellow: "Extermination!" Throughout the month of August 1853, war raged all along the valley of the Rogue River. The Indians suffered the most and so sought peace. First treaty negotiations opened near Table Rock on September 4. On September 8, an accord was reached: The Indians gave up their lands and their guns to settle on a reservation north of Table Rock (but the Indians had to pay the whites part of the money they were to get for ceding their lands—in reparations for their "attacks"). Another agreement was signed with other bands on September 10. The principle treaty (September 8) was never ratified.

The war in southern Oregon was seen by whites as independent of region-wide Indian-white relations. It was seen as a continuation of the Rogue River Indian troubles, rather than a sign of widespread Indian discontent with the white onslaught. Mary Ann Boatman would write from Southern Washington in September 1853, "The Indians Are very good and kind here. And they would not do enney thing to the Americans here. But the Rogue River Indians are At War with the Americans And the Miners, but that is three hundred Miles from here."[14]

Many of the Indians who lived near larger white settlements had already been displaced or were dead from disease. It was only in southern Oregon that the friction of contact had created war.

As the new treaty brought "peace," whites thought they had the instrument for regional safety with the Indians moving to reservations. Oregon Indian Superintendent Joel Palmer and the Washington Territory's new governor, Isaac I. Stevens, led the peace through treaty movement. As the Washington Territory's Indian superintendent, Governor Stevens would negotiate treaties with the tribes within his territory. And, that is what he sought to do: remove those who were there first to reservations, allowing newcomers to move onto the lands within the territories.

Chapter 2 notes

[1] The tribe spells its name as Yakama. However, historically, and geographically, the Indian nation's name was and is spelled with the "i," as in Yakima. In order to make it easier to find the geographic places associated with the tribe, the old spelling is used, while acknowledging that the Indians prefer Yakama.

[2] *A True Copy of the Record of the Official Proceedings at the Council in the Walla Walla Valley*, 1855, p. 80.

[3] Kowrach, *Mie Charles Pandosy, O.M.I.*, page. 63

[4] Trafzer and Scheuerman, *Renegade Tribe*, page 32.

[5] Ibid.

[6] Josephy, *The Nez Perce Indians and the Opening of the Northwest*, p.298.

[7] Kowrach, pages 49-50.

[8] Richards, *Isaac I. Stevens*, page 212.

[9] Ruby and Brown, *Indians of the Northwest*, page 67.

[10] Owhi was the Uncle of Kamiakin's Yakima wife.

[11] Trafzer and Scheuerman, page 36.

[12] America Butler, as quoted in Douthit, *Uncertain Encounters*, page 96.

[13] Beckham, *Requiem for a People*, pages 115-116.

[14] Schlissel, *Far from Home*, page 32.

Chapter Three

The Pressure Builds

Racial hatred was ever present in white-Indian relations, particularly on the white side. As one writer of the Indians in the Rogue River Valley noted, "…whatever is done by the Indians, though in self-defense, is published all over the land, as savage barbarity, for which nothing short of extermination is recommended and sought…"[1]

However, even without racism there still would have been a fight as the whites moved to displace the Indians. The whites wanted what the Indians had.

The Indians had already felt displacement. The Molalla Indians were related to the Cayuse and had once been living side-by-side with them. The Molallas had been centered near the Deschutes River of Central Oregon, while the Cayuse had lived on the John Day River. But, each tribe had been displaced when another, stronger Indian tribe[2] had rent the relationship by driving a wedge between the two nations. The Molallas fled to the west side of the Cascade Mountains, while the Cayuse moved east, into the Blue Mountains.

Now, as the whites moved into the Oregon Territory, the Indians felt the fear of displacement. What was sought by the whites was the best land, and that generally meant water. It was vital for Indians for fishing, crops, and as a highway. For whites, water was a vital for placer mining. More importantly, it was imperative for farming and ranching. Generally, the best locations close to water were where the Indians had established themselves. As the whites pushed west, the prime locations were Indian lands.

For example, the Yakima chief Kamiakin was rich by both Indian standards as well as white. He owned many horses, many cattle, and he had land. His home included irrigated gardens, the first in the Pacific Northwest. It was the water rich lands Indians owned and whites desired that helped drive the Rogue River Valley wars of 1850-1853.

But, as much as the whites wanted the land, equally true was the recognition (if in legal theory) that the land belonged to the Indians. From the start of our nation, it was determined that the Indians were to be fairly treated. The Northwest Ordinance Act of 1787 (that is, the *old* Northwest) was cognizant that the land was already occupied, and that in order for whites to obtain the land, the Indian claims to the land had to be extinguished through treaties. In dealing with the Indians, the Ordinance required that they be dealt with through the "utmost good faith." As one historian has written, "The federal government promised in each territory to acknowledge aboriginal land title, not to invade the tribes unless in 'just and lawful wars declared by Congress,' and from time to pass laws to prevent injustices being done to them."[3]

When Congress created the Oregon Territory (legislated on August 14, 1848), provisions of the Organic Act provided for the continuation of the "utmost good faith" of the Northwest Act. However, the good faith quickly dissipated.

In 1850, Congress attempted measures to stimulate the growth of the American empire while keeping faith with the Indians. First, it enacted the Oregon Land Donation Act. This forerunner of the Homestead Act gave 320 acres to every white male citizen (and an additional 320 acres if the man was married) who claimed and worked land within the Greater Oregon Territory. The act failed to recognize the pre-existing Indian land claims, unextinguished through treaty. White pioneers believed, not without justification, that the land was open and free, theirs for the taking. Recorded through the year 1855, nearly 2.5 million acres of Indian land had been claimed by nearly 8,000 settlers under the act, all without benefit of clear title through enacted treaty provisions (although it was never in doubt about the land claimed, at least not in white courts).

Recognizing the need to extinguish Indian land claims, in 1850 Congress also created the Willamette Valley Treaty Commission with Anson Dart as its head. His mission was to gain clear title to Indian land through negotiated treaties. As the whites poured into the Oregon Territory, they sought property to claim. Throughout 1851,

Dart would sign eight treaties. The problem with these treaties, from the white settlers' point of view was that Dart allowed the Indians to retain some portion of their tribal areas as reservations. These were often very desirable land tracts and that fact, coupled with the proximity of growing white populations, caused the Senate to ignore these treaties. In fact, the treaty commission was eliminated and the power to negotiate treaties was then placed with the Indian superintendents for each newly established territory.

The Senate ratified the first agreement with Pacific Northwest Indians: the September 10, 1853 treaty signed by the Cow Creek Indians of the Rogue River Valley. While the Indians of that tribe thought they had obtained land within their homelands, the treaty provided for a temporary reservation. It was up to the president or his designee to decide the best location for a permanent reservation. On November 9, 1855, President Franklin Pierce ordered a reservation created on the coast, centered on the Siletz River. He then ordered the Indians moved hundreds of miles to their new "home."

With so much unresolved, pressures grew. More settlers streamed along the Oregon and Applegate Trails and more mineral wealth was discovered, always on Indian lands. The whites who poured into the Northwest brought with them the means to clear the Indians from the land: germs. Measles sparked the Whitman Massacre and the Cayuse Indian war of 1847-1850. Now, starting with 1853, more illnesses swept the land. George Gibbs, a close associate of Isaac Stevens, documented the spread of smallpox throughout the plateau regions. Many tribes had "suffered severely" and whole villages had "been depopulated."[4] Fears of violent Indian reaction started to be noted.

Clearly, as the mix of whites and Indians grew to a level that would ignite conflict over choice lands, war became certain. The Rogue River Valley struggles set the pattern that would be repeated elsewhere in the Oregon Territory. Authorities started to note signs, and reported their concerns to higher command.

The Walla Walla Valley was one of the first areas that sent word of these concerns. After the Whitman massacre of 1847 and the ensuing Cayuse Indian War, most whites had fled the valley. But with the Oregon Land Donation Act, whites were starting to return to the lush valley with ample water. Moreover, the Army planned to send a survey party through the region. Cayuse raids on wagon trains had increased in 1852, and Indians saw army patrols often. As one Indian history has written,

> The Cayuses' memories of soldiers were never pleasant; whenever they saw one, they assumed he had come to fight, thus perpetuating the mutual ill feeling. Believing that their lands would soon be taken, the Cayuse sought to even the score...[5]

These "mutual ill feelings" were reported. Colonel B. L. E. Bonneville stated as early as February 23, 1853, that war was likely to break out as the Indians resisted white settlers moving into the Walla Walla Valley. The colonel feared that the triggering event *could* be the Saxton military road survey party, scheduled for the summer of 1853.

The Catholic mission serving the Yakima Indians sounded the next warning. Father Charles Pandosy wrote of the Indians gathering to plan their resistance to white intrusion. His letter of April 1853 warned of the "clouds...gathering upon all the lands, the winds begin to lower the tempest is pent up ready to burst."[6] His fears were more than Colonel Bonnevilles'. Not fearing a local outbreak, he was writing to warn of regional war.

> All the Indians on the left bank of the Columbia, from Blackfeet to the Chinook, inclusive, are to assemble at the Cayuse Country. All on the right bank, through the same extent country, are to assemble on the Simcoe (or the Yakima) including those from Nesqually and its vicinity. The cause of the war is, that the Americans are going to seize their lands.[7]

This was a vision of an Indian Armageddon. It seemed farfetched that all the Indians, even long-time enemies, could unite to fight white invaders. As an isolated warning, it could be easily dismissed, and it was.

But a third warning was sounded. On July 17, 1853, Major Benjamin Alvord informed his commanding officer, that he too had heard rumors that the Cayuse, Yakima, and Klickitat Indians were planning to resist white advances into their country. Alvord had apprised command that the need for treaties was imperative at the earliest possible opportunity, "...before the crowding in of the whites...produces collision and war."[8]

These fears would grow in 1854. When Governor Stevens arrived at Fort Dalles, Major Gabriel Rains greeted him with similar warnings of impending hostilities. But, what was the basis for these reports?

The first Indian "conferences" were initiated by the Cayuse over the winter of 1852 to the spring of 1853. They met with the Nez Perce, Umatilla, and Walla Walla, all traditional allies. Father Pandosy reported of one such meeting feasted by the Nez Perce:

Library of Congress

Major Benjamin Alvord went on to become a general.

> A chief of the Upper Nez Perce has killed 30 head of cattle at a feast given to the nation; and this number of animals not being sufficient, seven more were killed. This feast was given in order to unite the hearts of all Indians together, to make declarations of war against the Americans. Through the whole course of the Winter I have heard the same thing—that the Cayuse and the Nez Perce have united themselves for war.[9]

Other Indians called for united resistance. After the McClellan party had crisscrossed the Yakima area in the summer of 1853, Kamiakin told of his belief that McClellan was the advance party for invasion. Kamiakin's runners traversed the formidable Cascade Mountains to enlist the Nisqually in resisting the white onslaught.

In preparation for the coming war, Indians bought more powder and balls from the Hudson's Bay Company, and word reached many whites that the Indians were increasing their war stores by hording ammunition. And, as the hungry pioneers reached Oregon Indian territory, the Indians traded cattle for guns and ammunition from the desperate and starving immigrants.

It became clear by the summer of 1854 that something must be done to oppose the whites. Kamiakin turned to his friend, Father Pandosy, for advice. In a letter to his bishop (June 5, 1854), Father Pandosy related what he had said to the Yakima chief.

> It is as I feared, the Whites will take your country as they have taken other countries from the Indians....You and your lands will be seized and your people driven from their homes. It has been so with other tribes; it will be so with you. You may fight and delay for a time this invasion, but you cannot avert it.[10]

After many separate, smaller Indian councils, it was clear that the only hope was a united front against the whites. Runners were sent to all of the Northwest tribes, calling for a grand council in the summer of 1854. The place was the traditional council meeting grounds of the Grand Ronde River Valley, in Northeastern Oregon.

Was it to be war, surrender, or some other tactic? The debate was fierce. Many tribes, the Cayuse among them, wanted war. Others urged negotiations. The Yakima leader Kamiakin urged a peaceful alternative first. When the whites came to ask for a treaty, the Indians must state that they had no lands to give up, that the Indians already lived on their lands, needing the land for their cattle and horses. The Cayuse "...were opposed to it, believing the feather on an arrow to be mightier than that on a pen."[11] Each tribe advanced its position. But Kamiakin's will and oratory skills carried the day. "Whatever inter-tribal power plays may have taken place in the Ronde, Yakima Chief Kamiakin emerged as moderator, calling for the establishment of an Indian confederacy to oppose the whites."[12] His speech to his fellow Indians cried for justice and peace, but failing that, demanded war.

> We wish to be left alone in the lands of our forefathers, whose bones lie in the sand hills and along the trails, but a pale-face stranger has come from a distant land and sends word to us that we must give up our country, as he wants it for the white man. Where can we go? There is no place left. Only a single mountain now separates us from the big salt water of the setting sun. Our fathers from the hunting grounds of the other world are looking down on us today. Let us not make them ashamed! My people, the Great Spirit has his eyes upon us. He will be angry if, like cowardly dogs, we give up our lands to the whites. Better to die like brave warriors on the battlefield, than live among our van-

quishers, despised. Our young men and women would speedily be debauched by their fire water and we should perish as a race.[13]

Kamiakin recognized the real possibility that war would come, but he was chief and he knew the price his people would pay in war. He wanted peace, but it had to be a fair peace! Kamiakin's plan was for the Indians to claim their homelands. Each tribe settled on the land they saw as their ancestors' homes. "Thus, a circle was completed... thereby leaving no lands to treat for...now [if] asked for a council, it was agreed that they should consent, but should give up no land."[14]

Here then, was the Indian hope: Peace through treaties. When the whites called for treaties to take their lands, the Indians would agree that they had no surplus lands to give up.

And, as the Indians prepared their answer, the question was raised. Coming west was Isaac I. Stevens. Not only was he charged with conducting a railroad survey, he was to assume two assignments once he arrived in the newly created (1853) Washington Territory. His first assignment was to be the chief executive, or territorial governor. His second assignment was to be in charge of the Indians within the new territory, and he was also the superintendent of Indian affairs.

As governor, Stevens reported to President Franklin Pierce. As Indian superintendent, he reported to the Commissioner of Indian Affairs, George Manypenny. Naturally, Governor Stevens would work in cooperation with the territorial governor of Oregon[15] as the executives charged with the governance of their territories. And as the Washington official whose charge it was to sign treaties with the natives, Stevens collaborated with the Oregon Superintendent for Indians, Joel Palmer. Unlike Palmer, Stevens had no real background in dealing with Indians. Palmer had his experience from twice crossing the Oregon Trail, as well as having been a peace commissioner during the Cayuse Indian War. While both were appointed to deal with the Indians, Stevens' experience was limited to the decimated remnants of Maine tribes. It would rest on these two men's skill and compassion to peacefully resolve treaties with the Indians of the Northwest.

Palmer was kept busy in the summer and fall of 1854 addressing the continuous problems of the Southwestern portion of the state. As early as January of that year, tragedy required Palmer's attentions. Miners and settlers near the Coquille River on the Oregon Coast met to deal with the "Indian problem." Their specific complaints included such crimes as having an Indian ride a horse without consent of the white owner, blaming the Indians for a parted ferry rope, and the failure of the Indians to heed a call to meet with the self-appointed white leaders, no doubt for fear of their safety.

On January 28, 1854, a company of white volunteers under George Abbott attacked a sleeping Coquille Indian village at the dawn's first light. Taken completely by surprise, the village was quickly overrun, and fifteen men and one woman were murdered. The Sub-Indian Agent at Port Orford, F. M. Smith, wrote to Joel Palmer of the event.

> I grieve to report to you that a most horrid massacre or rather an out-and-out barbarous murder, was perpetrated upon a portion of the Na-son tribe, residing at the mouth of the Coquille river, on the morning of the 28th of January last, by a party of forty miners.[16]

Palmer faced the need to restore peace as the Indians had retaliated for the massacre. Two trappers, Elijah Burton and his partner, Venable, were killed, and James Lowe and his partner were waylaid in their canoe. More Indians were killed, and then more whites, and then the cycle repeated. Palmer would try to meet with the Indians in early May of 1854, but his efforts were futile as the Indians tried to avoid whites altogether. The rest of 1854 seemed to be a continuation of the long pattern of war between the miners and the Indians. This would remain a festering problem for Palmer, but he had agreed to join with Stevens and meet with the Indians of the eastern portion of both territories.

Governor Stevens needed treaties to settle the land claims for the Washington Territory. He divided his attention into three areas: the coast, Puget Sound, and the eastern half of the Washington Territory. His plan was to have as few treaties as possible, creating the fewest number of reservations, thus saving the government money. He sent runners to the various tribes, promising to start in December 1854 with the Indians nearest his capitol at Olympia. Then he would travel to the coast, and finally next spring meet with the Indians in the east.

Stevens called for a great council of Indians to meet with him and Superintendent Palmer in the spring of 1855. They would gather in the eastern part of the territory to sign treaties. It was when word of this proposed council reached the Yakima Indians that the Indians' recalled their apocalyptic prophecy.

When Owhi told Kamiakin about this threat [the call for a treaty council in the spring of 1855], he replied, "At last, we are faced with those awful people, the coming of whom was foretold by the old medicine man, Wa-tum-nah[17] long ago."[18]

The council was called and the Indians were ready.

Chapter 3 notes

[1] Beeson, *A Plea for the Indians*, page 20.

[2] While it is clear that this event occurred, what is less clear is which tribe caused the split. Some authorities believe it was the Tenino Indians, while others postulate it was the Paiute Indians. The event occurred before the arrival of the whites.

[3] Beckham, *Oregon Indians*, page 105.

[4] Trafzer and Scheuerman, *Renegade Tribe*, page 42.

[5] Ruby and Brown, *The Cayuse Indians*, page 179.

[6] Kowarach, Mie Charles Pandosy, O.M.I., page 74.

[7] Ibid., page 75.

[8] Josephy, *The Nez Perce Indians*, page 305.

[9] Trafzer and Scheuerman, page 75.

[10] Kowarach, page 78.

[11] Beckham, page 191.

[12] Ibid.

[13] Splawn, *Ka-mi-akin*, page 26.

[14] Ibid, pages 25-26.

[15] George Curry was either the acting governor, or the appointed governor from May 19, 1853 until Oregon became a state, in 1859. The exception was Governor John W. Davis, from December 2, 1853 to August 1, 1854.

[16] Beckham, page 132.

[17] Perhaps also Wat-tilki?

[18] Neils, *The Klickitat Indians*, page 76.

Chapter Four

Treaties

Pressures built: More pioneers moved into the Pacific Northwest and if treaties were not signed, and quickly signed, the wars of Southwestern Oregon would spread throughout the region. Both Palmer and Stevens knew this and felt driven to obtain the consent and the land of the Indians.

For Joel Palmer, his first concern was trying to contain the ravages of racial war in the Rogue River Valley. He appointed new agents to the various Indian tribes in his charge: Absalom Hembree, Edward Drew, Nathan Olney, and Ben Wright.[1] Having assigned his agents, Palmer rode south from his home in Dayton, Oregon for the Rogue River area on October 22, 1854. There, he met with various Indian tribes and they signed treaties that legally extinguished all Indian land title in southwestern Oregon. He did so by buying the land cheap. For example, the November 18, 1854 treaty with the bands of the upper Illinois River Valley cost only $30,000, or about five cents an acre.[2] By the end of November 1854, it seemed the longstanding Indian problems may have been peacefully resolved. The problematic peace was based on Indian confusion.

The Indian belief was that the Table Rock Reservation they occupied, even if it became more crowded with additional tribes moved onto it, was at least within their native river valley. However, Palmer had other ideas such as moving them east onto a reservation with the Klamath Indians or creating a coastal Indian reservation. What the Indians did not realize was that the terms of the treaty subverted their understanding with the phrase, "when at any time hereafter the Indians residing on this reserve shall be removed to another reserve."[3] It would be this confusion that would re-trigger war. While Palmer worked to create a coastal reservation in 1855, the Indians believed they would remain at Table Rock. Palmer let the Indians believe that Table Rock was theirs indefinitely. However, the new reservation was a fait accompli, as President Pierce signed the order creating the new reservation on November 9, 1855. "Three days after the presidential order was signed, it became federal policy to discontinue the Table Rock Temporary Reservation and remove the Rogue Valley tribes confederated there to the Siletz Reservation."[4]

Over the winter of 1854-55, Joel Palmer would continue with his efforts to peacefully resolve the Rogue River Indian situation. Soon, though, his attention would be drawn to the east, as he had already conferred with Governor Stevens about the need to resolve the eastern Indian land claims.

For Governor Stevens, his first efforts were directed to where the majority of the whites had settled: the Puget Sound area. While things were largely peaceful, the competition for choice lands created tensions, and pressure. Even near his capitol, Olympia, land demands were escalating the chance for conflict. To alleviate the risk, Stevens selected the neighboring Nisqually to entreaty for their land. A treaty council was called, to meet at nearby Medicine Creek, just before Christmas, 1854.

Medicine Creek Treaty

Gathering near the saltwater bogs of southern Puget Sound on Christmas Eve were representatives of the Nisqually, Puyallup, and Squaxin tribes. Most spoke the Salish language, as did the governor's chief Indian expert at the council, Benjamin F. Shaw.[5] Communications could have been more thoroughly completed using Salish, but the governor decreed that the trade jargon language of Chinook be used as the official language of translation for the treaty. This simplistic trade language had a very limited vocabulary, and was useless for conveying complex terms or ideas. Further, translator Shaw was not impartial; "Shaw argued that the United States…had erred in letting the Indians think they were equal partners in decisions relating to land disposal."[6]

From the start, Governor Stevens set the tone he would use with all Northwest Indians in his treaty negotiations. The contrast with Joel Palmer was stark. Superintendent Palmer would address the Indians at negotiations more as equals, or at least in neutral language, such as "my friends." Governor Stevens created an atmosphere from the start that put the negotiations on a different footing; he would address the Indians as, "My children."

Sincerely believing he was fair, Stevens started his negotiations from a position that he knew what was in the Indians' best interests, that they were not able to understand their best interests, and that he had to take care of them—to protect them. He had recognized earlier that his first thought, to move the Puget Sound and coastal Indians to one large, central reservation east of the Cascade Mountains would be impossible. The hunter-gatherer tribes of the rich tidal waters of Washington would perish in the alien and hostile world of Central Washington's semi-arid plateau country.

Library of Congress

Governor Issac Stevens, treatymaker and one of the most controversial figures in the history of the Pacific Northwest.

Recognizing that these tribes needed to remain close to their traditional sites, Governor Stevens selected reservations for the tribes near (but not on) traditional tribal lands. Thus, as he opened the treaty talks, his tone was dictatorial, not that of a bargainer. "One thing soon became clear: the Indians had not been brought to negotiate a treaty, but to sign it exactly as written."[7] This was made perfectly clear by Governor Stevens' own words: "You are about to be paid for your lands."

The Indians desired to hold onto traditional lands used to gather important foodstuffs, such as shellfish. Instead, each tribe was told that it would be given a reservation of 1,280 acres, and the sites were already laid out for them.[8] This quickly became a point of contention, lead by the Nisqually chief Leschi.[9] The chief wanted to keep traditional lands where for generations his tribe had fished along the river and where the tribe's horses had grazed the tidal plains. Stevens was steadfast in his denial of the Nisqually claims, and that they had to go to the reservation pre-selected for them (although along the river, Stevens selected the rocky lands unsuitable for white needs as the reservation site). Further, they were to reduce their herds to a more manageable size of 500 head, and ensure population control of the horses by making their prized stallions into geldings.

Tensions grew between the two sides. Demonstrating his frustration and anger, Leschi protested the lack of fair negotiations by taking his sub-chief certificate, issued by Governor Stevens' territorial Indian office, tearing it up, and working it into the mud beneath his feet. If he was a sub-chief, the ground was his home. If the earth was not his home, then the certificate was worthless.

These small tribes could not hope to force the changes they desired in the treaty. So, they finally agreed. The first were the Squaxin, which were to move to an island in the sound. The Puyallups received the land on the south side of Commencement Bay (where the city of Tacoma is located), and the Nisquallys' land on the Nisqually Flats, but not the tidal plains they had asked for first.

Fifty-nine Indians made their mark on the treaty. According to official records (that is, as recorded by Governor Stevens' secretary James Doty), the signatories included chiefs Sinawah of the Puyallups, and Quiemuth and Leschi of the Nisqually. However, Indian histories tell of a different ending. The Nisqually tradition says Leschi stormed out of the treaty grounds, refusing all gifts (calico and black strap molasses) offered, if he would sell his lands.[10] Some Indians contend fraud and forgery: "There are others who swear that he [Leschi] refused the gifts offered to him, and that he never signed. If there was a mark beside his name, they said, then it must have been forged."[11]

This treaty set the tone for all the rest of the Stevens' treaty efforts. On one side, "Stevens speculated that if the whole treaty program proceeded as smoothly as Medicine Creek….the next year would find the Indians from the Missouri River to the Pacific at peace."[12] For the Indians, there was the loss of their homelands, injustice, and the taint of fraud and coercion.

Point Elliott Treaty

After the Christmas treaty of Medicine Creek, Governor Stevens moved north intending to treat with the Duwamish, Snoqualmie, Skagit, Lummi, and (by proxy) the Nooksack Indians. As an opening note of disappointment, the Duwamish expressed a desire to meet on their homeland, east of Seattle. The governor's representative, his new secretary for the rest of the western treaties, George Gibbs, insisted on meeting at Point Elliott, and attributed the Indians' request to the evil influence from "cultus whites." In American eyes, "cultus whites" were those whites overly sympathetic to Indian interests, or, in other words, French Canadians (noted for having Indian wives) and Hudson's Bay Company employees, renown for their good relations with the Indians.

Edward S. Curtis Collection, Library of Congress
A young Yakima warrior.

When the governor arrived on January 22, 1855, the treaty basically replicated that of Medicine Creek, with the obvious exception that the reservation descriptions were changed to reflect the different tribes. And as he had before, Stevens opened his "negotiations" with his standard address: "My children! . . .You are my children for whom I will strenuously labor all my days of my life until I shall be taken hence."[13]

One historian noted that this was Stevens' favorite form of address to Indians and believed it to be the key to understanding his approach.

> He believed that they, like children, had not yet reached the status of adulthood with its rights and responsibilities, and that they needed care and guidance until they achieved full growth and maturity. He did not assume that they were inherently inferior, but that they had not yet reached the full potential of human development. Also, like children, they should obey their father...[14]

This treaty went as he had intended, with all chiefs signing in agreement and accepting their presents. According to the official transcripts, Chief Seattle of the Duwamish declared, "Now by this we make friends and put away all bad feelings, if we ever had any."

However, thirty years later, one of those present at the treaty signing printed a speech that he attributed to Seattle. While it is doubtful that it was ever given, it captures some of the spirit and intent of the Indians, particularly those at the Point Elliott Council. Among the moving passages of the speech, Seattle clearly recognizes the futility of resistance:

> The son of the white chief says his father sends us greetings of friendship and good will.
>
> This is kind, for we know he has little need of our friendship in return, because his people are many. They are like the grass that covers the vast prairies, while my people are few, and resemble the scattering trees of a storm-swept plain.

And if the numbers were overwhelming against the Duwamish, Seattle expressed the sense of hopelessness in resistance, "But let us hope that the hostilities between the red-man and his pale-face brothers may never return. We would have everything to lose and nothing to gain." And, what does the future of this tribe look like?

> The Indian's night promise to be dark. No bright star hovers about the horizon. Sad-voiced winds moan in the distance. Some grim nemesis of our race is on the red man's trail, and wherever he goes he will still hear the sure approaching footsteps of the fell destroyer and prepare to meet his doom, as does the wounded doe that hears the approaching footsteps of the hunter. A few more moons, a few more winters, and not one of all the mighty hosts that once filled this broad land or that now roam in fragmentary bands through these vast solitudes will remain to weep over the tombs of a people once as powerful and hopeful as your own.[15]

Perhaps Seattle never uttered these words, but if not, then at least they told the story of a people "once powerful and hopeful."

Point No Point Treaty

After a few days, Governor Stevens was ready for the next treaty. On January 25, he met with the Clallam, Skokomish, and Chimakim Indians. Fully anticipating another easy treaty, after giving his standard opening remarks the governor asked if the chiefs had anything to say. Standing up to speak, Chief Che-lan-the-tat of the Skokomish arose and objected:

> I wish to speak my mind as to selling the land[,] Great Chief! What shall we eat if we do so? Our only food is berries, deer, and salmon. Where shall we find these. I don't want to sign away my land. Take half of it and let us keep the rest. I am afraid that I shall become destitute and perish for want of food. I don't like the place you have chosen for us to live on. I am not ready to sign the paper.[16]

More and more chiefs spoke their objections. One Skokomish chief spoke that while most of the Indians were afraid to speak, he lamented, "It makes me sick to leave it."[17] The first day ended with Stevens making promises and asking for the Indians' signature.

The next day was dramatically different. The previous day had been stormy, and not merely with words. The weather had been frightful, raining with a blasting wind, but the new morning was spectacular, and Stevens said that the weather was a sign, blessing the treaty. And as the weather had changed, so did Indian resistance. The Indians did not renew their objections. Perhaps it was resigned recognition that their resistance was futile. No council ever had a better name. The Point No Point Treaty showed the Indians that there was no point in resisting; the whites would simply take the land they wanted.

Two more Treaty Councils

From Point No Point, Governor Stevens moved to the coast and by the end of January had signed a treaty with the Makah and Ozettes. From there, the governor moved to the Chehalis River for a council with the Indians of the Southwestern part of the territory, tribes such as Chinooks and Cowlitz. Stevens had predetermined that a single reservation would be adequate, one located on the Quinaults' homelands. With that selection, the Quinaults were easily persuaded to sign. The other tribes' objections mirrored and echoed those made at Point No

Point. As the treaty council continued, the Indians objections were repeated. No easy one or two day treaty council was in the offing here. After three days, with the Indians offering a compromise that they would sell some of their land in return for staying on their traditional homeland, Stevens was becoming frustrated and then angry. When a Chehalis chief, Carcowan, violated Stevens' rules regarding alcohol, showing up drunk, it was the final affront that Stevens would endure. With disobedient children not obeying their father, Stevens left, his first failure at obtaining a treaty.

While the last treaty was a failure, Governor Stevens had successfully taken care of the Puget Sound area and was now ready to undertake treaty efforts with the large tribes of the eastern portion of the territory. After joint planning with Joel Palmer, Stevens sent runners to the eastern tribes calling for a great council to be held in the spring. This would be the culmination of his efforts and the final push to secure Indian land titles from the Pacific Ocean to the Missouri River.

The Great Council of Walla Walla

With the Puget Sound area secured, Governor Stevens prepared for the next challenge by sending advance word of the council. Starting east in March, James Doty accompanied by two Indian agents — Andrew J. Bolon and Richard H. Lansdale—was to meet with the Indians and call them to a great council.

Appropriately, the advance party arrived at Father Pandosy's Yakima Mission on April Fool's Day. At first, Kamiakin was "either silent or sulky and declined meeting the whites or discussing the subject of a treaty."[18] Instead, not recognizing the internal politics of the tribal power struggle, Doty met with Te-i-as, Skloom, and Shumaway. This resulted in the call for a Yakima council meeting the next day.

At this meeting, witnessed by 200 Yakima, all the chiefs, including Kamiakin, attended. Doty again related Governor Stevens' desire to have a great council with all of the Indians, to which the Yakima agreed. Indeed, it was Kamiakin who suggested the traditional council site of the Walla Walla Valley and Doty seized this suggestion as a positive sign, agreeing to relay the suggestion again to the governor. Then, in closing, in an effort to show friendship, Doty offered presents of tobacco, clothing, and bolts of cloth.

Once more Kamiakin displayed his understanding of American methods. He angrily said he "had never accepted from the Americans the value of a grain of wheat without paying for it."[19] Further, he knew of the American trick that when Indians accepted gifts, the whites would later claim that the Indians had sold their land in exchange for that which was given to them. This stopped the other chiefs from taking any gifts for one day, when their greed overcame Kamiakin's cautions and they went to Doty to get their gifts—without, apparently, Kamiakin's knowledge. This was another sign of the internal political struggle for control of the tribe.

Library of Congress

Major Gabriel Rains

From the Yakima, Doty moved east and met with the Nez Perce, and then with the Walla Walla. The Nez Perce were a traditionally friendly nation, but it was with the Walla Walla that Doty met with more suspicion. Chief Peo-peo-mox-mox expressed his concerns and reluctance to enter into any agreement with the whites, but did allow that any agreement might be better than none as then the whites would merely move in and take the Walla Walla's land. Doty described Peo-peo-mox-mox as, "This is a shrewd old chief."[20]

Doty's report to the governor suggested success was possible. However, he also reported the latent hostility of the Cayuse and Walla Walla Indians, and suggested that troops accompany the governor to the council. Palmer and Stevens arrived at Fort Dalles en route to the council, and requested Major Gabriel Rains provide an army escort. Rains expressed his belief that the U.S. Army was not needed, but finally agreed to assign an escort. Stevens sent Doty to tell the Indians at the council site that he would be accompanied by a troop, and they were not to take this as a sign of intimidation by force. But, to the Indians what else could be meant by sending troops once more up the

Walla Walla Valley as the Americans had during the Cayuse Indian War?

Palmer and Stevens arrived at the council site on May 21, 1855. Stevens noted in his diary that there were some "malcontents" among the Indians and, "if not controlled, might embolden all not well disposed, and defeat the negotiations."[21] In other words, these would be disobedient children.

As the tribes gathered, the council grew to one of the largest meetings of whites and Indians ever held on the North American continent. Some Indians, such as the Spokane, came as observers, and others stayed away altogether, such as the Palouse.[22] Encamping in the verdant valley of the Walla Walla, were about 5,000 Indians.

Pre-council tensions

Between May 21, when the white party arrived and the official opening of the council on May 29, both sides sought advantage with posturing and gamesmanship. First, the Army escort under Lieutenant Archibald Gracie arrived two days after Stevens and Palmer. The troops arrived, set up a standard Army camp in impressive orderly fashion, making a statement of the Army's presence.

Next, the white party met to finalize their plans. Among the whites were Stevens, his secretary Doty, Doty's assistant, Doctor Lansdale, Palmer, and his Indian agent for eastern Oregon, Nathan Olney. The main point for discussion was really, how few reservations could they get away with in creating? How many tribes could be "confederated" on a single reservation? The original goal was to have two reservations: One just east of the Cascades, and one centered on the whites' strongest Indian ally, the Nez Perce.

The Indians practiced their own version of gamesmanship. On May 24, the Nez Perce arrived decked out in plumage and finery, showing their strength with almost 600 warriors. After their parade, complete with drums, the Nez Perce encamped and were visited by the white leaders. Here the Nez Perce made their opening move for position in the negotiations. As the whites conferred with the principle Nez Perce chief, Lawyer, Chief Utsinmalikin walked in and announced that Walla Walla chief Peo-peo-mox-mox, Yakima's Kamiakin, and others (notably the "malcontent" Cayuse) had approached him and other Nez Perce chiefs to come to their camp for a council. Utsinmalikin said he rejected their overture since they had not invited the Nez Perce headsman, Lawyer (notable as one of the most pro-white chiefs). At the very least, this move confirmed to the whites that there were malcontents, but the Nez Perce were their friends and allies in combating the negative forces arrayed against them.

The Cayuse made the next grand entrance on May 26. The tone of the Cayuse entrance with 400 mounted warriors was of a whole different tenor. The warriors rode around the white camp, as one observer said, like a war party. Their hostility was palpable, particularly toward the encamped Army troops. Finally, the chiefs rode up to Stevens and Palmer, where they were invited to dismount and smoke with the commissioners. They dismounted and shook hands, Doty noted, "in no cordial manner," and declined the offer to smoke. Instead, the Cayuse trotted off to their camp, one more distant camp than that of the nearby Nez Perce. Rumors, spread by some Nez Perce quickly reached the whites that the Cayuse were suggesting the best plan would be to kill the whites. In light of the Cayuse' entrance, it seemed at least possible. This concern was further supported with the arrival of two Catholic priests. Fathers Chirouse (who ministered to the Umatilla) and Father Pandosy (of the Yakima) who reported that while most of the Indians were well disposed to the whites, be wary of Kamiakin. They also confirmed that the Cayuse, Walla Walla, and Yakima had tried to get the Nez Perce to support their rejection of the treaty (but they did not report any indications of pending attack).

When the Yakima arrived on May 28, the Cayuse immediately called for an Indian council. But first Kamiakin greeted the whites. With Kamiakin came Peo-peo-mox-mox, his friend and ally. Doctor Lansdale noted Kamiakin as being "moderately friendly but still reserved."[23] In Peo-peo-mox-mox's demeanor, while outwardly friendly, the whites found him to be querulous. Why? He wanted additional translators, not just the designated white translators, so he could trust the translation. With that demand, things were ready for the official opening of the council.

The Council
First day: Tuesday, May 29

On the spring green grass stood the official council site. The stage was prepared. Near Stevens' tent, an arbor was erected to protect the participants from both the rain and the sun. Seated at the front on a bench, were Palmer and Stevens, and seated on the ground before them, as children before their father, sat the assorted chiefs, and behind them the spectator Indians.

The translators would work back and forth between the languages, each Indian language having their own set of translators. The pace of the translations allowed the secretary (and others) to record the council in detail. Governor Stevens' opening remarks were his classic form of address: "My children." And with that, he had the translators sworn in.

As a good host, the governor noted that the Indians were there as the invited guests of the whites, so the Indians would be supplied with food. When the governor offered the food, it was rejected by some. Chief Young Chief, of the Cayuse, replied, "We have plenty of cattle."[24] And when Joel Palmer offered the Yakima cattle, Young Chief simply noted that Kamiakin would dine at his camp. Further, Young Chief established that the Indians would not be rushed into anything, "We will talk slow, not all in one day."[25] The Indians were independent and not going to be rushed. This tense tone established, the first day's official proceedings ended. But, off the record it was noted that Palmer and Stevens asked Peo-peo-mox-mox and Kamiakin to dine with them, which they did. Little is known of the efforts the two whites made to convince these two "malcontents" but it must have been intense.

Second day, Wednesday, May 30

This was the beginning of the real negotiations. The historian Alvin Josephy has described the council as having an unintended transparency:

> The minutes of the proceedings are astounding to read. The transparency of the speeches of Governor Stevens and Super-intendent Palmer is so obvious that it is a wonder the commis-sioners could not realize the ease with which the Indians saw through what they were saying. One can only assume either that

their ignorance of the Indian's mentality was appalling or that they were so intent on having their way with the tribes that they blinded themselves to the flagrancy of their hypocrisy.[26]

Palmer opened the proceedings at least a little less condescendingly than Stevens, with a greeting of "My friends." His speech was not nearly as long as that of Stevens. The major thrust of his opening remarks was that what was being offered was really for the benefit of the Indians. That if the Indians would agree and move onto the reservations set aside for them then, the whites could protect them by "… an agent who shall be your brother and who shall protect you from bad white men."[27]

The Indians did not respond to the opening remarks and the council was adjourned.

Third day, Thursday, May 31

Again, Stevens started off with, "My children," and told the Indians how the whites wanted the Indians to sell them the land the Indians did not need. And in exchange, Stevens promised that the whites would pay and do much for the Indians, and if they did not, then the Indians could seek redress with their agent. Stevens continually referred to the wonderful gifts that the Indians would receive.

As for Palmer, his remarks did little to clarify the message the Indians were hearing. Stevens kept speaking of the things the Indians would gain by giving up their land to the whites, not what the Indians would lose. Palmer told the Indians of the history of white-Indian relations that was very one-sided. He described how some whites had tricked and robbed the Indians, and then asked the Indians, "It is these men I am told who would rob you of your property, who are giving you advice not to treat with us. Whose council do you prefer to take, these men who would rob you, or our's who come to befriend you?"[28] Once more, the Indians (the malcontents) were being influenced by bad whites, the "cultus" whites. Palmer went further, saying "These men who came here are strangers to you with smooth tongues, they care nothing for the truth."[29] One wonders how Palmer could think that the Indians would believe him in that he was a "good" white, and not one of the "bad" whites, who "care nothing for the truth." Palmer closed the day with a warning for the Indians. "These men you cannot tell always who they are, but all such men need watching. You will be able to judge who are your friends, such men, or myself and my brother, who have come here to act for your good."[30]

That evening, Young Chief sent word that the next day the Indians wanted to consider their words, and requested no meeting. However, the lobbying continued when Palmer and Stevens had the prominent Indian chiefs dine once again with them.

Fourth day, Saturday, June 2

Having sensed that their words were not moving the "malcontents," Palmer tried a different approach, that of showing the inevitability of the outcome.

> If there were no other whites coming into the country we might get along in peace....Can you stop the waters of the Columbia River from flowing on its course? Can you prevent the wind from blowing? Can you prevent the rain from falling? Can you prevent the whites from coming? You are answered no! Like the grass hoppers on the plains, some years there will be more come than others. You cannot stop them...[31]

It was as if Palmer were describing a plague of locust moving over the land. But, it was with words of trust that Palmer ended his speech. "If we make a treaty with you and our Great chief and his council approves it, you can rely on all its provisions being carried out strictly."[32]

And it was then that Stevens told "his children" that it was now time for the whites to listen to the Indians.

At once, the Indians' frustration came forth. Five Crows started, "Do you speak true that you call me brother?" He then related his connection to the earth, loved by the Indians as their mother, and he deferred to Peo-peo-mox-mox, who clearly was angry.

> We have listened to all you have to say, and we desire you should listen when any Indian speaks. It appears that Craig[33] knows the hearts of his people, that the whole has been pre-arranged in the hearts of the Indians, that he wants an answer immediately without giving them time to think, that the Indians have had nothing to say so far it would appear that we have no chief. I know the value of your speech from having experienced

Edward S. Curtis Collection, Library of Congress
Yakima mountain camp.

the same in California,[34] having seen treaties there. We have not seen in a true light the object of your speeches….Look at yourselves: your flesh is white, mine is different, mine looks poor. Our languages are different. If you would speak straight then I would think you spoke well…..From what you have said I think you intend to win our country, or how is it to be? In one day the Americans become as numerous as the grass….I know that is not right, you have spoken in a round about way. Speak straight, I have ears to hear you and here is my heart. Suppose you show me goods, shall I run up and take them? That is the way we are, we Indians, as you know. Goods and the Earth are not equal… We require time to think, quietly, slowly….you have spoken in a manner partly tending to evil. Speak plain to us.[35]

After that speech, Stevens needed to break the Indian momentum. He suggested that the session was over, and they would not meet the next day, the Sabbath. It was in dramatic contrast to Peo-peo-mox-mox's demand that, "We have listened to all you have to say, and we desire you should listen when any Indian speaks." But, more drama occurred that night. What is known is that after midnight, Lawyer came to Governor Stevens' tent with word that the Cayuse were leading a plot to massacre all of the whites the next day. To protect the whites, Lawyer said, "I will come with my family and pitch my lodge in the midst of your camp, that those Cayuse may see that you and your party are under the protection of the head chief of the Nez Perces."[36]

Was there a plot? Did the Cayuse finally persuade the Walla Walla and Yakima to join in a plan to kill the whites? Or was this merely a shrewd ploy on the Nez Perce Lawyer's part to ingratiate his tribe further into the good graces of the whites, ensuring better treatment for the Nez Perce? It is impossible to know. But, there was no attack on Sunday, June 3, and there was no council either.

Fifth day, Monday, June 4

The next council opened with Governor Stevens asking for more Indian comments. The first to respond was Lawyer. His speech was a careful oration designed neither to offend the whites, or the Indians. He basically asked that the Indians be seen as a poor people and for the whites to listen to what the Indians had to say.

But most of the chiefs had little to say. Kamiakin issued a challenge for the whites to demonstrate their honesty. "I have been afraid of the white man. Their doings are different from ours. Your chiefs are good. Perhaps you have spoken straight, that your children will do what is right. Let them do as they have promised. That is all I have to say."[37]

Repeatedly, the Indians asked that Stevens and Palmer be honest, to speak straight. The Cayuse chief Stickus stated, "I ask you my friends to speak straight and plain to us." Peo-peo-mox-mox noted that the commissioners had not told them yet what lands were to be considered as reservations.

> I do not know what they [the interpreters] have said. My heart was heavy, my heart was to separate so, that was my heart. I do not know for what lands they [the interpreters] have spoken. If they had mentioned the lands that had spoken of then I should have understood them. Let it be as you propose so the Indians have a place to live, a line as though it was fenced in, where no white man can go. If you say it shall be so, then all these Indians will say yes. Although that you have said the whites are like

the wind, you cannot stop them. You make good what you have promised. You have spoken for lands generally. You have not spoken of any particular ones....The manner in which you have addressed the whole of us has made my heart heavy.[38]

Another chief asked, "I wonder if we shall both tell the truth to each other?" But then a Nez Perce chief, Eagle From the Light spoke, relating his own history, how the whites "hung my brother for no offense." He noted that the Indians had sought to understand the whites, that they had gone "hunting for someone to teach them to go straight." He ended with his charge to the commissioners: "Look at that, it is the tale I had to tell you and now I am going to hunt friendship and good advice. We will come straight here, slowly perhaps, but we will come straight."[39]

Now it was time for Stevens to "come straight." He answered Peopeo-mox-mox's question of where the reservations would be, and how many. He told them that there were to be two reservations, one centered on the Nez Perce, and one centered on the Yakima. He offered one to his strongest ally, the Nez Perce, and one to buy the silence of his greatest malcontent, Kamiakin. He did speak straight in one sense, admitting (if not in these terms) the reason for two reservations was economy. "You may ask, why so many tribes on one reservation, and how is it proper to place them on the reservation? We want as many tribes together as can be taken care of by one agent."[40] And with little more, the council was adjourned for another day.

Sixth day, Tuesday, June 5

The commissioners spent the sixth day detailing the reservations. Maps were shown, with the boundaries clearly delineated. Excluded from the reservations were choice valleys, wanted by the whites, such as the Walla Walla Valley and the Yakima River Valley, the route Stevens wanted his northern railroad to take. After four hours of explanation, the Indians had little to say. However, Chief Stickus of the Cayuse did note that his tribe would be moved away from their homeland.

> My friends I wish to show you my mind. Interpret right for me. How is it I have been troubled in mind? If your mothers were here in this country who gave you birth and suckled you,

and while you were sucking some person came and took away your mother and left you alone and sold your mother, how would you feel then? This is our mother, this country, as if we drew our living from her. My friends, all of this you have taken.[41]

The council ended that day with Five Crows saying, "I am as it were, without thinking yet. I require time to think and then I will answer." [42]

The next day the Indians talked amongst themselves, discussing what they had been presented with by the whites. One chief, though, conferred with the whites. Nez Perce Lawyer went to the whites and spoke privately. Certainly having his tent right next to Stevens' was an advantage. In return for receiving additional payments as a chief, Lawyer agreed to accept the reservation for the Nez Perce, and promised to bring the rest of his tribe in agreement, and work to bring the other tribes into line.

Seventh day, Thursday, June 7

And that is what Lawyer did in the opening remarks of the day's council. Lawyer supported the whites, and encouraged the other Indians to do so, too. "The President has sent you here to us poor people. Yes! The President has studied this and sent you here for our good."[43] To this Governor Stevens replied, "We have the heart of the Nez Perces through their chief. Their hearts and our hearts are one. We want the hearts of the other people through their chiefs."[44] But it became apparent with the next Indian that Stevens had not yet gotten their hearts.

"I wonder if this ground has anything to say," asked Chief Young Chief. "I wonder if the ground is listening to what is said. I wonder if the ground would come to life and what is on it. Though I hear what this earth says. The Earth says, God has placed me here. The earth says that god tells me to take care of the Indians on this earth….I am as it were blind. I am blind and ignorant. I have a heart but cannot say much. That is the reason the chiefs do not understand each other right. They stand apart. Although I see your offer before me I do not understand it. Lawyer understood your offer and he took it. I do not understand it and do not take it."[45]

Joel Palmer called on Peo-peo-mox-mox. The chief's words echoed the Indians' dissatisfaction, and he asked for a postponement for future consideration. "Treating us as children, giving us food, I do not know what is straight....If you were to repeat as we are now and appoint some other time, we shall have no bad minds. Stop the whites from coming up here till after this talk, not to bring their axes with them....The whites may travel in all directions through my country. We shall have nothing to say to them providing they do not build houses on our land." If given time to consider the treaties, Peo-peo-mox-mox said, it would give time for the whites to prove their words were true.

But he then addressed the actions of Lawyer, and what that meant for the Walla Walla. "Now I will speak about Lawyer. I think my friend has given his lands, that is what I think from his words....I only request another meeting, whenever it shall be. It is not only by one meeting that we can come to a decision."[46] In essence, Peo-peo-mox-mox was offering a compromise: adjourn to give time to consider, and reconvene at a later time. Chief Owhi, of the Yakima, seconded this call, "This is the reason I cannot give you an answer...shall I steal this land and sell it? Or what shall I do? ...My people are far away. They do not know your words. This is the reason why I cannot give you an answer now."[47]

To this suggestion of compromise, the whites displayed irritation and impatience. Palmer chastised the Indians for their "blindness," but, it was Palmer who was blind.

> We have listened and heard your chiefs speak. The heart of the Nez Perce and ours are one. The Cayuses, the Walla Wallas, and these other people say they do not understand us.....How long will this people remain blind? We come to try to open their eyes. They refuse the light....How long will you listen to this bad council and refuse to receive the light? ...We don't come to steal your lands, we pay you more than it is worth....What is it worth to you or us? Not one half of what we have offered for it.[48]

This was the crisis point for the whites. To the call for another meeting, Palmer threatened bad things would happen if the decisions were postponed. "Pe-pe-mox-mox says 'let us part and appoint another day.' Before that day would arrive we might have a great deal of trouble." The threat was that the whites would overrun the Indians

Raven Blanket, Nez Perce.

without the protection of the reservations. Palmer was pushing for fear of having the Indians walk out.

The fear was real. Chief Camasspello replied, "How do you show your pity by sending me and my children to a land where there is nothing to eat but wood?"[49] Another Cayuse, Howlish Wompoon, told the commissioners, "The Nez Perces have already given you their land...Your words since you came here have been crooked."[50]

Trying to control the council, both Stevens and Palmer responded to the Indians, promising that they had spoken straight. They called on the Indians to be of one heart. But the call for Indian unity (and agreement with the Nez Perce position) failed. Chief Five Crows responded, "Listen to me you chiefs. We have been as one people with the Nez Perces heretofore. This day we are divided. We ...will think over the matters tonight and give you an answer tomorrow."[51] With but a few words more, the council adjourned.

Throughout the council grounds, things were tense that night. Making their usual rounds, Lieutenants Gracie and Lawrence Kip went to the Cayuse camp. As Kip noted,

> There is evidently a more hostile feeling towards the whites getting up among some of the tribes, of which we had tonight a very unmistakable proof. The Cayuse, we have known, have never been friendly, but hitherto they have disguised their feeling. Tonight, as Leiut. Gracie and I attempted, as usual to enter their camp, they showed a decided opposition; we were motioned back, and the young warriors threw themselves in our way to obstruct our advance. To yield to this, however, or show any signs of being intimidated, would have been ruinous with the Indians, so were obliged to carry out our original intentions. We placed our horses abreast, riding round the Indians, where pos-

sible, and at other times forcing our way through, believing that they would not dare to resort to actual violence. If, however, this hostile feeling at the Council increases, how long will it be before we have an actual outbreak.[52]

Tensions were at a breaking point.

Eighth day, Friday, June 8

While tensions were high, there was movement. Young Chief brought forth a problem and a compromise.

> The reason why we could not understand you was that you selected the country for us to live in without our having any voice in the matter....You embraced all my country. Where was I to go. Was I to be a wanderer like a wolf without a home, without a home I would be compelled to steal, consequently I would die. I will show you lands that I will give you....We will see when you make another offer whether we can agree to it.[53]

Joel Palmer quickly took up this compromise. He told the chiefs that as a result of their words yesterday, the whites had heard them, and decided that it was right to create a third reservation, just as Young Chief had said. It appeared that this compromise had moved the Indians to the point of agreement, with only the Yakima (and Kamiakin) possibly holding out. But even Kamiakin was giving in. He explained to the whites that he had wanted to speak with his people prior to committing to anything. But he, too, would sign: "I do not speak this of myself, it is my people's wish."[54] The internal politics of the Yakima had forced him to give in, as Owhi and Te-i-as "are the chiefs." But Kamiakin wanted it known that he did not agree. "I Kamiakin do not wish for goods myself. The priest knows me. He knows my heart. He knows I do not desire a great many goods. All that I wish is for an agent, a good agent who will pity the good and bad of us and take care of us. I have nothing to talk long about. I am tired. I am anxious to get back to my garden. That is all I have to say."[55]

So, it was possible that everything could be settled, but then, a development arrived, unforeseen and explosive. It was the voice of a runner, saying that the Nez Perce Chief Looking Glass was coming. They decided to adjourn and await Looking Glass's arrival. Still, Stevens announced the treaties would be signed tomorrow.

As Looking Glass rode into the council grounds, he carried a trophy of his hunt across the mountains: A staff that had a scalp of a Blackfoot dangling from it. As Stevens and Palmer strode to greet the chief, his disdain was palpable. Instead of addressing the whites, he turned to his fellow Nez Perce chiefs and cried out, "My people, what have you done? While I was gone, you have sold my country. I have come home, and there is not left me a place on which to pitch my lodge. Go home to your lodges. I will talk to you."[56] Was this the end of the success Stevens and Palmer just achieved?

Ninth day, Saturday, June 9

Prior to the council starting, the whites started lobbying the Indians. Stevens met with Lawyer, who said that Looking Glass would calm down, providing the whites did not reduce the Nez Perce reservation to accommodate the new reservation for the Umatilla, Walla Walla and Cayuse. Once more Lawyer shrewdly bargained for his people.

Then the governor met with Peo-peo-mox-mox and Kamiakin, to hold them to their word signing pledge, as they had promised yesterday. The two agreed, with Kamiakin saying he could sign only for the Yakima and the Palouse tribes, as was recorded by Secretary Doty.

The council did not reconvene until the afternoon. It opened with the governor presenting the final versions of the three treaties, going over the points agreed on, while ignoring other changes not mentioned to the Indians. For example, instead of the two tribes Kamiakin had said he was able to represent, the treaty now identified him as chief of the fourteen nations that Stevens wanted to move onto the confederated reserve called the Yakima Reservation. This part of the treaty was never read aloud. Instead, Stevens told the Indians, "Shall it be read over in detail? You have already heard it not once but two or three times."[57]

But now Looking Glass spoke. "I am going to talk straight....I am not like those people [pointing about to other chiefs] who hang their heads and say nothing."[58] After hearing Young Chief protest that he had asked for more time and another meeting, Looking Glass continued. He pointed out the reservation he wanted on the map. It was the outline of the land the Indians, that is Kamiakin, Peo-peo-mox-mox, and himself, had agreed to in their long ago council creating a strategy to deal with the whites. Each tribe would claim their homeland, saying all the lands were used, and none was left over to sell.

The internal politics of the Nez Perce came into view. A supporter of Lawyer called out, "This is just putting it off further," but he was put down by another Nez Perce, Three Feathers: "Looking Glass is speaking, we look upon him as a chief."[59]

Tension rose anew. Both Palmer and Stevens tried to argue Looking Glass out of his position. The arguments went back and forth, with

Smithsonian Institution
Nez Perce chief, Looking Glass

Stevens appealing to those chiefs who had indicated their readiness to sign. Instead, they supported Looking Glass. Anger was evident. Palmer told Looking Glass, "We did not come here to talk like boys… The Nez Perces, the Walla Wallas, the Cayuses, and the Umatillas agree to the boundaries as we have marked. Do you wish to throw all we have said behind you. Shall we like boys say yes today and no tomorrow! Peo-peo-mox-mox, Young Chief, and the Nez Perces say yes! None of their people say no! Why do we talk so much about it. I have done."[60]

The Nez Perce were done for the day because Looking Glass needed more time. But Peo-peo-mox-mox signed the treaty for the Walla Walla.

As for Kamiakin, another controversy arose. Stevens recorded that Kamiakin signed the treaty. What is not recorded in the official minutes are remarks Stevens made, but noted by others present. According to Andrew Pambrun[61], one of the official translators, when Kamiakin started to show reluctance to sign, to support Looking Glass, Stevens turned to Kamiakin and said, "If you do not accept the terms offered and sign this paper, you will walk knee deep in blood."[62] Kamiakin signed last. "Kamiakin was the last and as he turned to take his seat the priest hunched [sic] me and whispered, look at Kamiakin, we will all get killed, he was in such a rage that he bit his lip till they bled profusely."[63] As presents were handed out to the chiefs, Kamiakin once more refused to accept gifts from the whites. According to one text, "Kamiakin apparently feared that accepting gifts for signing the treaty, even token ones, would make it more binding."[64]

That night, Stevens met with Lawyer, to finalize their plans for the Nez Perce. Stevens said that the council would recognize Lawyer as the chief of the Nez Perce, and accept his signature as binding on all of the tribe. From this meeting, Lawyer went to a council of Nez Perce, and through a stormy session prevailed in the tribal politics to ascend over Looking Glass.

The next day, the final day, Monday, June 11, the council reconvened for the Nez Perce signing. With Lawyer leading, all of the Nez Perce signed the treaty. Having eliminated the last of the Indian holdouts, Stevens then turned to the Cayuse, the original "malcontents," and they, too, signed the third treaty. The council was over.

Treaties

[1] Several of these would be controversial or problematic, the chief of which was Ben Wright. Ben Wright had earned a reputation being an Indian fighter against the Cayuse, and most particularly, the Modoc. His reputation included absolute racial hatred of the Indians.

[2] Schwartz, *The Rogue River Indian War and its Aftermath*, page 70.

[3] ibid.

[4] Berg, *The First Oregonians*, page 164.

[5] Eckrom, *Remembered Drums*, page 4.

[6] Richards, in *Isaac Stevens*, page 198.

[7] Ibid, page 5.

[8] The treaty also included a standard phrase that if the President later decided to remove the Indians to a different reservation, it was within his authority to do so.

[9] While Leschi was a Nisqually, he did have a grandmother who had been a Yakima, and this connection remained, allowing the Nisqually and Yakima to have cross-mountain relations.

[10] Carpenter, *The Nisqually*, page 170.

[11] Eckrom, page 12.

[12] Richards, page 202.

[13] Richards, page 204.

[14] Ibid.

[15] Seattle's speech is from Furtwangler, *Answering Chief Seattle*, pages 13-17.

[16] Richards, page 205.

[17] Ibid.

[18] Josephy, in *The Nez Perce*, page 314.

[19] Ibid.

[20] Richards, page 214.

[21] Josephy, page 315.

[22] Although Trafzer and Scheuerman, in their book, *Renegade Tribe, The Palouse Indians and the Invasion of the Inland Pacific Northwest*, write that three Palouse chiefs (Kahlotus, Slyotze, and Tilcoax) attended as non-signatory observers (page 49).

[23] O'Donnell, *An Arrow in the Earth*, page 199.

[24] Stevens, *Official Proceedings*, page 36

[25] Ibid, page 37.

[26] Josephy, page 318.

[27] Stevens, page 41.

[28] Ibid., page 50.

[29] Ibid.

[30] Ibid.

[31] Ibid, pages 51-52.

[32] Josephy states," Indians have never forgotten this false statement, typical of those which have been responsible for characterizing so many government officials in their eyes—even to this day—as men with 'forked tongues.'" Page 322.

[33] William Craig the Nez Perce translator, was married to a Nez Perce woman. Peo-peo-mox-mox is in effect accusing Craig and the Nez Perce of having a pre-arranged agreement with the whites.

[34] It should be recalled that Peo-peo-mox-mox was well traveled, and his son had accompanied John C. Fremont to California, only to be killed by a white, without legal recourse.

[35] Ibid, pages 55-57.

[36] Richards, pages 322-323.

[37] Stevens, page 59.

[38] Ibid, page 60.

[39] Ibid, pages 62-63.

[40] Ibid, page 64.

[41] Ibid, page 72.

[42] Ibid.

[43] Ibid, page 76.

[44] Ibid, page 77.

[45] Ibid, pages 77-78.

[46] Ibid, page 79.

[47] Ibid, pages 81-82.

[48] Ibid, pages 82-83.

[49] Ibid, page 84.

[50] Ibid, page 86.

[51] Ibid, page 87.

[52] Kip, *Army Life on the Pacific*, page 18.

[53] Stevens, pages 88-89.

[54] Ibid, page 93.

[55] Ibid.

[56] Josephy, page 328.

[57] Stevens, page 98.

[58] Ibid, page 99.

[59] Ibid, page 100.

[60] Ibid, page 104.

[61] Another interpreter, William Cameron McKay, wrote, "…when the Indians hesitated, the Governor said to tell the chief, "if they don't sign this treaty, they will walk in blood knee deep." …When he [Kamiakin] returned to his seat, his lips were covered with blood, having bitten them with suppressed rage. Father Chaurause [Chirouse], the Catholic Priest was standing by me at the time, and he drew my attention to the blood, remarking, I am afraid we will all be murdered before we leave these grounds." As quoted in Ruby and Brown, *The Cayuse Indians*, pages 203-204.

[62] Pambrun, in *Sixty Years on the Frontier in the Pacific Northwest*, page 95.

[63] Ibid.

[64] Ruby and Brown, *The Cayuse Indians*, page 203.

Chapter Five

The Summer of Discontent

T he treaties had been signed. One provision of those treaties was that the Indians would have time to move on to the reservation lands, that the whites would be kept out, and this was to remain so until the treaties had been ratified by the Senate. Joel Palmer had assured the Indians, "If we make a treaty with you . . . you can rely on all its provisions being carried out strictly."

Instead of keeping the whites out, Stevens and Palmer had published in regional newspapers that the lands east of the Cascades were open for white settlement. Only twelve days after the council adjourned, a jointly signed statement encouraged whites to move onto the lands currently held by the Indians, if outside the reservation boundaries. Within days, or at best weeks, whites moved east looking for land, looking for gold, and moving on Indian lands with little or no distinction made by the whites as to where future boundary lines might be drawn.

From Walla Walla, Stevens moved north, to the Spokane country and then east to Flathead and Blackfoot areas, to make similar treaties. Palmer set off for central Oregon to enact treaties with the Deschutes, Wascos, and Warm Springs tribes, among others. Despite Stevens' feeling of total satisfaction at gaining signed treaties, other voices within the white community were not sure a true victory had been won. "George Gibbs, a former secretary of Stevens, told a friend that the 'greatest single blunder' committed by the governor 'was in bringing together the Nez Perces, Walla Walla, Yakamas...and others into one council, and cramming a treaty down their throats in a hurry.'"[1]

The Indian signatories of Walla Walla had a range of feelings. Many Indians came away from that parlay feeling as if they had been forced to sign or to "walk knee deep in blood." "Even the Nez Perce…. had lost some of their pride and self-respect."[2] Worse, the Indians who had not been there, but who were included felt worse than coerced; they felt that their homes had been stolen from them. At the Catholic mission in the Yakima country, Fathers Pandosy and Joseph Brouillet met with the various tribes to explain what the treaty required. Here, tribes from the Canadian border to the Columbia River found out that Kamiakin had signed the treaty as their chief. Kamiakin protested that he had not agreed to be their chief, saying he had said he would sign for the Yakima and Palouse alone, but he was confronted with his mark on the treaty showing he had signed for a vast number of Indians outside of those two tribes. The tribes became angry.

The angriest were the Sinkiuse and their chiefs Quil-ten-e-nock and Que-tal-a-kin.[3] How could Kamiakin let himself be duped by the whites, they demanded? In response, the Sinkiuse said they would fight any white who tried to take their land. But even the Palouse, who had agreed to let Kamiakin sign for them, were now willing to fight.

Other voices were also calling for war. As noted by one of the translators at Walla Walla, Doctor William C. McKay, "I am familiar with the chiefs and head men of these tribes. They have frequently told me they were opposed to the treaty…they contended with earnestness the treaty was forced upon them by the commissioners."[4] Thus, Father Joseph Joset was able to report that he had heard the Indians "…agreed to make a mock treaty. In order to gain time and prepare for war."[5]

While cooperating with the whites, the Cayuse started to think of war. Five Crows, a signatory, protested to other Indians that the treaty was a bad thing, forced upon them. Other Indians counseled peace. The Yakima Te-i-as wanted to abide by the treaty, while his brother Owhi wanted to wait to see if the whites would live up to their agreements. Kamiakin, feeling betrayed by the whites and unjustly attacked by the other Indians for being a dupe, commenced to speak of war. When the whites started to be seen moving across the passes into the Indian lands east of the Cascades,[6] they told the Indians they met that the land was no longer Indian land. This seemed to be the last betrayal that Kamiakin could endure. The great chief of the Yakima once more sent runners to the various tribes, seeking counsel from them. Runners went from the Nisqually of Puget Sound to the great tribes farther east.

This sense of betrayal was felt everywhere. On Puget Sound, Leschi heard from Indians near Olympia that he had been identified as a troublemaker and was to be arrested and jailed, perhaps hanged. He traveled as far south as Albany, Oregon (visiting a relative to assist him in his protest against the whites), and there he heard of more Indian troubles, in the southern and western part of the Oregon territory.

Despite the treaties of 1854, the Rogue River Valley was not peaceful. In June 1855, two companies of volunteers,[7] seeking to avenge the death of a miner, hunted the Indians of the Illinois River. Hearing of the movement of volunteers, Indian agent George Ambrose warned the tribes to move to the Table Rock Reservation. Most were able to, but five men and a woman were killed.

More violence broke out in July. A white, angry over an Indian being drunk, shot the Indian, but failed to kill him. The Indian shot truer, killing the white. The white's friends killed two Indians, and that was followed by the Indians killing ten whites. The whites quickly claimed the guilty tribe as being Rogue River Indians and volunteers swiftly marched to Fort Lane and to the Table Rock Reservation where they knew they could find Rogue Indians, even if innocent of any crimes.

The volunteers accused Agent Ambrose and the Army under Captain Andrew Jackson Smith of harboring the guilty Indians. They demanded that seven Indians be turned over to them for "justice." If not, the volunteers proposed to ride in among the Indians and take the "guilty." In turn, Ambrose and Smith knew the Indians would defend themselves, and there would be open warfare again throughout the valley.

The army was seen as overly sympathetic to the Indians, and at times almost allied with the "savages." *The Oregonian* newspaper editorialized, "It is a fact well known throughout the country that the citizens generally accuse the government officers with sympathizing with the Indians in all their difficulties with the whites [September 15, 1855]."

George Crook, a soldier who fought along the Rogue River, described the problem as,

The trouble with the army was that the Indians would confide in us as friends, and we had to witness this unjust treatment of them without the power to help them. Then when they were pushed beyond endurance and would go on the war path we had to fight when our sympathies were with the Indians.[8]

Captain Smith tried to keep the situation calm. While refusing to let the volunteers trespass, he did place two suspects most likely to be among the guilty into irons, agreeing to turn them over to proper authorities,[9] but not to the volunteers to be murdered. One citizen decried this in a letter to a local paper, denouncing Smith as he had "utterly refused to accede to the reasonable request of an injured community" by giving up the guilty.[10] Tensions were high now not only between the whites and Indians, but between the white settlers and the Army.

Throughout the southwestern portion of the Oregon Territory, tensions remained high in the interior valleys. One of the most feared band of Indians was of the murdered Chief Tipsey. He had hated not merely the whites, but also his fellow Indians who had signed treaties with the whites. While Tipsey had died in 1854, his band continued to attack whites. Throughout August and September 1855, Tipsey's warriors pillaged the valleys of the Siskiyou and Cascade Mountains. On September 25, a wagon train of supplies for miners was attacked, with two whites killed. Another miner was killed on September 26, and word spread of Indians raiding the valleys. The Yreka volunteers rode north to revenge the attacks.[11] The commander of the troops was Major James Lupton (formerly with the U.S. Mounted Rifles Regiment, and had fought with the Oregon Rifles). Tensions increased on both sides. As *The Oregonian* newspaper saw it, the southern Oregon "...citizens...shall rise in their might and with their own hands inflict the punishment these 'red devils' so richly deserve [September 8, 1855]."

Joel Palmer arrived in this growing caldron of conflict intending to settle more treaties. He signed a treaty with Umpqua and Coos Indians on August 17, and with the Coquilles on August 23. Palmer's goal was to clear the coast of Indian land titles, as he had the interior valleys in 1854. But, as he met with Indians at the mouth of the Rogue River, in present-day Gold Beach, the Indians fled into the surrounding forests.

What had caused the Indians to flee was an incident which resulted in the death of five men. An Indian was arrested on suspicion of assaulting a white. The Indian agent, Ben Wright, believing that the local sheriff was untrustworthy, asked the army to provide an escort to the court trial. As the troopers did so, the aggrieved white man and his associates attacked the party. As the soldiers paddled their canoe down stream, the whites pulled alongside in another canoe, and opened fire. The soldiers quickly returned fire, and a naval battle then raged. In the ensuing gunfight, two Indians were killed, as were three whites. Such incidents confirmed a sense that the Indians were planning something and that the U.S. Army was untrustworthy.

Edward S. Curtis Collection, Library of Congress
Yakima mat lodge.

Nevertheless, Palmer persuaded the Indians to return to his council, and by September 8, he had completed his mission to clear Indian title to the coast. He had purchased not quite 5.9 million acres for a trifle. His costs of $90,000, over sixteen years, came to less than a penny and a half per acre.[12]

However, Palmer's peace problems did not perish. His agent in the valley, George Ambrose, reported more Indian problems, and wrote that if the Indians were not removed from Table Rock soon, "I fear they will plunge the whole country in a war...already the people talk of waging a war of extermination."[13] It seemed that the southwestern part of the territory was once more on the verge of total war.

But, this fear was not limited to the southwestern part of the Oregon Territory. It seemed everywhere there were rumors of impending wars. On the Puget Sound, a Hudson's Bay employee reported that he had seen the Nisqually, under Leschi, being drilled like soldiers.[14] Others reported the Indians were trying to buy more gunpowder and shot from the Hudson's Bay Company or any other source possible. The Nisqually chief was going from tribe to tribe, warning "...that the reservations were a clever prelude to complete annihilation."[15] Things were tense.

In the interior, war was ready to flare into a complete conflagration. One Catholic priest reported to his superiors, "the savages seem resolved to maintain the struggle to the death, convinced that the treaties of the government for the purchase of their lands are nothing but frauds."[16]

Other reports started to come in to authorities. George Gibbs, returning to Olympia, Washington reported great unrest among the Indians. Nathan Olney, the Oregon Indian agent at The Dalles, wrote to Major Haller at the fort in mid-September that he had word of a plan that the Yakima "and other Indians on the North side of the Columbia to commence a war on the Americans."[17] Word reached settlers that miner Henry Mattice had insulted[18] an Indian woman and had been killed by four Sinkiuse Indians. Then word of seven more slain miners felled by Yakimas (led by Qualchan, the son of Owhi), was received. These acts prompted Father Padnosy to hurry over the mountains to confer with Acting Governor Charles Mason.

Reaching Olympia by September 22, the good father reported that Kamiakin was urging the Indians to war. This report was seemingly supported by Andrew Bolon, Indian agent for the Yakima. Prior to heading to the Spokane area, he had met with the Yakima about the whites moving unharmed throughout the area. "Father Louis J. D'Herbomez wrote that Bolon was a man of 'little prudence and wisdom' and that many 'Indians hated him for the manner in which he treated the Indians.'"[19] He had told the Indians if they did not behave, he would have Army troops come to their country. The treaty the Yakima had signed promised no troops would enter their lands. If the Yakima had not been angry before, this threat of violation was another betrayal sure to fuel their discontent.

But, with the most recent death of miners, Indian Agent Bolon decided he had to confer with the Yakima again to learn what had occurred and to bring the guilty to justice. On September 20, Bolon left Fort Dalles on the Columbia River and headed north into Yakima country. Relying on his misplaced trust of a sound relationship with the Yakima, he traveled alone.

As he reached Toppenish Creek,[1] he encountered Shum-away (also known as Ice), a younger brother of Kamiakin. Telling Shum-away why he was going to see Kamiakin, Bolon was warned he should turn back as the young warriors were angry, that they would kill any whites who were found on their lands. Ignoring the warning, Bolon continued to the Catholic Mission.

Reaching it, he found that the chiefs had left. Staying only long enough to write a letter for Father Ricard asking him to make inquiries, Bolon mounted at three in the afternoon, and told Father Durieu he hoped to be back to The Dalles by late in the morning the next day.[20] He would make camp that night in the Simcoe Mountains.

The next day Bolon overtook a party of Indians whom he knew. The principle Indian of the group was Mo-sheel, son of Shum-away, and Bolon knew him from the time Mo-sheel had studied at a mission school in the Willamette Valley. They exchanged friendly greetings, with Bolon shaking each Indian's hand. But to his party, Mo-sheel said, "This is the man who hanged my uncles and cousins at Wallula."[21] He was referring to the Indians who had been hanged for the Ward Massacre.[22]

As the Indians argued amongst themselves, they rode together with Mo-sheel wanting revenge. As several argued to let Bolon travel in peace, Mo-sheel finally said, "I am going to kill him the same as he killed my poor people."[23]

At noon, the group stopped, made a fire, and tried to warm and dry themselves, in the cold drizzle of the mountains. Bolon, unsuspecting, unsaddled his horse, leaving his pistols still in their holsters on the saddle and walked away to stand near the fire. As Bolon extended his hands to warm them by the fire, the Indians continued to argue, trying to convince Mo-sheel that it was not a good thing to kill the white. But the hate flowed.

Coming up from behind, one Indian, Wah-pi-wah-pi-lah, grabbed Bolon behind the knees, and threw him to the ground. So-qiekt and Mo-sheel pounced on Bolon, who cried out in Chinook, "Do not kill me! I did not come to fight you!"[24]

Stak-kin, another of the party, grabbed Bolon's beard, turned his head while the others held him, and sliced his throat, letting the blood flow into a puddle on the ground. To cover up their crime, Bolon's horse was killed, and both bodies burned and then buried.

When Bolon failed to return to The Dalles, many became worried. Nathan Olney sent a Deschutes Indian to look for Bolon. Within a day, he returned with word that Bolon had been murdered. This crime could not go unavenged. Discontent had ignited into violence.

Chapter 5 notes

[1] Trafzer and Scheueman, *Renegade Tribe*, page 61.

[2] Josephy, in *The Nez Perce*, pages 333-334.

[3] Who later came to be known by the white name, Chief Moses.

[4] Ruby and Brown, *The Cayuse Indians*, page 205.

[5] Ibid, page 206.

[6] The July 5 issue of the *Puget Sound Courier* reported on a gold strike found near Colville, prompting a large wave of whites to head east, across the Cascade Mountains.

[7] Stimulating the volunteers was the fact that the federal paymaster was there to finally distribute back pay to the volunteers for their efforts during the hostilities of 1853. About $221,600 was distributed for either wages or supplies, at a time when drought was limiting the ability to earn wages outside of fighting Indians.

[8] Crook, in *General George Crook, his Autobiography*, page 16.

[9] Captain Smith did turn these two Indians over to civil authorities, who held them pending a grand jury ruling. When the grand jury ruled that there was no evidence of guilt for these two Indians, the sheriff released them, and the mob outside immediately seized them, hanging them.

[10] Schwartz, *The Rogue River Indian Wars and its Aftermath*, page 80.

[11] The mining operations had been halted with a severe drought that curtailed placer mining. One of the few ways to earn money was as a "volunteer," fighting Indians.

[12] Ibid, page 82.

[13] Ibid, page 83.

[14] Eckrom, *Remembered Drums*, page 20.

[15] Burns, in *The Jesuits and the Indian Wars of the Northwest*, page 125

[16] Ibid, page 124.

[17] Bischoff, in *The Yakima Indian War*, page 62.

[18] The common term used for rape.

[19] Trafzer and Scheueman, page 62.

[20] Ibid, page 64.

[21] McWhorter, in *Tragedy of the Whk-shum*, page 26.

[22] Mo-sheel's father was Yakima, his mother Palouse, and his wife was Klickitat. It is unclear as to which tribe's set of relatives were hanged as the killers of the Wards.

[23] Ibid, page 27.

[24] Ibid, page 28.

Chapter Six

The War Begins

To the Army, it did not seem as if the murmurs of discontent had changed into the alarms of war. Instead, what was called for was a show of force to suppress Indian activity, and to capture the guilty, not war. It was a police action, not total war.

Before the news of Bolon's death had reached population centers, newspapers such as *The Oregonian* were lighting the tinder for the flames of war. A September 22, 1855 editorial led with the headline of "More Indian Murders—Prospects of a General War," and then followed with, "The Isledeperies, Yakimas, and Palouses, it is supposed, have combined together for the purpose of preventing the whites from traveling through that country occupied by them. They repudiate the treaty recently made with Governor Stevens and are preparing for a general war."

Events progressed rapidly with Bolon's murder. Acting commander of the Eleventh Department, Major Gabriel Rains, ordered a two pronged response. He told Brevet Major Granville Haller, in command of Companies I and K of the Fourth U.S. Infantry at Fort Dalles (The Dalles, Oregon), to take a detachment north to investigate Bolon's murder and apprehend, if possible, those responsible. Rains then ordered Lieutenant William Slaughter to take other Fourth U.S. Infantry troops stationed at Fort Steilacoom (near present-day Tacoma, Washington) and march across the Cascade Mountains on the McClellan Military Road and enter the Yakima Valley from the northwest.

The plan was not to engage in outright war, but to impress the Indians with the Army's strength, and to arrest the men who murdered Bolon. In fact, the Army was afraid it might be difficult to find enough Indians, scattered as they were, to impress. The Army was always fearful the Indians would slip away into the wilderness, and did not even think of preparing for war.

At once, Army plans went awry. A friendly Tenino, Old Yice, was their scout. He rode to Fort Dalles with word that "many warriors were collected together in the Yakima Valley."[1] So frightened by the prospect, Old Yice refused to march with Haller's command as it entered that same valley. Haller would write later of the warning that Old Yice had foretold, "…it would be out of the power of the soldiers, with double their present force, to escape destruction, if they once encountered Kamiakin's warriors."[2] The two understrength companies of soldiers, tired from a summer of patrolling the Oregon Trail, marched out of Fort Dalles on September 30. As Major Haller 's force of eighty-six men entered the Yakima Valley, he used a standard movement formation "…with guards deployed in front, and rear, and on both flanks…"[3]

The troops moved north as hostile Indian scouts kept watch. As soon as the Army crossed the Columbia, a rider took off for the Indian village. The sentinel arrived at Kamiakin's camp by October 3, and the chief, recalling the promises made at Walla Walla, saw the Army's movement "…as the final betrayal of the Walla Walla treaties that the Indians had fearfully come to expect."[4] Couriers summoned reinforcements, signal fires were lit, and more scouts posted to keep the chiefs informed of the Army's progress.

The Indian versions of the events have Kamiakin moving forward to ask Haller to withdraw, but was fired on instead.[5] As the command neared the Toppenish Creek ford, nearly 500 Yakima and Klickitat Indians opened fire on October 6, 1855.[6] One historian wrote that Haller's troops triggered the battle by being anxious to try out their new Minie ball ammunition: "Appearing on a high point, a chiefly [Kamiakin?], gesticulating figure presented a fair target. The new rifle's custodian let fly and missed, sounding, said Haller, 'the tocsin of war…'"[7]

At first, the Indian's cries and gunfire rattled Haller's raw Michigan recruits. But, they soon rallied as Lieutenant Gracie (the same who had been at the Walla Walla council) pulled the mountain howitzers from the mules, and fired spherical case shot into the tree line, where the Indians had taken cover. Rushing forward to push Indians away from the ford and secure it, Sergeant James Roper became cut

Newspaper drawing depects Oregon Indians collecting their annual supplies at a government agency before going on the war path.

off, wounded twice, and forced to retreat from the ford. The Indians moved along the hills to get behind Haller's soldiers to attack his halted pack train. To stop that flanking attack, Captain Russell led his company in a charge, forcing about 200 Indians to fall back. This allowed the command to move to a more secure area near the stream as night fell.

Dawn broke and the Indians opened fire, hitting with (as Haller reported), "surprising accuracy." But, for the white warriors their new Minie bullets were experimental and because of an initial design flaw they quickly fouled the rifle grooves, making the guns useless. It was impossible to advance, so Haller prepared a message for the fort, which had been left in the command of Lieutenant Edward Day (Third U.S. Artillery), reporting his situation, and sent the letter with a messenger through Indians' lines on the command's swiftest horse. In the message was Haller's stated intention to retreat, but he did not express the need to be reinforced or rescued.

Captain Russell swung the cannon around the perimeter to repel Indian concentrations. With some muskets fouled beyond use, Sergeant Mulholland cleared one threat by ordering part of I Company to charge with him, using nothing but bayonets to move the Indians.

Throughout the day, Haller saw the numbers of Indian attackers swell. In addition to Yakima and Klickitat Indians, Cayuse Indians under Weatenatenamy and Five Crows were there, as were Walla Walla's led by Peo-peo-mox-mox.[8]

By the end of the second day, the command had suffered two dead, and thirteen wounded. With darkness, the command started its retreat, but within the darkness, the forty-man rearguard became lost, and now Haller's force was in two parts, wandering out of touch from each other. As the fighting retreat raged on, Major Haller ordered his howitzer spiked and buried. The command's sole Indian guide was able to elude the surrounding Indians, and rode off to request a relief column.

The third day found the Indians pushing hard against Haller, threatening to overrun him before help arrived. Haller, with Captain Russell and Sergeant Mulholland, again made a bayonet charge, which bought time, but at the lost life of the sergeant, who finally succumbed to his third and fatal wound. Needing mounts to carry the wounded, Haller stripped the mules of all supplies, loaded the wounded, and made another night march.

Haller was met by a relief column of forty-five men of the Third U.S. Artillery, under the command of Lieutenant Day, who had rode north when friendly Indians brought word of Haller's battle. Haller reported five infantry men killed and seventeen wounded, a casualty rate of about twenty-six percent.

Lieutenant Slaughter's unit of fifty men had made it to the Natches Pass when word reached him of Haller's defeat. Fortunately, one of Slaughter's scouts had married Yakima chief, Te-i-as' niece, and as this scout named Edgar crossed the pass, he met Te-i-as. The Indian told of Haller's defeat, and that Kamiakin was now headed toward the pass to wipe out the soldiers there.[9] Prudently, Slaughter retired to Fort Steilacoom to await further orders.

In praise of the enemy, Haller wrote:

> In regard to the enemy before us, it is due them to say that they fought with a courage far beyond my expectations and continued their efforts without intermission for such a protracted period as to suggest unpleasant ideas.[10]

Nothing succeeds like success, and news of Kamiakin's defeat of Haller brought many new Indian allies. Major Rains, fearing a widespread uprising, asked the two territorial governors to summon militia for federal service. Rains requested four companies from Oregon and two from Washington. *The Oregonian* newspaper, reporting Bolon's death by September 29, helped to fuel the fire. It reported, first the headline:

Startling News—More Indian Depredations
Mr. Bolon, Indian Agent, Killed

The headline's story reported that, "The Indian Agent Mr. Olney sent out, reports that seventeen whites had been murdered by these Indians, and that the reason they killed Bolon was, that hereafter they should kill friends and foe alike, that they regard all whites their foes. That the design was to attack the whole lower country first, and that a war of extermination had been decided upon."

Washington's Acting-Governor Mason[11] placed the first two militia companies raised under federal authority and asked for additional volunteers to protect the Puget Sound settlements. Mason also called on the United States Revenue Cutter (the forerunner of the modern Coast Guard) *Jefferson Davis* for munitions and for protection against water-borne Indian raids. The citizens of Puget Sound were treated to the growing concern from the local papers. The *Pioneer and Democrat* reported the following on October 12:

The Indians—East and West

Bolon…murdered….When Indians so far forget their friendly relationship or their treaty stipulations with our people and government, as to kill the agents sent amongst them to protect their rights or punish their offenses, there is left with our civil and military authorities but one only alternative—the extreme measure…..Instead of individual members of the bands being responsible for the recent outrages committed, the evidence is ample that the tribes *entire* are to be held accountable…..Chastisement can now justly be visited on the *tribes*…The inhabitants along the Willamette and Columbia rivers appear to be in a state of considerable alarm….

Oregon's Governor Curry exceeded the army's request, calling up eight militia companies. Within the month, he would call out an additional nine companies. He placed the Oregon Mounted Volunteers Regiment under the command of Colonel James Nesmith who had served with the Oregon Rifles during the Cayuse Indian War, and with General Lane in southern Oregon in 1853. It is worth noting that Governor Curry refused to place the Oregon militia under federal command. Not only were the federal troops seen as inept, they were perceived by the settlers as lacking the élan to close with the enemy. Nesmith assembled his men and marched to Fort Dalles.

Governor Curry's orders to Colonel Nesmith included cooperation with Major Rain's forces in the field, but went beyond that, to independently seek out the enemy. The Yakima were thought to be calling for their allies, particularly the tribes at the Walla Walla council to support them in war against the whites. Cayuse chiefs such as Wiecat and Umhowlish were reportedly raising warriors to attack whites.[12] Andrew Pambrun sent word of the warning given him by the Cayuse chief Weatenatenamy that something was about to happen, but did not know of the outbreak of war until Nathan Olney, the Indian agent at The Dalles, arrived at the Hudson's Bay Company fort near the Wallula bend of the Columbia to assess the situation there.[13] What Olney found led him to believe that the Indians in that area (mostly Cayuse, Walla Walla, and Umatilla) were ready to join against the whites. When he tried to visit Peo-peo-mox-mox's camp, he was refused, but found the Walla Walla warriors dancing a scalp dance, displaying in triumph what were reported to be American scalps.[14] In addition to reporting that to Army command, he sent letters to the white settlers in the Walla Walla and Umatilla valleys. His October 12 letter summed up the situation:

> I am of the opinion that the Indians in this vicinity are about to join in the war commenced upon the whites on the north side of the Columbia by the Yakimas and others. In view of such an event, I have written to the commanding officer at The Dalles for a military force to escort you out of the country.[15]

The U.S. Army, busy raising additional troop strength to go after the Yakima, did not have resources to protect those in the Walla Walla Valley. Thus, with reports such as Olney's and Pambrun's, Governor

Curry's orders to Colonel Nesmith included sending troops to that area to assist settlers and deter hostile Indians.

War elsewhere—The South

On the southern front of what was now a regional war, the first battle was fought two days after the start of Major Haller's defeat. Settlers heard rumors that hostile Indians of the late Tipsey's band were camped on the banks of Butte Creek and were planning to raid the valley. On October 7 a meeting held in a church quickly turned into a hate-filled recitation of Indian "crimes." The only dissenting voice was that of John Beeson. He wrote, "As there was a Methodist Quarterly Meeting to assemble…I hoped there would be heard in that religious assembly some expression of brotherly kindness, and charity for the poor doomed outcast…I arose and spoke with all the feeling, and all the power I had, in the behalf of the poor Indians."[16] His words fell on ears deafened by racial hatred.

A quickly mustered company of Oregon Volunteers, under the direction of Major James A. Lupton, proceeded from Jacksonville to the Indian camp. As the morning of October 8 dawned, volunteers quietly surrounded two camps, and opened fire. Twenty-three Indians were killed (more possibly, as many wounded were carried off with the escaping Indians), but upon entry into the camp, they discovered that most of those they had killed were old men, women, and children. As one pioneer chronicler (and quartermaster for the volunteers), Charles S. Drew, wrote, "The attack was commenced while it was yet too dark to distinguish one Indian from another, and by this reason it so happened that several squaws and children were killed. None were killed after it became light enough to distinguish the sexes."[17] In the fighting, an arrow struck Major Lupton killing him and his promising political career as the representative of Jackson County in the Oregon Territorial Legislature. The second company's attack was less bloody, killing one woman and two boys. One of the shooters expressed the regret of many that so few Indians had been killed.

However, this was not Tipsey's band. Two villages had been attacked: Chief Sambo's and Chief Jake's. These bands were, in theory, under the protection of the Indian agent, George Ambrose. His report on the attack noted the Indian men, fearing the whites, had fled to the Table Rock Reservation on October 7, so as not to provoke an attack on their villages. What were left were women, children, and old men. Ambrose saw some bodies floating down the river, but "Of the twenty-three dead bodies he counted, fifteen were women and children, and four were old men."[18] When news of the massacre reached Table Rock, the warriors of those two villages, plus many others, streamed off the reservation and joined non-treaty Indians in what they now viewed as a fight for their lives. It was not as if the Indians had not thought or prepared for white attack. According to Captain Smith, "A large majority of the Indians are well armed with good rifles, of different descriptions…"[19] With the reservation being vacated, Indian agent Ambrose failed to see the real reason (self-defense) and instead, blamed the Indians. He wrote, "No longer any doubt exists but that this must be a war of extermination against all the chiefs and leaders of these hostile bands."[20]

Lupton's attack drove Indians throughout the valleys of southern Oregon to arms. Indian raiding parties revenged the Lupton Massacre and by October 9, had killed sixteen white men, women, and children in isolated settlements. One farm was occupied by Jacob Wagner, his wife, daughter, and a visiting temperance lecturer, Miss Sarah Pellet. With no knowledge of the events, they were totally surprised by the Indians. Miss Pellet escaped with the news of the attack, while the others were found in the ashes of the burnt cabin when a relief column arrived and fought an Indian rearguard.

The press reported the situation in the south as part of a planned, coordinated Indian uprising. *The Oregonian* newspaper reported the killings on October 20 with the headline:

Great Indian Fight at the south!—Over 100 Indians Killed—Escape of Miss Pellet.

And then gave its editorial point of view:

There can no longer be a shadow of a doubt in the mind of a single individual throughout the length and breadth of Oregon but that we are now in the midst of an Indian war. The fact that all of the Indian tribes, north, south, east, and west, have combined together in a war of extermination against the whites is well settled. They have already, by concert of action, commenced burning the dwellings of our citizens, murdering our women and children indiscriminately, shooting every man or small body of men they can find, stealing and driving off the stock of the inhabitants wherever they can find it, and doing every other act of violence that blood-thirsty, cruel, and inhuman barbarians could do. Many of these tribes have long been engaged in this mode of warfare, but now all the tribes who can number a respectable force have engaged to exterminate the whites from the country west of the Rocky Mountains. *War!* Aye, a War of *extermination* has been declared by the combined Indian Tribes against the whites on the Pacific slope!

More Indian attacks were reported. The George Harris farmstead suffered. When the Indians attacked he tried to fight back, but was gunned down. His eleven year-old daughter, Sophie, was shot through the arm, but Mrs. Harris was able to load and fire a pair of pistols, keeping the Indians from breeching the cabin door, but she watched her husband die and the rest of the farm burn. Their hired hands, Frank Reed and David Harris (unrelated) were gunned down in the fields while working.

Many farms were ravaged. The Haines farm had four killed, Isaac Shelton and a man named Hamilton died at a ferry crossing, and four teamsters were gunned down while their mules were carried off, still with the apple saplings tied to the pack frames.[21]

In the north, the *Pioneer and Democrat* newspaper kept readers informed about the violence to the south:

Rogue River War

From Rogue River, the news is truly startling. Report says that some 20 or 30 families have been murdered and dwellings burned....It appears that the miners and settlers have turned out to a man, almost, and have commenced a war upon the merciless and troublesome Indians in earnest—killing every Indian that fell in their way—man, woman, or child.

It is impossible to tell, at present, how many whites have been killed. The citizens had already killed one hundred and six Indians—sparing neither age nor sex.

With only three units of regular Army in southern Oregon for protection,[22] Governor Curry[23] called for nine more companies of militia to be formed into two additional regiments. The governor charged them to stop the Indians "menacing the southern settlements with all the atrocities of savage warfare."[24] By October 20, fifteen companies had been recruited (Colonel John Ross, commanding) for the unit now called the Ninth Regiment of Oregon Militia, but arms and ammunition were very scarce. Oregon's governor requested supplies from the Army, but the Army refused to supply or support the state unless its militia was placed under federal command. This hampered the Oregon companies from quickly taking the field, and created local hostility toward the federal government and the U.S. Army. Nevertheless, cooperation between militia and federal troops was common once in the field.

Action came faster in the south, as the white population was greater and the threat more immediate. On October 16, militia (Company E) under the command of Captain William B. Lewis arrived at the mining camp of Galice Creek, with Indian women and children hostages, and awoke the next day to find themselves surrounded by Indians. The troops took cover in the Chinese miners' cabins as the Indians launched burning arrows into the camp, lighting a house on fire. After a twenty-four hour battle, the larger Indian force retired, leaving four militiamen killed and eleven wounded.[25]

Meanwhile, Lieutenant August Kautz of the Regular Army had a party of soldiers who were finally establishing a route through the Coast Mountains to connect Fort Orford with the main valley trail. When the command neared a junction with the Oregon-California Trail on October 24, they were surprised by the Rogue Indians. Lieutenant Kautz was seemingly struck down by an Indian bullet. Seeing their commander fall, the troops panicked. However, the bullet had lodged itself in a small book inside his coat. Kautz got to his feet and ordered a counterattack. Repelling the Indians, the party reached Fort Lane with two dead. With his retreat, Kautz brought news to the fort of his inadvertent discovery of the Indian gathering place. He had stumbled on the main concentration of Rogue Indians.[26]

Fights broke out as the volunteers hunted for any Indians to kill. On October 25, a company of volunteers found a peaceful village of Indians along the Umpqua River in the area known as Looking Glass Prairie. Among the volunteers was Indian agent George Ambrose, who described the villagers as being about thirty in number, "who were friendly disposed." Ambrose described the volunteers' onslaught as "follow up their plan of extermination." In the attack on the tranquil village, four men and a woman were killed before the Indians could escape into the surrounding trees. Ambrose's conclusion was "I have not been able to learn that these Indians were charged with any crime."[27] The pressures of war continued in the southern part of the territory.

Puget Sound

But, southern Oregon and the Yakima Valley were not the only theaters of war. Puget Sound found October to be significant, too. It started with the Nisqually Indian agent, James McAllister being visited by Chief Leschi. The two had been friends for some time, so it was not surprising that in early October the chief stopped by the Indian agent's farm. What was alarming was Leschi's warning to McAllister: He planned to fight the whites and if McAllister joined in the fighting, Leschi would kill him, too.

As a result of this meeting, McAllister wrote to Acting Governor Mason on October 16 that he had "…information and are satisfied that Leschi, sub-chief and half Clikitat [sic] is and has been doing all he could possibly do to unite the Indians of the country to rise against the whites."[28]

No white could have envisioned a more dramatic move than when on October 22, Leschi walked into the governor's office. Leschi told the governor that war might be coming and the governor believed he had persuaded Leschi to come into town and surrender to the protection of territorial forces. When after two days of waiting, Leschi had not surrendered, Governor Mason ordered Captain Charles Eaton and his rangers to find and escort Leschi into custody.[29]

The nineteen man patrol accompanied by the "embedded" press (the *Pioneer and Democrat* newspaper editor, James Wiley) rode east into the foothills of the Cascades. One of the lieutenants for the Rangers was James McAllister. As the rangers reached Leschi's farm, they found it had been abandoned in a hurry as the plow stood mid-furrow. The troops confiscated fifteen horses to re-mount themselves.

On October 25, the rangers crossed the Puyallup River and started to move east along the McClellan Military Road. After three days of fruitless searching, the command reached the summit of Elhi Hill and looked down onto what was called Connell's Prairie, named for

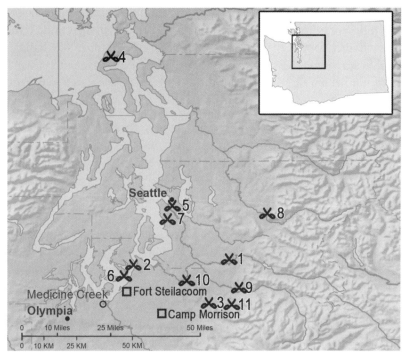

Puget Sound Front
1855-1856

1. Green River	November 4, 1855	
2. Tacoma Narrows	November, 1855 (Traveller)	
3. Slaughter's Death	December 5, 1855	
4. Whidbey Island	January 19, 1856	
5. Seattle	January 26, 1856	
6. Fox Island	January, 1856	
7. Dumwamish River	February 23, 1856	
8. Snoqualmie Falls	February, 1856	
9. White River	March 1, 1856	
10. Connell's Prairie	March 7, 1856	
11. Carbon River	March 21, 1856	

Michael Connell, the settler who farmed there and who was also one of the rangers. From this strategic point, Eaton established a camp and sent eight of his troops back to Olympia for supplies and reinforcements.

While they awaited the return of the detachment sent to Olympia, word was received that the Indians for whom they were searching were located about three miles away along the White River. Eaton sent out a scouting party of four: McAllister, Connell, and two friendly Indians (including Stahi, a relative of Leschi who had agreed to act as a scout for Eaton). Eaton, meanwhile, was checking on a portion of the military road nearby that would require repairs if wagons were to use it for re-supply.

As Eaton, with the newspaper editor Wiley riding with him, moved along the road they heard a musket shot followed by another and then by several more. Crying, "My God! Our boys are gone!"[30] he and Wiley spurred their horses back to the crest of the hill.

As he rode back into his camp, he ordered, "Boys, saddle up your horses, get your baggage in readiness, and above all things, keep cool."[31] The troops moved to a nearby Indian longhouse, and made that into a redoubt. Inside were Indian food supplies, and with water, the whites were ready to withstand a siege. They prepared a clear field of fire, and waited.

They did not wait long. One of the two Indians in the scouting party ran into the clearing with word Stahi had switched sides, joining Leschi. McAllister was reported killed in the opening musket fire of the ambush and Connell was said to be wounded, but able to ride off to cover. He did not ride far, but fell dead of his wounds. On October 27, the opening battle in the new theater was over and now war had spread to Puget Sound.

The Indian version of the opening battle has Leschi ordering the ambush, with a particular order to kill McAllister, the man he had warned not to carry arms against the Indians. The Nisqually warrior Tooapyti aimed at McAllister, killing him with a single shot and knocking him from his saddle.[32]

As night gathered the area into gloom, so did the whites' mood as the Nisqually's attacked. The Indians started to infiltrate into the trees surrounding the Eaton Rangers' defensive position. One ranger, Andrew Laws, recalled his first sight of his enemy:

> They were painted up fine and wore something that reached from their waists to about halfway between their hips and knees, but otherwise were naked. Their faces and breast and legs had a great deal of red paint. They had black hair that was pretty

long and combed straight down. The three that stepped out of the brush were big fellows.[33]

Laws opened fire, killing one of the three. Returning fire, the Indians shot from all parts of the woods, clearly having the longhouse surrounded. One spent musket ball ricocheted and hit Private Edward Wallace. While the force was sufficient to cause the bullet to penetrate the skull, it did no other damage, leaving Wallace a life-long souvenir.

Near dawn on October 28, George McAllister, the slain lieutenant's son, volunteered to get help and rode to Fort Steilacoom for a relief column. With dawn and no sign of Indians, Eaton moved toward his rescue, and the remaining rangers retreated without incident.

But the end of Eaton's battle was not the only incident of October 28. As the Indians moved away from Eaton's soldiers, they rode through the White River Valley. Reaching the King farm about breakfast time, the Indians happened upon Mrs. King and her three children eating (Mr. King was bed-ridden with pleurisy). As she opened her front door to the sound of someone arriving, she was confronted by red-painted Indians, one of whom pointed his musket at her. Slamming the door, she pushed the children to the floor, grabbed her husband's revolver, and started firing out a window. Outside were more than a dozen Indians.

Once she had emptied her pistol, the Kings were defenseless. The Indians entered the cabin, and removed the children to the woods. In the confusion, the three children, led by seven year-old Johnny, wandered off further into the woods, and once things quieted, they moved back toward their home.

There, they found their cabin burning, and their mother dying, laying in the mud in front of the home. Speaking with almost her dying words, the mother told the children to run to a neighbor's cabin. They found it deserted. Unable to reach the distant settlement, they would have perished except for the kindness of two Indians who had not joined the warpath. The two took the children to Seattle, leaving them with a white family.

In Seattle, the King children added their tale to refugees who had fled the rampaging Indians. Other settlers were wounded and still others missing. The whole event was now being referred to as the White River Massacre.

While real news was scarce, rumors sufficed. *The Oregonian* would report of the Puget Sound front:

Latest news from Puget Sound
SEVERE BATTLE WITH THE INDIANS
Several Whites Killed

"…The people were leaving the back settlements along the Sound for places of safety. Many had taken shelter in the military barracks at Steilacoom. Olympia was being fortified, and the citizens were flocking there for safety."

Displaying the confusion from which this type of warfare suffers, a patrol of six soldiers was near Connell's Prairie on October 31, when they met a band of friendly Indians. Greetings were exchanged and items traded, allowing the Indians to move on. As the patrol continued, it rode off the prairie and into the woods. Another ambush was sprung by different Indians, killing one white, and mortally wounding another. The party spurred their horses and rode for succor.

They galloped into another band of hostile Indians. Only four whites were still alive, but they closed with the Indians, using pistol and knives to overcome the Indian attack. With another of their party gone, the three avoided all other hostile contact until they reached safety.

Meanwhile, a relief column had been dispatched on October 29 to retrieve settlers. Captain Christopher Hewitt marched with a company of forty volunteers and four Indian scouts, to bring the settlers in from the outlying farmsteads.

By October 31, the Hewitt command had reached the King farm, where they buried Mrs. King. They found the King's hired hand, a man named Cooper, about 150 yards away, dead with a bullet in his chest. At the next farm they reported finding Mrs. Brannon and her infant dead at the bottom of the well. William Brannon had died quickly from wounds he had sustained in the fight.

They reached another family farm belonging to a King family, unrelated to the other Kings. They found a grisly scene, with the Kings dead and their bodies partially eaten by animals. The son, George, was not found, but was reported to have been taken hostage.[34]

The *Puget Sound Courier* newspaper filled townsfolk in on the tragedies of the war:

Outbreak of the Indians west of the Cascades —Murders Committed

....On Monday last, a dispatch was received from Capt. Sterritt of the Decater, stating that the Indians had committed several outrages on the settlers living on the Deawamish River, and that Capt Hewitt had proceeded to the field with fifty-five men.

The specter of widespread war kept regional newspapers full with tales of the seemingly endless Indian carnage. How could any citizen not demand protection from the authorities with news so bloodcurdling? *The Oregonian*, in Portland, reported of Puget Sound:

Latest from Puget Sound

"...down the sound the Indians were laying the country waste, murdering men, women, and children, and burning the houses, barns, etc. On the Puyallup River, near Seattle, several had been killed—among them were H.H. Jones and wife, G. King, wife and two children, W. H. Baunan and wife, Mr. Cooper and others. One woman was said to have killed with her own hand three Indians before she was killed."

November was relatively quiet along the shores of Puget Sound. One combined command of fifty men moved out from Fort Steilacoom on November 3 to search for hostiles. Lieutenant William Slaughter, regular Army, joined with Captain Gilmore Hayes, Washington Volunteers to search for Indians. Marching up the White River Valley and crossing to the Green River, the command had not seen any Indians, but felt they were nearby. On the morning of November 4, a tree was felled to use as a bridge across the Green River, a rifle shot roared out and an axe-man fell dead. Here the river kept the two sides from closing with each other, instead each side kept up rifle fire, as well as warming campfires, across the swollen river as the rain fell. Two more whites were wounded. Captain Hayes, deferring to the regular army officer's experience, let Lieutenant Slaughter take overall command of the battle. Hayes would note, "Lieutenant Slaughter deserves credit for his deliberation and his remarkable efficiency."[35]

Unable to get to the Indians across the river, Slaughter waited for reinforcements. Captain William Wallace arrived the next day with another volunteer company. With no Indian gunfire coming from the far bank, the soldiers moved across the bridge. Slick with moss and rain, some troopers fell in, while others lost their rifles.

Moving up the valley, Slaughter spread his force as an extended skirmish line, with a squad protecting each flank. However, all they found was an Indian sniper's occasional rifle shot. When they made camp that night, the soldiers were wet, tired, hungry, and frustrated. One soldier climbed a tree and starting yelling in Chinook to the Indians he knew were there, but could not see. The Indians yelled back their desire to drive the whites from their land.

On November 6, the whites pushed on to Carbon Creek, running high by all the rain and once more attempted to cross the rushing water. To the volunteers, this made being a soldier so much less fun than they thought it would be when they volunteered. As the whites started across, the Indians opened fire. One Indian hit Private John Edgar[36] in the lung, but the bullet kept going and hit Addisom Parham. Finally, knowing where the enemy was, Slaughter ordered some men to hold them while demonstrating as if they were crossing the creek. Then, he ordered two wings of nearly fifty men each to try and trap the Indians in an envelopment. Instead, as the soldiers broke through the brush, they were met with rifle and shotgun fire, resulting in more wounded, but no trapped Indians.

Weary and frustrated, the command limped on home. Meanwhile, other official efforts were spent in either mustering in volunteers and training them, or in unsuccessful sweeps to find hostile forces. One company of volunteers under Captain John Carson moved up the Puyallup River for a six-day patrol, returning to Olympia on November 14 without firing a shot. Their sole contribution was the destruction of one canoe, the capture of one horse, and the discovery of a dried salmon cache.

However, the most dramatic event of November did not occur on land. The steamer *Traveler* was headed south through the waterway known as the Tacoma Narrows. With strong currents as the tide reached maximum influence, it was best to traverse the area at slack water. Because of the depth of the water when slack water occurred at night, Captain J. J. G. Parker felt comfortable ordering up steam. As the vessel chugged along, Captain Parker saw some logs ahead and prudently ordered a slight change in course to avoid them, but strangely, the logs moved with his course change.

Suddenly the logs moved toward the steamboat and two canoes full of Indians came alongside. Boarders were attacking his boat. With good fortune, the *Traveler* had a dozen Army infantrymen on deck and they began shooting. Rifle fire dropped some, while others were hit with bayonets and axes. Easily repulsed, the Indians clambered back into the canoes. The next day found the decks stained with blood, and four fingers left from one Indian's grab at a railing guarded by a crewman with an axe.[37]

Now the entire Puget Sound area appeared to be the next target for Indian attack. Seattle was turned into an armed camp. As one resident, the wife of a local minister wrote, "I can assure you that our little town has something of a martial appearance. Twice a day the Co. of volunteers assembles at the fort…and answers to roll call and go through their drill. Then almost every man carries his gun."[38] Blockhouses were quickly erected, and supplies sought. Cannon from the Revenue Cutter *Jefferson Davis* reinforced one fort, and supplies from the Hudson's Bay depot at Victoria brought the steamer *Beaver* laden with ammunition, rifles, and money to support the Americans in their time of need. Reinforcements disembarked November 21 when the *California* berthed. One company of the Third U.S. Artillery, Captain Erasmus Darwin Keyes commanding, arrived from San Francisco. It would be a long winter.

As the war started in the north, other areas suffered from continued fighting.

War in the South

Fort Lane quickly became the center of military activity in southern Oregon. By the end of October, 300 militia had arrived to augment the ninety troopers of the First U.S. Dragoons, under the command of Captain Andrew Jackson Smith. Among his command was Lieutenant George Crook, who was to gain his greatest fame as an Indian fighter after the Civil War.

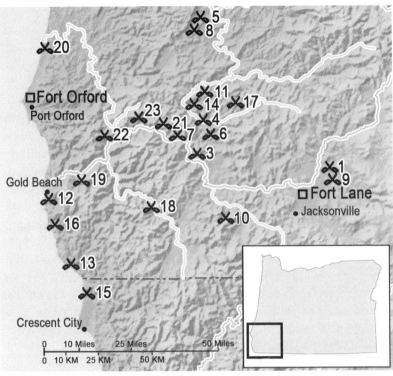

Southern Front
1855-1856

1.	Lupton's Massacre	October 7, 1855
2.	Table Rock	October 8, 1855
3.	Galice	October 16, 1855
4.	Kautz's fight	October 24, 1855
5.	Looking Glass Prairie	October 25, 1855
6.	Hungry Hill	October 31-November 1, 1855
7.	Battle Bar	November 26, 1855
8.	Olalla	December 5, 1855
9.	Butte Creek	December 24, 1855
10.	Applegate Valley	January 5, 1856
11.	Cow Creek	January 23, 1856
12.	Gold Beach	February 23 to March 21, 1856
13.	Chetco River	February 23, 1856
14.	Cow Creek	March 14, 1856
15.	Tolowa	March 14, 1856
16.	Pistol River	March 18, 1856
17.	Labon's Battle	March 23, 1856

18.	Illinois Valley	March 25, 1856
19.	Skookum House Prairie	March 26, 1856
20.	Coquille River	April 1, 1856
21.	Big Meadow	April 27, 1856
22.	Big Bend	May 27-28, 1856
23.	Augur's attack	June 2, 1856

After more volunteers arrived, it was decided to attack the main camp of the Indians who, after Lieutenant Kautz's discovery, were known to be concentrating at Grave Creek. The plan was to split the white force into three divisions and attack the camp from the front and rear simultaneously. One of the repeated criticisms made by pioneer militia of army troops was that they did not know how to fight Indians. This battle reinforced the civilian conviction that the regulars were weak Indian fighters.[39] October 31 was a cold, fall day. As Captain Smith's force arrived early at the rear of the Indians' camp, they grew cold. To take the chill off, Smith had fires lit. Thus, the command forfeited any chance for surprise and spurred the Indians to evacuate their camp and prepare for combat. The first salvo of the battle came from about four miles north. The Indians, seeing Captain Smith's fires, had retreated to what became known as Hungry Hill. It was a hill with a bald top, making an ideal defensive position for the Indians.

The volunteers advanced at around ten in the morning. Captain T. S. Harris ordered his men to attack and cover the movement of Colonel Ross' force and the supposed movement of Captain Smith's dragoons. Harris' men dropped their packs and ran toward the top of the hill, firing their weapons. But, as they slowed in their uphill charge, they made targets for the Indian rifles and arrows, which finally stopped them in their tracks. One of the attackers, Luther Hawley, described the charge as being led by the "fleetest on foot." But, as they neared the Indians, "they poured a deadly fire into our ranks."[40] The whites retreated.

With Ross' arrival, Captain Smith finally ordered his dragoons forward. Ross and Smith's forces united in a frontal assault on the ridge top. After taking heavy casualties, they cleared the ridge. Pursuing the Indians into the valley on the far side, the troops entered thick woods only to be pinned down by heavy fire. Every advance was repulsed with the wounded left to their own salvation. Thirsty, the wounded crawled to the valley floor seeking water, thus giving the canyon the name of Bloody Springs, for the number of wounded trapped. All that night the white troops were trapped. The next morning, All Saints' Day, the Indians attacked. More losses were taken. As Hawley recalled, the Indians "surrounded our camp and made a general charge upon us, which was repelled in a manner which does credit to the officers and men under their command."[41] Dragoon Lieutenant Horatio Gibson was shot in the leg, one of the twenty-six wounded in the fight. When the Indians retired, twelve white troops were dead or dying. The soldiers left the field to the Indians. This was the third battle of the war in the south since Lupton's surprise attack, and all three had been Indian victories.

Library of Congress

George Crook, a lieutenant during the 1850s, went on to become one of the Army's best Indian Fighters after the Civil War.

The defeat prompted a call for more troops. Regular Army reinforcements arrived at Six Bits House (now called Wolf Creek Tavern, an Oregon State Park). Among these troops was George Crook, who described the situation thusly:

> It seemed that the day previous to our arrival here, Capt. A. J. Smith, 1st Dragoons, in command of Regulars and Volunteers, had had a fight with the Indians some miles southwest of where we were, and if the troops did not get the worst of it, it was a drawn battle, and the troops withdrew to the settlements, and left the Indians monarchs of the woods, and no one knew where they were liable to attack next.[42]

November 26, 1855, saw a battle in the south with yet another Indian victory. Three hundred and eighty volunteers (Major James Bruce, commanding) and fifty regular U.S. Army troops (under the command of Captain Henry Judah) attempted to capture 200 Indians at Black Bar, on the Rogue River. Mountain snow a foot deep slowed the troops, giving warning to any Indians who were in the area. The troops failed in their objective when they were unable to cross the river under intense Indian fire. The plan had the two forces divide to catch the Indian village in between. Hauling cumbersome howitzers, the regulars were delayed in their advance on the north side of the river. Finding the Indians on the other side of the river, the volunteers started to chop down trees to build rafts. However, the sound alerted the unsuspecting Indians. Catching the troops exposed on the opposite, south shore, about to launch their rafts, the Indians opened fire. After six hours, the expedition retreated a short distance with one dead and four wounded. For three days, the two sides kept the other from advancing in a snowy standoff. Finally, the whites, cold and hungry, retreated. As one participant wrote, "Major Martin and Major Bruce seeing that we were in danger of being bound in here by snow deeming it unwise to remain here longer, ordered their forces to march back for the settlements."[43] Once again, the Indians had repulsed a white force, this time twice their size.

War in the East

At The Dalles, Oregon, Major Rains was gathering his force of regulars and volunteers to march into the Yakima country to avenge Haller's defeat. In addition to those Washington Territory volunteers under his direct command, the First Regiment of Oregon Mounted Volunteers (First Oregon) was mustering, to act as an independent force, under Colonel Nesmith.

Rains was preparing to march when he met with Nesmith. He wanted to place the Oregon volunteers into federal service, and thus, under his command. To do so, he refused to supply the Oregon troops with supplies from the federal depot at Fort Dalles. Nesmith was under orders from the governor not to allow his troops to be placed under federal command. He refused Rains' ultimatum. One result was the delay in the First Oregon taking the field for want of supplies and equipment. Another consequence was that the ranking officer at The Dalles was Nesmith. That was unacceptable to Major Rains. Contacting Acting Governor Mason to change his role, he requested a higher rank in the Washington Volunteers.

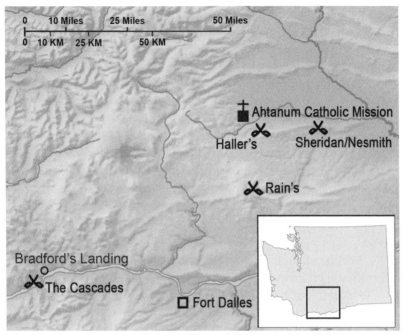

Eastern (Central) Front
1855-1856

1. Haller'd defeat	October 6-8. 1855
2. Rain	November 8, 1855
3. Sheridan/Nesmith	November 8, 1855
4. The Cascades	March 26-28, 1856

On October 30, Major Rains, now a brigadier general in the Washington Volunteers (appointed by Acting-Governor Mason) marched north from Fort Dalles with a force scrapped together from every nearby post. This group included parts of Companies G, H, I, and K of the Fourth Infantry, Companies B, L, and M of the Third Artillery, and a detachment of First Dragoons under the command of Lieutenant Phillip Sheridan (who gained fame during the Civil War). In addition to the 200 regulars, two companies of Washington Territorial Volunteers accompanied Rains in federal service, bringing Rains' total strength to 350 men. Lastly, to act as a blocking force, Rains ordered two companies of infantry, under Captain Maurice Maloney, and one company of volunteers under Captain Gilmore Hayes, to march from Fort Steilacoom east, over the Naches Pass.[44]

Acting as an independent command, Colonel Nesmith marched north on November 1, with five companies (C, D, E, F, and G) of Oregon militia, representing another 450 troops invading the Yakima Valley. While not in coordination, both forces remained in close contact, which developed as a two-pronged advance. The First Oregon caught up with the regulars by November 5.

Kamiakin's Indian scouts reported a much larger force than Haller's. It became apparent that the Indian coalition could not defeat such a large force. The Cayuse chose to retreat to defend their homeland, and the Walla Walla decided on another area to attack. "It was reported that Peopeomoxmox and his forces would cut off Governor Stevens' party in that direction as it returned from the Blackfoot council."[45] Kamiakin decided to conduct holding fights of small hit and run battles in order to give the women and children time to retreat.

The morning of November 8 was frosty. The regulars led the way and were about two miles in advance of the First Oregon. While attempting to ford the Yakima River near Toppenish Creek, Major Rains' command was attacked by a force of fifty warriors, led by Kamiakin. Unable to repulse the attack with his force divided by the river, Rains summoned reinforcements from Colonel Nesmith. Two companies of Oregon Mounted joined with Sheridan's dragoons to make a mounted attack into and across the river, clearing the ford for Rains' advance.[46] The young lieutenant of dragoons recalled the action in his memoirs:

> About 1 o'clock we saw a large body of Indians on the opposite side of the river, and the general commanding made up his mind to cross and attack them. The stream was cold, deep, and swift, still I succeeded in passing my dragoons over safely, but had hardly got them on the opposite bank when the Indians swooped down upon us. Dismounting my men, we received the savages with a heavy fire, which brought them to a halt with some damage and more or less confusion...As they numbered about six hundred, the chances of whipping them did not seem overwhelmingly in our favor, yet Nesmith and I concluded we would give them a little fight...but all our efforts were in vain.[47]

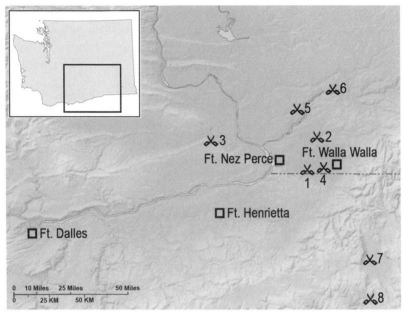

Eastern Front
1855-1856

1. Frenchtown	December 7-9, 1855
2. Touchet	November 8, 1855
3. Cornelius	April 7, 1856
4. Stevens'	September 1856
5. Snake River	February 1856
6. Tucannon	March 13, 1856
7. Shaw's	July 17, 1856
8. Burnt River	July 15-16, 1856

The next day, near Twin Buttes, the command was again met with small-arms fire. Seeing the Indians on the ridge, General Rains' howitzers opened up, and his men charged the ridge. Running forwarded were two regular companies, at the head of which were Major Haller and Captain Ferdinand Augur, as well as three volunteer companies led by Captains Cornelius, Hembree, and Bennett. At the top they found abandoned stone rifle pits from behind which the Indians had fired. The ridge was successfully cleared without loss of life (none were reported by either side). Leaving the ridge, the troops returned to camp, allowing the Indians to return. Their harassing rifle fire prompted another charge, this time clearing the ridge for good.

Sweeping the valley plains, the two forces made no more contact with enemy forces, but upon reaching the Catholic mission at Ahtanum Creek, they burned supplies much needed by the Indians to survive the winter, and killed 100 Indian horses and mules. Here, adding to the hatred, the volunteers desecrated the mission, stealing religious items, and finding a buried half keg of gunpowder. Many of the Oregon troops were of the political party known as the Know-Nothings, who practiced an intense hatred of, among other things, Catholics. With the priests' journals of expenses, and the discovered gunpowder, many choose to believe they had found proof that the good fathers were the abettors of the Indian war.

Kamiakin, recognizing the overwhelming firepower facing him, led his people across the Columbia to safety. But before leaving, Kamiakin had asked the Catholic priest, Father Pandosy, to write a letter for him, explaining why they were fighting. Dated October 7, he had dictated it right after the Haller battle. It was left for the Americans to find. In part, Kamiakin first explained the treaty was a problem:

> If the governor had said to us, my children, I am asking you a parcel of land in each tribe for Americans, but the land and your country is always yours, we would then have given with good will what he would have asked us and we would have lived with you all as brothers. But he has taken us in small groups and thrown us out of our native country, into strange land among a people who is our enemy (for between us we are enemies) in a place where our people do not even have enough to eat for themselves.

But Kamiakin then listed more wrongs done to Indians:

> Then we said, now we know perfectly the heart of the Americans. For a long time, they have hanged us without knowing if we are right or wrong, but they have never killed or hanged one American. We are therefore as dogs….at the same time the Americans chase us from our native lands…You Americans want, therefore, to make us die of famine little by little. It is better for us to die at one blow.

Decrying more injuries, Kamiakin protested white rape of Indian women. But he also talked of Bolon, whom Kamiakin said threatened

Edward S. Curtis Collection, Library of Congress
Sons of a Yakima chief.

the Indians, and for whose death Kamiakin, as chief, took responsibility. Kamiakin announced the Indian offer of peace, but their willingness to fight.

> If the soldiers and Americans, after reading this letter and learning about the motives which bring us to fight, want to retire and treat us in a friendly way, we will consent to put down our arms and to grant them a parcel of land from each different tribe, as long as they do not force us to be exiled from our native country. Otherwise, we are resolved to be cut down and if we lose the men who keep the camp in which our wives and our children we will kill them rather than see them fall into the hands of the Americans to make them playthings. For we have hearts and self-respect
>
> Write this…so that they can give you an answer and let us know what they think. If they do not answer, it is because they want war.[48]

Thus, here was a written declaration for peace or war.

More sweeps failed to find any Indians. Believing this meant they had ridden to the west to attack Maloney troops at the pass, Rains ordered mounted troops to push in that direction. Moving up the valley toward Naches Pass, Colonel Nesmith and Lieutenant Sheridan failed to find any hostile forces. Finally, the two frustrated white forces pulled back to Fort Dalles. Haller would later remark, "Again Kamiakin had the greatest satisfaction of seeing the Whites withdraw from his domain—this time an overwhelming force—without sustaining any serious loss of life among his braves."[49]

Walla Walla Indians under Peo-peo-mox-mox returned from the Yakima country, exploiting what the fleeing white settlers left behind. The Hudson's Bay Company had abandoned Fort Walla Walla and Peo-peo-mox-mox plundered it.[50] Meanwhile, led by Wiecat, Cayuse Indians burned the old fort at the site of the Whitman mission and massacre. At the abandoned Catholic mission on the Umatilla, the buildings were burned as Tenino (Des Chutes) Indians under Chief Stockwhitley moved east to join their traditional allies, the Cayuse.

In accordance with Governor Curry's orders, Major Mark Chinn had taken two companies of the Oregon Mounted into the Des Chutes Indian country in early November to compel peace. Chinn heard from other Indians that the Cayuse, traditional allies of the Des Chutes, had been attempting to bring them into the war, notwithstanding the treaty recently negotiated by Joel Palmer, Indian Superintendent of the Oregon Territory. With Chief Stockwhitley already gone, Chinn's two companies passed through the Des Chutes country unmolested, and marched east.

On November 18, Major Chinn arrived at the destroyed Catholic mission (located in the present-day town of Echo, Oregon), and decided to use it as a base of operations. The Oregon Mounted Volunteers immediately started to construct a fort, complete with bastions at opposite corners, 100 feet by 100 feet square. While the federal forces were officially prohibited from supporting the volunteers, it did not prohibit private donations. In addition to other supplies, Major Haller's wife donated a wagon to the troops, and in her honor, the fort was called Fort Henrietta.

As the fort was being built, Chinn ordered scouts out to keep informed of where the hostiles were hiding. On November 19, Indians ambushed a four-man scouting party. On November 20, another scouting mission saw Indians and promptly attacked them before the Indians got the jump. Yet another patrol found abandoned settlers' cabins ablaze.

The War Begins

On November 21, a large party of Indians approached the fort and drew in the sand. When the Indians left, the whites went out to see what had been drawn. Their interpretation of the signs as a message from Peo-peo-mox-mox that he had a large force of five tribes allied under him and were ready to fight.

Another patrol, riding to the old Fort Walla Walla on November 27, was surrounded by a group of Indians and held at bay overnight. A relief column rode out the next day, and the two groups returned to Fort Henrietta on November 30.

Meanwhile, on November 28, fort sentries saw signal fires burning along the hills. Uncertain if these fires were to report an Indian victory over the two overdue patrols, the fort was glad to find that the flames had been used to warn other Indians that reinforcements were arriving. On November 29, Colonel James K. Kelly, the new commanding officer of the First Oregon,[51] arrived with the rest of the regiment, along with Nathan Olney, Indian agent (and Indian "expert") with his six Tenino Indian scouts. Olney described Kelly as being "…determined on pushing the war forward and pressing the enemy as hard as possible while provisions and ammunition lasts…the blow must be struck while the men are eager for the fight and have the means of fighting."[52]

The newly arrived troops raised Fort Henrietta's combined strength to 350. However, garrison duty would greatly reduce the force when the Oregon Mounted moved out in pursuit of the enemy.

Now, after two months of war the whites were confronted with fighting to the north, to the south, and to the east. And, everywhere, every time that they had fought the Indians, the Indians had either won, or the whites had fled. The war appeared it would be very long.

Chapter 6 notes

[1] Jackson, in *A Little War of Destiny*, page14.
[2] Bischoff, *The Yakima Indian War*, page 84.
[3] Ibid.
[4] Josephy, in *The Nez Perce*, page 346.
[5] Splawn, *Ka-mi-akin*, page 46.
[6] Other estimates ranged as high as 1,500 warriors, including other tribes such as Cayuse and Walla Walla Indians, led by Peo-peo-mox-mox (*Ruby and Brown*, 207).
[7] Guie, in *Bugles in the Valley*, page 7.
[8] Ruby and Brown, in *The Cayuse Indians*, page 207
[9] Richards, in *Isaac I. Stevens*, page 241.
[10] Ibid, page 12.
[11] By law, whenever Stevens was outside the territory, as he was at the Blackfoot Council, the

authority of the governor resided in the Lieutenant Governor, Mason.

[12] *Ruby and Brown*, page 208.

[13] Pambrun, in *Sixty Years on the Frontier in the Pacific Northwest*, page 96.

[14] *Ruby and Brown*, page 210.

[15] Victor, in *The Early Indian Wars of Oregon*, page 435.

[16] Beeson, *A Plea for the Indians*, page 50.

[17] Douthit, in *Uncertain Encounters*, page 134.

[18] Ibid.

[19] Ibid, page 136.

[20] Ibid, page 138.

[21] Beckham, *Requiem for a People*, pages 153-154.

[22] Fort Lane had two under-strength troops of dragoons, a small detachment was at Fort Orford, and one unit of infantrymen escorting a railroad survey party in the Umpqua River Valley.

[23] Governor Curry had been made even more concerned when on October 16, he had encountered a band of Klickitat Indians near Corvallis. The band seemed to be aware of Haller's defeat, but took no aggressive actions themselves.

[24] Schwartz, in *The Rogue River Indian Wars*, page 87.

[25] Ibid, pages 92-93.

[26] Beckham, pages 157-158.

[27] Schwartz, page 94.

[28] Eckrom, *Remembered Drums*, page 22.

[29] Ibid.

[30] Ibid, page 26.

[31] Ibid.

[32] Ibid, page 35.

[33] Ibid, page 27.

[34] George King would eventually be released, but lived long enough with the Indians to be found speaking more Salish than English. Eckrom, page 39.

[35] Beeson, page 51.

[36] Edgar would hold on to die an awful death from gangrene.

[37] Ibid, pages 57-58.

[38] Ibid, page 59.

[39] There was some justification to the belief that the Army did not know how to fight Indians. All of the volunteers were pioneers, usually recently arrived after gaining experience crossing on the Oregon Trail or other pioneer routes. The Army's fighters were often green. For example, when the Ninth U.S. Infantry was created in 1855, the field grade officers (major and above) were experienced: Colonel George Wright came from the Fourth U. S. Infantry, Lieutenant Colonel Silas Casey from the Second U.S. Infantry, the Third U. S. Artillery contributed Major Edward Steptoe, while the First U.S. Dragoons contributed Major Robert Garnett. In contrast, the company grade officers (captain and below) were about half political appointees directly from civilian life, without prior military experience, and the raw troops were raised primarily from Maine, Connecticut, New York, New Jersey, Pennsylvania, Virginia, Ohio, and Tennessee.

[40] Schwartz, page 99.

[41] Ibid.

[42] Crook, His Autobiography, page 26.

[43] Schwartz, page 104.

[44] Maloney would never reach the pass, instead retreating to Fort Steilacoom, as he received word that there were "two to three thousand Indians well armed, and determined to fight in my front." Bischoff, page 116.

[45] Ruby and Brown, pages 213-214.

[46] Rains suffered its only dead at this point, when two soldiers were swept away in the strong current and drown.

[47] Sheridan, Indian *Fighting in the Fifties*, pages 44-45.

[48] Kowrach, *Mie Charles Pandosy, O.M.I.*, pages 95-96.

[49] Bischoff, page 129.

[50] Ruby and Brown, page 214.

[51] Nesmith had resigned to pursue his political aspirations.

[52] Jackson, page 114.

Chapter Seven

A Bleak Winter

As the weather turned cold, so did the prospects for the white pioneers. For the last two months, all of the news had been bad. Every battle and skirmish had been an Indian victory. Every tribe, it seemed, was in arms against the whites. Every part of the two territories had seen bitter engagements. The newspapers carried the names of those killed.

Adding to the bad news, two more sources of discontent made things even bleaker and both centered on politics. First, were party politics.

Three political parties were contending for dominance. The oldest struggle for power was the Democratic Party with its traditional rival, the Whig Party. But in the 1850s a third contender had come forward in a new faction based on intolerance and even hatred, called the American Party, better known as the Know-Nothing Party. This coalition was against anything "un-American," such as foreigners, Catholics, and Negroes. These three parties contended for power.

Party loyalty meant reward once power was obtained, therefore the last thing a political boss wanted was for patronage to be given to a rival party or to their henchmen. Thus, Democratic politician Governor George Law Curry wanted to reward his fellow party members and help keep his faction in power. In October, after calling for the creation of the Ninth Regiment of Oregon Volunteers, the members of that regiment voted for their officers (as all volunteer regiments did, up to the rank of colonel). What dismayed Governor Curry was that the soldiers voted in Whigs and Know-Nothings as the officers. This was unacceptable, so after only five days of service the governor used as his excuse to order the companies disbanded the charge that the troops

Library of Congress
General John Wool

were "waging a war of extermination against the Indians."[1] Making sure that this time the new regiment had the correct political alignment, the "proper" officers were elected, but the new regiment's ardor for extermination was no different than that of previous units.

The political shenanigans continued. Democratic Party member Joel Palmer owed his position to party loyalty and his appointment by Democratic President Franklin Pierce was pure patronage. But, early in 1855 rumor had it that Palmer had switched to become a Know-Nothing. One trait of the Know-Nothings was their reluctance to publicly acknowledge their membership, so when Palmer said nothing, it could be accepted as evidence of his being a Know-Nothing. If the war was not enough, political posturing added to the turmoil.

Indian Agent and stalwart Democratic Party man George Ambrose sought advancement, remarking that it was the Whigs and Know-Nothings who had started the war by telling the Indians "that just as soon as winter should set in they would all be killed."[2] The two parties provoked the war, stalwarts elected fellow sectarians to lead the fight, and they then gained all political advantage, including the distribution of federal monies. Ambrose was charging that the Whigs and Know-Nothings were buying the population's sympathy for killing Indians.

This power struggle continued when Governor Curry expressed his dismay that Joel Palmer was employing Know-Nothings, and the Salem *Statesman* newspaper called for the removal of all Know-Nothings from the Indian superintendent's employ--code for the removal of Joel Palmer. The Democratic caucus in the legislature forwarded a letter of complaint to President Pierce, and this dissatisfaction finally culminated in the Oregon Territorial House calling for the removal of Palmer based on three issues: his inclusion of illegitimate Indian chiefs in signing treaties, his desire to remove the Indians to a western reservation too close to whites, and finally his membership in the Know-Nothings.[3]

Contributing to the problems was that even the federal authorities were adding to the sense of abandonment felt by the territorials. The problem rested with General John Wool, Pacific Division commander. Wool believing the war had been started by the white greed, ordered his forces not to support the two territories' volunteer forces. Bolstering Wool's belief in who started the war was Joel Palmer (adding to his internal political problems). These two men saw the cause and the solution to the Indian war in the same light. After Wool's fall visit to the field, he concluded, "In Oregon...many whites are for exterminating the Indians....As long as individual war is permitted [that is, by the two governors] and paid for by the United States, and what is expected by all the citizens....we shall have no peace, and the war may be prolonged indefinitely, especially as it is generally asserted that the present war is a God-send to the people [because of a recession]."[4]

Both governors Curry and Stevens were outraged by Wool's comments, and by his refusal to support territorial forces in the field. In Oregon, the Legislature sent a memorial to President Pierce, which noted that the Indians started the war, "unprovoked on the part of the whites," and it was volunteer forces who were valiantly fighting. They further charged that General Wool withheld Army protection from the settlers or failed to provide them with the means to defend themselves by failing to supply weapons and ammunition, and thus the legislature demanded his recall from the post of pacific commander.[5]

Wool was not well received in the Washington Territory either. Governor Stevens came to believe that Wool would do nothing to support the territory or Stevens. Wool responded to Governor Stevens by writing, "Unless the friendly Indian can be protected against the very frequent attempts made to deprive him of his life and property this war may be protracted to an indefinite period of time, for he will be driven to hostility, if not from a sentiment of revenge, from sheer desperation."[6] Soon, both Stevens and Wool took to the press to criticize each other, and Stevens wrote to the Secretary of War supporting the legislature's call for the removal of Wool.

However, Wool had been selected by President Pierce for very good reasons. Indian troubles in the Northwest were not the only thing occupying Wool's attention. The United States was negotiating with Mexico for the acquisition of more land that would come to be known as the Gadsden Purchase, and Wool was instrumental in securing the border to prevent an "incident" triggering another war with Mexico. The calls for his removal fell on ears deafened by politics.

But whatever the political issues, whatever the relationships between the governors and the Army's field general, the war raged on and both the Indians and the troops in the field felt the war and winter's penetrating chill.

To the South

It was a cold winter throughout the Pacific Northwest. Snow started to fall with the beginning of December and by Christmas more than a foot of snow rested on the Rogue River Valley floor. The residents of Jacksonville found sleigh rides an enjoyable distraction. But, to the Indians, cold meant death. The specter of mortality came either directly by the white volunteers or through hunger, as the whites raided the camps and destroyed winter food supplies.

December started off with the Indians continuing their string of successes. On the First of December, the Umpqua Indians raided a settlement of six settlers' cabins along Looking Glass Creek. When the homesteaders fled, the Indians helped themselves to chickens and hogs, mounted the horses and mules left behind, and then torched many of the buildings. But when word reached the Indians of approaching troops, they took off into the hills, riding the captured mounts.

The volunteers pursued the attackers, finally finding their camp. Using an early morning surprise, on December 4, a company of Second Oregon Mounted Volunteers attacked the raiders near Olalla. Clearing the hostiles, the whites found but two Indian bodies but supposed that an undetermined number of Indians had been wounded.

The cold kept most of the troops in bivouac. But, sporadic patrols were sent out and if a camp was detected, more troops would ride out. Two such encampments were reported to Fort Leland and in a reconnoiter, Captain E. A. Rice (Company D, Second Oregon) and Captain Miles F. Alcorn (Company G, Second Oregon) rode out to the Indians' location on December 23. They entered the villages professing their friendship, expressing peace, but took careful note of the camps and the surrounding country. The two officers returned with full companies the next day and attacked the villages, located along Butte Creek not far from where Lupton had massacred other Indians. Nineteen Indian men were killed in the surprise raid, and all of the winter stores were destroyed, leaving the women and children to starve in the cold.[7] The volunteers returned to the fort to celebrate Christmas.

After the holiday, Captain Rice moved D Company to Fort Lane, in response to word of Indians in the Applegate Valley. With the New Year, Rice scouted into the hills to flush the Indians into the valley where other troops could attack. As the command moved forward, the Indians sprang an ambush, firing shots into the column in a classic "hit and run" attack. The only man killed was Martin Angel, the man who had urged the mob to kill an Indian boy several years earlier, yelling "nits to lice! Kill them all!" Despite the death, D Company pressed on and as they moved on narrow, ice-covered trails a mule slipped and fell down the cliff, causing the loss of ammunition (most critically, for the howitzer being carried on other mules).

The volunteers pressed on to find Indians dug in inside abandoned settlers' cabins. On January 5, the whites opened their siege of the Indians. However, without the howitzer, the whites could not press forward. The Indians had dug rifle pits inside the walls of the cabins, and carved rifle slits near the ground, thus limiting their exposure to white fire.

As soon as more ammunition for the howitzer arrived the cannon roared, but still the whites could not force a breach in the Indian defense. That night, the Shasta Indians slipped out into the woods, leaving three dead.[8]

The volunteers and regular Army forces continued to search for Indians during the rest of the month of January. One search effort was made by Company A, Second Oregon, under the command of Captain Joseph Bailey. Searching along Cow Creek, the weary volunteers made camp on the night of January 23. So tired were they that officers failed to post sentries, and as the cold men drew near to their camp fires for warmth, they made perfect targets, back-lit by the fires. Umpqua Indians sprang an attack, firing into the mass of men huddled for warmth, and then they fled before effective return fire could hit any Indians. Thomas Gage of Camas Valley and John Gardiner of Eugene were shot down in the fusillade.

A different band of Indians made an attack on January 25 on the camp of Company K, Second Oregon. Captain John Poland led a scouting party up from the mouth of the Rogue River, and camped near Big Bend (near Illahe, Oregon). From the camp, Poland ordered two troopers, plus an Indian scout named Enos, to move out to look for the hostile Indians.

Enos is a character of note in the history of southern Oregon. A half-caste, Enos moved back and forth between the world of the whites and that of his mother's Indian world. It is believed that Enos was one of John C. Fremont's guides as the Pathfinder moved into Oregon in 1846. With his reputation as a guide well established, Enos was thought to be the perfect scout to find the hostile tribes, while avoiding being surprised in return.

On the morning of January 25, Enos led his two companions into a trap from which neither emerged. Moving down river, he reached the settlements at the mouth of the Rogue and told the settlers that Captain Poland had sent him to get more ammunition. Rejecting offers of help with the ammunition, Enos headed up river, but he never reached Poland's command.[9]

From Fort Orford, Lieutenants John Chandler and John Drysdale led regular Army forces in search of Enos, now suspected of complete treachery. In addition, the army was trying to get as many tribes as possible to surrender, and be removed from the war zone. In the first part of their mission, Chandler and Drysdale failed to find the renegade, but they did persuade some Indians to surrender to the army. They were moved for transshipment to a new reservation. For the time being, Enos remained free.

Meanwhile, the Army was finally moving on Palmer's plan to remove all the Indians of the Rogue Valley to a great coastal reservation. Some would march to the coast and be transported by ship to the Siletz Reservation, while others were ordered to march north 300 miles through the deep winter snows. The concentration of reservation Indians started in late January, and by February 23, 1856, the march north started. Four hundred eighty Indians started north. Many died of the cold, others starved. Angry whites and disease took a toll as well. As one historian wrote, "Removals to the Reservations were brutally inhumane."[10]

The Indians moving north were accompanied by Indian agent George Ambrose, fresh from his efforts to kill the Indians. He kept a diary, and noted within the first week how some Indians had been killed by angry whites, while "Today we had another Indian to die the first by disease on the road, although many are very sick."[11] So many Indians died on the march, other alternatives were tried. Some Indians were moved to temporary camps, such as at Yachats. One Indian historian described the place: "Yachats was nothing more than an extermination camp."[12] The choices for the Indians were stark, indeed. Capitulate and die along the way to the camps, die when you reach the camps, or die fighting the troops raging through your homeland. Some would surrender, while others continued to fight, but either choice, it seemed, ended in death.

As the removal of Indians from the valleys started on February 22, the night saw many whites celebrating George Washington's birthday. It was a festive occasion, with settlers coming for miles around to join in the bright celebration in the dark of winter. One such party was held in the community of Gold Beach at the mouth of the Rogue River. Many settlers planned to spend the night to avoid traveling home in the dark, so the party continued until the early hours of morning, almost to dawn.

While the party persisted, some of Captain Poland's men were released from guard duty to join the gaiety. Fourteen men of Company K remained on watch. However, word reached Indian agent Ben Wright that Enos was across the river at a village of the Tutuni Indians and wanted to talk. Wright asked Poland to accompany him, and so the two missed the party going to the river's south shore to speak with Enos.

With the commanders removed from the troops, the settlers celebrating, and everything seemingly peaceful, Enos ordered his warriors to attack. First among those attacked were the guards on duty. Of the fourteen, nine were killed immediately. Of the five remaining, one soldier ran for two days, bringing word to Fort Orford of the complete surprise.[13]

Next to die were Poland and Wright. Wright was particularly singled out by Enos. Earlier, Wright had "punished" an Indian woman named Chetco Jenny by stripping her naked and whipping her through the streets of Port Orford.[14] It is believed Enos knew Chetco Jenny and knew of Wright's humiliation of her. When the bodies of Poland and Wright were found, they were so severely mutilated they could not be easily identified.

The Indians stormed throughout the area. Twenty-three settlers were killed. The rest fled to a partially built fort (called Fort Miner) that acted as their sanctuary from the rampaging Indians. One hundred and thirty men, women, and children were packed into the redoubt, on the north side of the Rogue River. Besides a stockade, the fort had cabins and an earthen wall surrounding the three buildings.

The Indians had the whites corralled; consequently, the surrounding area was theirs to command. Virtually all of the buildings were burned and many of the outlying farms attacked. John Geisel and his three sons were killed and his wife and their two daughters were taken prisoner.

Word reached Port Orford and its weak army command. Those settlers, fearing they were next, retreated to their stockade which was quickly expanded to accommodate the entire Port Orford population. The people of Port Orford could imagine that all whites to the south had been killed. As the army post's surgeon, Rodney Glisan wrote, "We feel much anxiety to hear from Rogue River, as large columns of smoke are plainly to be seen rising up from the vicinity of the fort erected there by the whites of that place."[15]

If the Port Orford people could not know what was happening, they could imagine the worst, and feared it would happen to them. But inside the fort along the Rogue River, the settlers held on. The men fired their long guns at the attackers while women still in their festive dresses reloaded the muskets, keeping the men armed and ready. Tending the fires, the ladies not merely cooked, but melted lead to be poured into bullet molds. Outside, Enos could be seen riding back and forth on a white stallion directing the Indian attack. Not knowing if anyone outside the fort grasped their plight, the settlers created a large sign painted on cloth, spelling "HELP," in the hope that a passing ship would see their plea for relief. The first the people knew of the outside world coming to their assistance was from an ill-fated marine reconnaissance from Port Orford, literally washing on to the shore.

Eight brave men rowed a whaleboat down the coast seeking survivors at the Rogue River community. Nearing the surf line, they saw an American flag still flying, as well as the sign beseeching help. They decided to land, instead of rowing back to Port Orford. As the boat came toward shore, the breaking waves tossed the boat, capsizing it. Six men drowned, and two were saved only when armed men from Fort Miner came out with cover fire to rescue the floundering men. The saved men told the trapped whites that help was coming. The question was, would it arrive in time?

Library of Congress
Major John Reynolds

Hunger was a crisis. Desperate for food, eight men sortied from Fort Miner to gather potatoes from a nearby field. As they ventured forth, the Indians waited until the settlers neared the food and then opened fire. Six of the men died in the crossfire, while the other two made it back under the direct covering fire of other men in the fort.

Major John Reynolds,[16] the commanding officer at Fort Orford, sent word out via steamer, requesting help from the south and north. More help was being mustered from the east. Brigadier General John Lamerick reported that he had 478 men in his northern battalion and 387 men in his southern battalion preparing to march from the interior valley to the coast, ready to kill all hostiles. At Cow Creek, on March 14 the Indians assailed Captain Laban Buoy's Company B, Second Oregon. Despite superiority in numbers, the volunteers were stopped and Lamerick's command was forced to regroup.

Meanwhile, more troops had arrived at Fort Orford (forty from San Francisco). Major Reynolds was prepared by March 14 to march south with 102 regular troops and fifteen scouts. The largest regular army relief force was gathering at Crescent City, just below the border in California. Lieutenant Colonel Robert Buchanan was gathering a combined force of regulars and volunteers, organized to march north for the besieged settlers. Already at Crescent City were troops stationed there under the command of Captain Delancey Floyd-Jones. Joining him from Vancouver Barracks were seventy-four troops under the command of Captain Christopher C. Augur. Arriving from San

Francisco were forty more troops under Captain Edward O. C. Ord.[17] The two-pronged relief effort was under the direction of General Wool. While he had hoped to rescue the settlers by March 15, that was not to be. As noted, Major Reynolds was unable to even start the relief column (under Captain Augur) south until March 14 and Colonel Buchanan met with unanticipated resistance before even reaching Oregon. As the army moved north from Crescent City, the soldiers found that the Tolowa Indians had joined in the uprising and had to be fought in order to push north.

At the Chetco River, the troops found nothing but dead settlers or burned cabins. They did manage to scrounge food from the unattended gardens, which Edward Ord wrote was welcome: "This was a Godsend to us poor soldiers, for Uncle Sam doesn't furnish them with anything of the sort better than rice and tough old beans."[18]

As was frequently the case, the volunteer troops felt the army was not aggressive enough. Not wishing to dawdle, the volunteers of Crescent City, under Captain George Abbot, punched ahead of the slow-moving regulars. On March 18, the volunteers rode into a carefully planned ambush at Pistol River. Here the volunteers were trapped by the Indians until the regular army moved up to their relief. Together, the force resumed its march toward the relief of the Rogue River settlers.

Nearly a full month had gone by since the original attack, when on March 21 Colonel Buchanan's command finally lifted the siege. Later that same day, Captain Augur's troops arrived from the north. As the settlers celebrated their deliverance, the soldiers buried the mutilated bodies of the whites killed and left in the open. Now, concentrated on the coast were sufficient regular army forces to take the offensive. And that is what was planned: A spring offensive to end the war in the south.

War in Puget Sound

The winter in the north seemed as dismal as in the south. Nowhere could the whites achieve victory against the Nisqually. Just as reinforcements had arrived, Lieutenant Slaughter has decided to take to the field. He felt that if the Indians were not controlled soon, the entire area would suffer a loss of heart that could soon spread into a financial depression if the settlers were unable to plant their crops with spring weather. Thus, Slaughter was determined to take the war to the Nisqually.

A week after he had marched out, the army suffered another casualty. On the morning of November 28, as camp stirred, Private Elijah Price was shot as he walked back from the spring having filled his pot with water for coffee. A sentry returned fire at the Indian sniper, killing him. This was the type of war being fought in the rain forests of the hills east of Puget Sound: Indians could be a mere feet away, unseen through dense underbrush, announcing their presence by a gunshot ringing out.

As the troops marched through the thick brush, they became weary. Besides the difficulty of the terrain, the almost constant rain and drizzle kept the soldiers' clothing, bedding, and even gunpowder wet. And, they still were unable to close with the elusive Indians. While the whites might have cannon as an advantage, the Indians had an overriding advantage: they knew the ground so well as to avoid the whites except to set up ambushes.

On the first of December, William Slaughter called for a three-day rest along the Stuck River. The men spent some of the time making their campsite secure, calling the locale "Camp Morrison." On the third day, Lieutenant McKeever led a company of reinforcements in to the wilderness outpost. Finally, between regulars and volunteers, Lieutenant Slaughter felt he could take the battle to the Indians.

On the evening of December 4, a council was held in an abandoned cabin at Brannon Prairie. Slaughter laid out his plan: he had left a secured base of operation at Camp Morrison. Lieutenant More had that location amply protected with strong defenses and forty infantrymen. Next, his troops rendezvoused with Captain Christopher Hewitt's company of sixty-five men from Seattle. Slaughter was to create a hammer and anvil approach.

The anvil would be More at Camp Morrison, as well as Captain William Wallace encamped in a Puyallup Valley strongpoint. Captain Gilmore Hays held Muck Prairie along the Nisqually River, while many smaller volunteer posts would be manned at critical points. Having established the anvil, now Slaughter formed his hammer. Two columns would move up the White and Green River valleys. Slaughter would lead one and Hewitt the other. It was a good plan. The hammer

Library of Congress
Captain Edward C. Ord

would strike the Indians and force them against the anvil, crushing them.

The council broke after agreeing to the plan and the men started to return to their campfires, seeking what warmth they could in the soggy environment. Lieutenant Slaughter stood in the cabin's door, watching his fellow officers walk away. Behind him the fire in the hearth gave off a glowing warmth that filled the cabin.

But, the fire also backlit Slaughter. As he stood in the doorway, a single shot rang out and an Indian's bullet crashed into Slaughter's chest, penetrating deep into his heart. It was said the bullet could have been fired by Kanasket, the Klickitat Indian war chief leading the attack, but no one knows for sure.[19] Quickly, soldiers grabbed their rifles in readiness to repel the attack. Whites opened fire, indiscriminately pouring fire into the woods all around. More rifle fire came from the Indians, and then they slipped away. Two more whites lay dead, and five were wounded, one of which would not live long enough to reach medical help. The hammer had been destroyed.

Word quickly spread as the forlorn company marched back to civilization with their fallen leader. Lieutenant Slaughter had not been merely an energetic leader of troops, but a popular figure in peacetime. His wife and he had been welcome guests and company in many settlers' homes. Things seemed truly desperate. One pioneer woman, Margaret Chambers said that she was "about as badly frightened as I ever was in my life."[20] Captain Guert Gansvoort of the *U.S.S. Decatur* summed up the feeling of many when he wrote, "the number, valor and prowess of the Indians has been greatly underrated."[21] What more could go wrong?

After Christmas, six inches of snow fell, adding to the general misery. Isolated incidents of Indian snipers shooting at soldiers or set-

110

tlers reported missing continued through the end of the year. Even Fort Steilacoom was not immune from attack. On the night of December 28, an Indian raiding party tried to sneak past the sentry, but a shot stopped them. The morning found no bodies, but blood was in the snow. Thus ended the old year.

The New Year of 1856 started on a hopeful note for the beleaguered whites. Captain Keyes, now in command at Fort Steilacoom, received word that Leschi with thirty-three warriors in six canoes had landed on nearby Fox Island, an Indian reservation. Some reports had Leschi contacting whites he had known in a peace gesture, since Leschi had let the Indian agent send word of his arrival to Fort Steilacoom. Other settlers said he was trying to recruit more warriors for future attacks. To Keyes it did not matter. If he could check Leschi through surrender or death, the war would be a long way toward ending.

Keyes started the steamboat *Beaver* toward Fox Island. On board were thirty armed men, under the command of Captains Maloney and Balch, but the Hudson's Bay boat was no longer the armed tender it had been in its heyday. The cannon had been removed to fortify a Hudson's Bay post. As the *Beaver* reached Fox Island, the Indian Agent John Swan rowed out to report that not only was Leschi there, but so was the Klickitat warrior chief Kanasket. Swan reported they sought peace.

Meanwhile, Captain Keyes was trying to get more help to capture the two war chiefs. He sent word to Captain Gansevoort that he needed the Navy's *U.S.S. Decatur*, its boats, and, as importantly, its marines to capture the Indians. When told that it was not possible for the *Decatur* to leave its station, Keyes turned to the U.S. Coast and Geodetic Survey steamer, *Active*. While the *Active*'s boats were too small to hold sufficient men, if the *Decatur* lent its boats and marines, then the *Active* could bring them to Fox Island, and between the *Beaver* and the *Active*, Keyes would have Leschi trapped.

However, intra-service disputes resulting from a perceived slight to Gansevoort by the *Active*'s captain, Lieutenant James Alden,[22] concluded in Keyes' inability to complete his entrapment, and Leschi with his warriors paddled their canoes back to the main land. A chance to end the war had sailed with Leschi. Time would tell if Leschi had been seeking peace, or war.

January 19 saw a continuation of the war and hope that leadership to end it had returned. The first news was the disconcerting report that Whidbey Island had been attacked. With complete surprise in the dark of pre-dawn, a five o'clock attack brought the shout, "Indians, Indians! The yard is full of Indians!"[23] Attacking were the Haidas, of Vancouver Island. Their object was the Revenue Cutter *Rival*, which they boarded and stripped of such items as sails, oars, compass, and other stores. The Indians took their plunder into their canoes and started north. The settlers piled into the *Rival*, giving chase. Overtaking the Indians, the heavily armed whites forced the Indians to give back much of their plunder, and the least bloody battle of the entire war was over.

The other news January 19 was the arrival of Governor Stevens from his councils in the east with tribes such as the Blackfeet. Narrowly escaping Indian attack, Governor Stevens returned to take command from acting governor Mason. The newspaper *Pioneer and Democrat* put it simply in their headline: "The Governor is Back!" He reported to the territorial legislature that he was unwilling to wait for summer to end the war. If they waited for good weather, as the Army wanted, the Indians would simply dissipate into the mountains. Instead, Stevens promised, "The war shall be prosecuted until the last hostile Indian is exterminated."[24] Therefore, Stevens requested the authority to raise more territorial troops, and the legislature answered in the affirmative.

It was good timing, as many of the volunteer units formed in October had either expired enlistments or were soon to be discharged. Most had signed on for ninety days, but some were formed for as short a time as two months. For example, Captain Hewitt's Seattle Guards were disbanded from an expired enlistment on January 25, 1856. While many of the same troops would turn around and re-enlist, there were periods when areas were relatively unguarded. In the case of the Seattle Guards, they were replaced with U.S. Marines from the *Decatur.*[25]

The Indians were not idle. After his close call on Fox Island, Leschi had gone to the Yakima tribe and asked chief Owhi for assistance in a plan he had for attack. Agreeing, Qualchan came over the Cascades with Leschi with 100 Yakima warriors.

Leschi had seen an opportunity. The beached *Decatur* lay on its side with its cannons unable to be brought to bear on anyone attacking. The Indians were armed at least as well as the settlers, with cannon the only weapon they could not counter. Here, then, was a chance to attack an enemy strong point without risk of being exposed to cannon fire. Leschi brought his warriors, and Qualchan's Yakima, to the edge of Seattle, and prepared to attack.

Timing is everything in war. The week before, the repairs had been completed and the *Decatur* refloated. When Leschi had sought to send scouts down to report on Seattle, a patrol by Hewitt's Seattle Guards from Fort Duwamish (about six miles east of Seattle) had found the canoes to be used, and destroyed them. If Leschi had attacked then, he would have found the town largely undefended. Without up-to-date information, Leschi nevertheless decided to press ahead with the attack. The day after the Seattle Guards were discharged, Leschi attacked Seattle.

With the dawning of a new day, the Marine guard on duty no longer seemed to be needed, so they marched to the water's edge, loaded in their boats, and rowed to the ship for breakfast. At first, things were quiet, but that quickly changed.

Henry Yesler spotted the Indians dressed for war approaching Seattle. He jumped in his rowboat, and headed for the *Decatur*. The time was eight o'clock. He reported to Captain Gansevoort of the impending attack, pointing out where the Indians were last seen gathering. As a means to signal the alarm, as well as repulse the Indians, the captain had one of his cannon fire a shot into the trees where he believed the Indians were. Thus, the U.S. Navy fired the opening round of the Battle of Seattle.

The Indians quickly moved toward the town, firing as they came. The marines spread out to defend the town as they landed on the shore. Louisa Denny, seeing marines charge, stopped her biscuit making to see what the commotion was about. She saw the Indians charging toward the waterfront, and grabbing biscuits and her daughter, ran for the blockhouse, located where Main and South L streets are in today's Seattle. Most sprinted for the blockhouse built by the marines, referred to as Fort Decatur (Front and Cherry Street). Once inside, rifle fire through the slits thwarted the Indian attack.

While the Indians fanned out surrounding the town, the sixteen cannon from the *Decatur* kept up a steady stream of fire, effectively denying the Indians the ability to close with townsfolk. When the Indians made a charge at the main wharf, they were repulsed by a counter charge, with Lieutenant Phelps leading the U.S. Marines against the Indians. Not as fortunate was Navy Lieutenant Francis G. Dallas. He and his party of sailors were defending the southeast section of the town. He was attempting to direct the naval gunfire, using his spyglass to look for targets. As he stood up, a bullet passed beneath his upraised arm, and into his chest, stopping his heart.[26]

Although the Indians could not press home their attack, they could pillage and plunder. Homes and businesses had supplies seized and then the buildings torched. The Indians even had time to roast a stolen ox for their dinner that afternoon. But, finally, unable to defeat the Navy, the Indians retreated.

"The battle at Seattle was the psychological low point of the war for the whites on Puget Sound."[27] As a Washington paper reported the events, it did seem bleak:

Pioneer and Democrat
The Indian War!!
The Ball Opened at Seattle

…This attack upon Seattle, and that, too, in broad day-light, is decidedly the boldest move that has yet been made by the redskins….thus far in the war, they have not only held their own, but obtained the advantage….with savage war-hoops, as it were, at the doors of every town and settlement within our borders.

The war could not get worse than this, many said to themselves. Others feared that the end was near. The Reverend John Devore wrote to a friend of what many citizens were feeling after Seattle. "Have you one consoling word to utter in our behalf? Our country is laid waste. We hear nothing but the clangor of arms and the war whoop. We lie down at night bidding each other farewell and resign ourselves to the God of battles, not knowing that we shall ever behold another day."[28]

But, good news was soon reported. On January 30, the Ninth U.S. Infantry Regiment arrived as reinforcement for the beleaguered pioneers. When the steamer *Republic* arrived, it brought Lieutenant

Colonel Silas Casey with 200 regulars to take command of Fort Steilacoom, and the war in the north. Once more, it was hoped that the Army, coupled with territorial volunteers, could take the war on the offensive.

One of the first ideas was to fight the Indians with their own methods. Three companies of friendly Indian mercenaries were raised: Pierre Charles led the Cowlitz Indian company, Sidney Ford had a company of Chehalis Indians, and Wesley Gosnall commanded a similar force of Squaxin Indians. To differentiate the "good" Indians from the bad, the territory's first lady, Mrs. Stevens led the ladies of Olympia sewing special caps to be worn to distinguish the good Indians.[29] Even more valuable was the group of Snoqulamies (numbering seventy-five) led by the chief Patkanim. This group promised to track down Leschi.

Meanwhile, the Army was trying to find a peaceful way out of the conflict. Lieutenant Colonel Casey sent the (now) former Indian Agent from Fox Island, John Swan, to find Leschi, and gain his surrender. Swan moved up the Green River, under observation by Nisqually scouts, but he was allowed to proceed into the foothills, almost to the very Cascade Mountains themselves. Finally reaching Leschi, Swan reported back to Casey:

> The number of warriors present was about one hundred and fifty, and these, with the small number of spies out, undoubtably [sic] comprise all the force in arms. Leschi is anxious for peace, but wishes a guarantee that his people shall receive no punishment, and that a new reservation shall be set aside for their use. He fears that if his people lay down their arms, private citizens may take their lives for what they have done in war.[30]

Without the guarantees, peace remained elusive. To Nisqually, the forts built by the territorial forces seemed to surround them, and the news that the Ninth Infantry had arrived seemed to foretell of a white offensive.

But the first offensive was led by Patkanim. He was acting under a government offer of $20 per severed head of a Nisqually warrior and $80 for a chief's head. Patkanim moved into the foothills, and captured one Indian camp with eighteen people in it, eleven being women and children. Three Klickitat warriors after surrendering lost their heads to the government bounty.

Looking for more money, Patkanim moved further into the Cascades. Shortly after John Swain left Leschi, Patkanim used that information to move on the Nisqually camp. But, instead of a dawn surprise attack, the Nisqually were ready. Michael Simmons, a white observer with Patkanim, recorded the moment when Leschi turned the element of surprise around on Patkanim. Leschi yelled out to his would-be killer, "I have understood that you were coming to attack me, and I prepared for you. I think I will have your head before tomorrow noon."[31]

Instead of the surprise attack, a ten-hour battle raged. Both sides fired back and forth, and shots from Patkanim's men killed many Nisqually women and children, who were trapped in their longhouses. That evening, Leschi led his band out of the battle, but lost more kin when they forded the swift-flowing Green River. Among the other side's casualties was a wounded Patkanim. With supplies running low and their headman wounded, the Skyhomish and Snoqualmie Indians brought Patkanim out of the woods on February 20, along with word of the first significant Leschi defeat.

More events indicated a turn in the tide of war. On February 23, volunteers ambushed Duwamish Indians on the river of the same name. The Indians had three canoes filled with supplies, reportedly heading for Leschi's new camp. Instead of relief for Leschi, two Indians were killed, and one canoe full of supplies was destroyed.

Another piece of good fortune came the whites' way when Casey's Ninth Infantry was camped near Elhi Hill, not far from the battles of last October. Led by Captain Erasmus Keyes, their mission was to sweep forward and push the Indians deeper into the mountains. Once camp was set, Keyes would send out small ambush patrols, often with as few as three men.[32] The night of February 28, as campfires burned brightly, one patrol was set outside the camp to spring a trap on any approaching Indians. As the ambushers waited, Private Kehl saw a group of Indians moving single file. Biding his time until he could not miss, the soldier fired at the Indian in the lead, scattering the rest. The corporal of the patrol, O'Shaughnessy helped drag the mortally wounded Indian back to camp. There, Captain E. Keyes came to the fire to speak with the Indian. The wounded Indian was none other than

Kanasket, the Yakima chief who had crossed the mountains to support Leschi. Keyes ordered the Indian to be hanged, but while the noose was being prepared, Kanasket yelled to his companions, and rifle fire came from the tree line. Not waiting for the rope, Corporal O'Shaughnessy put his rifle to Kanasket's head and scattered his brains across the clearing. Keyes later wrote, "Regarding the carcass of the dead chief as that of an unclean animal that men hunt for the love of havoc, we left it in the field unburied, and went on our way to fight his people."[33]

Library of Congress
Lieutenant August Kautz

Among the soldiers now in the field was recently transferred Lieutenant August Kautz, fresh from his experiences fighting Rogue River Indians. Kautz was leading a company of fifteen men to secure a crossing of the White River, near Stuck Valley. On March 1, waiting for Casey's arrival, Kautz once more was attacked by Indians. Moving back into the woods, Kautz was clearly outnumbered, with two of his men wounded. All Kautz could do was send for help, and hold on.

Receiving word of Kautz' situation, Captain Keyes led two companies of men up the White River, fording the snow-fed waters reaching to their arm pits, but finally forcing the relief of the beleaguered Kautz by three that afternoon. The now united command needed to clear the Indians from the crossing, so Keyes ordered a bayonet charge. The frontal attack worked, forcing the Indians to flee the crossing to a nearby hill. There was but a single white casualty. August Kautz, shot in the chest while fighting the Rogue Indians of Oregon, was once more wounded by a bullet in the leg.

But the nearby Indians still posed a threat, so with the setting winter sun low in the western sky, Keyes order yet another frontal attack. Lieutenant David McKibben led a charge, this time uphill against a dug-in Indian foe. About halfway up the hill, the Indians opened fire, but the whites carried the crest, forcing the Nisqually to flee. This time, the whites suffered two dead and eight wounded.

Dodging the forces led by Colonel Casey, the Indians used hit-and-run tactics. One white settler, William White, was killed coming from church service on March 2. On March 4, not far from present-day Spanaway, Washington, the John Bradley farm was attacked. While none were killed, two of the Bradleys were wounded, but held off the attacking Indians from inside their cabin.

The war seemed to be going well for the whites by the end of winter. The tide had turned it seemed and success was near. Leschi and his warriors were now fleeing for their lives.

Winter War in the East

After the Walla Walla Council in June, Governor Stevens had moved first north and then east to negotiate treaties with other tribes. When Haller suffered his defeat, no one knew exactly where the governor was within the territory. Messengers were sent to find him, as well as an escort of Washington Territorial troops under Colonel B. F. Shaw. Shaw never did find the governor, but messengers did. However, Governor Stevens had already left Fort Benton with an escort of twenty-five men on October 28. The messenger reached Stevens on October 29. With word of the outbreak of hostilities, the governor was encouraged to proceed east, down the Missouri/Mississippi to New Orleans, and then by boat to Olympia. In the field and the capitol, people were afraid it was too dangerous for Stevens to cross through warring Indian nations. Stevens was determined to return to his capitol in the most direct route and take command.

His party traveled 230 miles through the Bitterroot Mountains in four and a half days, despite three feet of new snow in the passes. As he did so, he found friendly Nez Perce Indians who provided an additional escort. The Nez Perce knew of the war, and gave Stevens more details; They told Stevens that Peo-peo-mox-mox and Kamiakin had marched east with warriors to intercept and kill the governor. Here was information from friendly and trusted Indians.[34]

The governor reached the Coeur d'Alene Catholic mission, and there was able to muster another company of miners whom he dubbed the Spokane Invincibles. But prior to leaving, he received one more word of warning from the Indians at the council: "Peo-peo-mox-mox was said to have boasted that he would take Stevens' scalp himself."[35]

Spokane warriors from Chief Garry's band.

Wishing to keep the Indians around Spokane out of the war, Governor Stevens held another council, at the Spokane Indian camp, starting on December 4, promising the Indians, "I have said to every Indian—I say it to you—nothing will be done without your full consent. I trust you will ever remain my children, that you will look to me as a father."[36] Among the Indians present were a tribe that had never been at any council, but, from whom Stevens had taken their land. The Isle des Pierres, or Sinkiuses had not been invited to the Walla Walla council, but had been one of the fifteen tribes the whites had assigned to Kamiakin's signature. Their hostility put Stevens in the difficult defensive position. Furthermore, the Sinkiuses told Stevens of the Battle of Twin Buttes, and how Kamiakin had crossed the Columbia headed toward the Spokane country.

With the council now focused on the war, Stevens urged the Indians to remain friendly to the whites. Garry, a chief of the Spokane, promised his pledge of peace, but also counseled justice. "You want peace here—good—but also make peace in the Yakima country."[37]

But Garry also reported to Stevens that Kamiakin's emissaries had visited his camps just five days prior, seeking allies.[38]

But, Stevens was not interested in peace with the Yakima. He had already determined his course of action: punish the Indians who had broken their word at the treaty council. Stevens had sent an express rider to Fort Dalles with his recommendation that the Army bring the Indians to terms through action. Chief Garry's words fell on deaf ears.

So did the rest of Garry's talk. He spoke further of the reservation being created for his tribe. The chief spoke of how white settlers had already started to pour onto his lands, even before a treaty had been signed. Garry wanted to know who would protect the Indians from white crimes, noting how whites had killed Peo-peo-mox-mox's son and the murderers were never brought to justice. Stevens had no ready answer but to adjourn.

As Stevens listened the next day, he heard many objections to white conduct, but also a general willingness to abide by fair treaties, fairly enforced. However, Garry rose up to give a clear statement of the Indians' position:

> Governor. See the differences there is between these Indians and you. See how everybody is red and you are white. The Indians think they are not poor. When you look at yourself, you see you are white. You see the Indian is red, what do you think? Do you think they are poor when you look at them that way? When you look at those Red men, you think you have more heart, more sense than these poor Indians. I think the difference between us and your Americans is in the Clothing; the blood and the body are the same. Do you think because your mother was white, and theirs black that you are higher or better? We are black, yet if we cut ourselves, the blood will be red—and so with the whites it is the same, though their skin is white...When I speak you do not understand me...Since we have been speaking, it is as if we had been talking for nothing....If you take those Indians for men, treat them so now. The Indians are proud, they are not poor. If you talk truth to the Indians to make peace, the Indians will do the same for you....On account of one of your remarks, some of your people have already fallen on the ground. The Indians are not satisfied with the land you gave them...If all those

120

Indians had marked out their own reservation, this trouble would not have happened…If I had the business to do I could fix it by giving them a little more land.[39]

Here it was again: The unfair treaties and treatment of the Indians caused the war. Here it was again: Stevens would (or could) not hear the Indians speak. Finally, there were two agreed points that all Indians made to Stevens. First, end the war with the Yakima by reopening and negotiating a fair treaty, and second, no soldiers north of the Snake River could enter into the Indian reservation created for these tribes. Chief Garry demanded the right to draw the boundaries of his reservation. Stevens' tactic, the one he had objected to when tried by the Indians at Walla Walla, was to call for time to consider, to meet at a future date to settle these issues. The Spokane Council ended, with Stevens making promises. The council might have been ended, but, "Every Indian present had known that Stevens had talked with a crooked tongue."[40]

Having failed to settle the northern Indians' issues, Stevens now hurried as fast as he could to the war. His force of two companies (the Spokane Invincibles and the Stevens Guards) trudged through snow drifts pushing hard for the safety of friendly Nez Perce at Lapwai. Reaching Lapwai, Governor Stevens was welcomed by the Indian Agent William Craig, and then met with the leaders of the 2,000 Nez Perce encamped nearby. Old friends such as Lawyer greeted Stevens as did other chiefs, Looking Glass among them. Here, Stevens heard more of the war, such as the raid of the Hudson's Bay Fort Walla Walla. The next day, word came of the big fight held in the valley of the Walla Walla, between the Indians and the First Oregon Mounted Volunteers. Stevens now felt he had to get home and so headed toward the Walla Walla on December 15. In addition to his fifty-five white troops, Stevens was protected by ninety-five Nez Perce warriors.

The First Oregon Mounted Volunteers
On the 2nd of December, in the valley of the Umatilla, the First Oregon Mounted Volunteers moved out from Fort Henrietta heading for the Walla Walla River. The first order of business was to seize the abandoned Hudson's Bay post of Fort Walla Walla. Colonel Kelly ordered his troops to move in two columns. The plan called for a night

approach. As the columns enveloped the fort, there was a chance to surprise the hostile Indians still plundering the fort.

However, these were volunteers, not disciplined regulars, so a night march resulted in nothing but confusion and chaos. Equipment was lost, as officers were separated from their commands. Moreover, the troops were noisy. Their unsecured equipment rattled in the night and they shouted to one another trying to find friends or lost comrades. During the night, Captain Bennett had to blow a dinner horn to rally his men.

Still in darkness, the command halted three miles from the fort, and immediately started fires for warmth, and cooking their breakfast. Any remaining hope for surprise was lost as 350 men made fires and talked amongst themselves.

As dawn broke on December 3, the Oregon troops found the Hudson's Bay fort empty. James Sinclair, the former chief trader at the fort, showed the troops where he had buried his howitzer, adding more fire power to the white command. Nearby, some Indians were seen driving a herd of cattle across the river. Reports of Indian theft of white cattle had been received, so a company of volunteers forded the Walla Walla River, loaded a cannon, and opened fire on the Indians, who returned fire, with no injuries noted to either side. But, these shots opened the campaign up the Walla Walla River.

A patrol up the river east of the Columbia encountered a party of forty Indians and gave chase. Long distance rifle fire was exchanged, but again it seemed as if the war in the East would be bloodless. Major Chinn led a scouting unit into the same party of Indians, who turned out to be Cayuse. They professed peace and proved it by telling the whites where the main village of Walla Walla Indians was located. The Cayuse said those Indians were the ones who were hostile.

Meanwhile, December 4 saw action elsewhere. A supply train had left Fort Henrietta, bound for Colonel Kelly's command. An ambush on the train resulted in some of the pack mules being run off. The attack was attributed to Deschutes and Cayuse Indians, under the direction of Chief Stockwhitely. The column sent a rider back to the fort to request support.

Unfortunately, the fort had been attacked, too. Guarding the supplies and the remounts kept at the fort was a company of volunteers. In a surprise raid the first white killed was Private William C. Andrews.

He was scalped; his head skinned by the removal of his scalp and his beard. The rider seeking support returned to the supply train without help, but with word of Private Andrews' mutilation.

On the same December 4 morning, Colonel Kelly, acting on the information obtained from the "friendly" Cayuse, rode with the main column to the confluence of the Touchet and Walla Walla Rivers, with the expectation of finding the hostile Walla Walla Indians. For some of the troops, it was their second trip up the Walla Walla River in war. They had marched in the 1848 Cayuse War in the dead of winter to reach the scene of the Whitman Massacre. Upon reaching that site they had found a grisly scene of bodies disinterred, and gnawed on by wolves and other scavengers. Veterans told the tale to the young volunteers around each night's campfires.

Meanwhile, Major Chinn would follow with the supply train from Fort Henrietta and those companies with horses already tiring from chasing reports of Indians. With him came word of the mutilation of private Williams.

By December 5, Kelly had marched with his main force fifteen miles up the Touchet River, when his scouts, under the command of Captain Narcisse Cornoyer encountered a party of seventy Indians led by Peo-peo-mox-mox himself and advancing under a white flag of truce. As the captain watched the Indians approach, he sent a rider back to Kelly. Telling them to stop before they got too close, he noted that the Indians all seemed to be dressed in brand new Hudson's Bay blankets.

Colonel Kelly arrived, dismounted, and the two war chiefs, one red, the other white, shook hands. The great leader of the Walla Walla demanded to know why the soldiers had entered his lands. Colonel Kelly said it was for the wrongs the chief had done against the whites. Peo-peo-mox-mox denied any wrongdoing and professed his desire for peace. He said to the colonel, "I see your boys are like mine. They are keen for a fight. But us old men have better sense."[41]

In response to the Indian's denial of wrongdoing, Kelly detailed the various white ranches raided and burned in the Walla Walla Valley, and the plundering of Fort Walla Walla. The chief denied this, but Kelly stated they had the testimony of the Cayuse chief, Howlish Wampool, who had witnessed Peo-peo-mox-mox hand out Hudson Bay goods stolen from the fort, in an effort to induce the reluctant

Cayuse to join in the fight against the whites. Admitting he had at one time advocated war, Peo-peo-mox-mox said he had come to realize that war was wrong[42]. Further, the Walla Walla chief agreed to try and recover the property his warriors had stolen and offered to sign a new treaty. Kelly demanded more, basically the surrender of the tribe. Peo-peo-mox-mox agreed, asking until the morning to deliver up his arms and ammunition. In addition, he invited the Oregon troops to enjoy his hospitality by camping in their village.

Kelly asked Nathan Olney, an Indian agent, for his opinion; could the colonel trust Peo-peo-mox-mox? Olney was convinced the Walla Walla chief was stalling to gain time to fight, and if they moved into the village, it would be a trap. Further, of what use would another treaty be, when Peo-peo-mox-mox had just signed one treaty professing peace last June?

As Kelly later noted, "we concluded that this was only a ruse for gaining time to remove his village and preparing battle. I stated to him that we had come to chastise him for the wrongs he had done our people, and that we would not defer making an attack upon his people unless he and his five followers would consent to accompany and remain with us until all difficulties were settled. I told him that he might go away under his flag of truce if he chose, but that if he did so, we would forthwith attack his village."[43] Peo-peo-mox-mox reluctantly agreed, asking only that he could send one of his sons to ride ahead to tell his people to kill five cows to celebrate with the whites.

As the column moved toward the village, the soldiers could see many Indian warriors riding along the ridges, and these warriors grew ever closer, as the Touchet River flowed through rugged hills which narrowed ahead where the Indian village was located. Again, Nathan Olney told Kelly that he feared the column was riding into a trap. Seeing the canyon narrow to a point where no more than three could ride side-by-side, Kelly ordered a halt, and in the late afternoon sun, ordered his command to make camp, moving back two miles to a more defensible locale. Peo-peo-mox-mox asked for permission to send another messenger with word that the whites would not be at his village that night. The request was granted, with the stipulation that the messenger be told to return. The messenger never was seen again.

All night long, sentries kept vigil, no longer needing the attention of the sergeant or the guard's reminders to stay watchful. Others huddled around campfires, trying to keep the cold out. Veterans' tales of Indian treachery, mutilation of captives, and how some of these same troops had discovered the bodies of the Ward party gave shivers worse than any caused by the cold.

The next morning, the command found out how the Walla Walla had spent their night. The soldiers formed on the morning of December 6 and resumed their march up the Touchet toward the village they had seen the day before. In the snow that had fallen all night was the clear evidence that the Indians had spent the night packing their camp and moving off so as to be out

Edward S. Curtis Collection, Library of Congress
Son of the great Walla Walla chief Peo-Peo-Mox-Mox.

of white reach. Along the crests of the canyon, armed warriors were mounted on painted ponies watching the movement of the volunteers. Kelly ordered emissaries to ride toward the Indians, flying a flag of truce, seeking to fulfill Peo-peo-mox-mox's promises, but the Indians just moved off. By mid-afternoon, Kelly ordered his column to retire to where the Touchet flowed into the Walla Walla River, so he could gain supplies brought up by Major Chinn.

As the reunited Oregon troops encamped that night, they heard drums from the hills. More tales were told, and those coupled with the cold and the rhythm of the drums kept the men restless.

The morning found the hills around the volunteers' camp alive with more armed Indians, their numbers greater than the day before. During the night, one of the hostages attempted to escape. Peo-peo-mox-mox had not been put under restraint, but merely guarded, so when the attempt was thwarted, the six Indians were bound. On the morning of December 7, Colonel Kelly ordered the ropes undone. He told Peo-peo-mox-mox that he believed the chief had used the messengers to alert his people and to have them prepare for war. He further warned that if he or any of his fellow Indians held by the whites attempted to escape, they would be shot.

Seeing the Indians, Kelly attempted to get them to surrender, but instead, they sent back word that they wanted Peo-peo-mox-mox released and if the Americans moved further up the valley, it meant war. With that warning, Kelly ordered his men to mount and move east up the Walla Walla River Valley.

The battle started at a little after eight o'clock in the morning. Indians opened fire on the soldiers herding the cattle. Kelly ordered three companies of troops, B (Captain Orlando Humason), H (Captain Davis Layton), and I (Captain L. B. Munson) to clear the ridge of snipers. The Indians slowly gave ground as the whites gave chase. Guarding the pack train were companies A (Captain E. J. Harding) and F (Captain Charles Bennett), with the rest of the command riding up the valley floor. This phase lasted for about ten miles when the force suddenly found themselves confronted by a large number of Indians. Here, two miles west of the old Whitman Mission were the buildings of the abandoned La Roche farm. The Oregon pioneer historian Frances Fuller Victor estimated the Indians facing the First Oregon ranged from 600 to as many as 2,000 warriors, with 1,000 the most likely number.[44]

The advance had brought the volunteers to a point in the valley with the hills to the Oregon's left (north), and the Walla Walla River to their right, with about one mile of level ground between the two geographic features. At the La Roche farm the Indians swarmed down the hills and west from their strong point, effectively stopping the volunteers' advance. From the slopes as well as from the thick brush along the river, the Indians poured in rifle fire. The Indians had a destructive cross fire converging on the head of the white column.

With rifle fire coming from three sides, Kelly ordered elements of F and I companies to charge the brush on their right and clear it. Meanwhile, Kelly ordered Company A to reinforce his front.

Preparing to charge, Captain Munson grabbed a flag, stood before his troops, and yelled, "Company I, charge! Follow me boys!"[45] As the charge started, Lieutenant A. Fellows (F Company) was killed, and Captain Munson (I company) was wounded, sapping the charge of leadership before covering the ground. Then Captain Alfred Wilson arrived with his A Company. Ordering his men to dismount and fix bayonets, he led them across the open ground. This charge pushed the Indians back a little, but it too seemed on the verge of failing, when F

Company, Captain Charles Bennett, resumed the attack. This forced the Indians to retreat about a mile, to the cabin of the Tellier farm, but at the cost of a private and Captain Bennett killed.

With the Indians in one cabin, Captain Wilson brought up the howitzer recovered from Fort Walla Walla. He aimed it at the cabin, and opened fire. However, the piece was defective, and instead of giving effective fire, the barrel exploded after the third shot, wounding the captain of A Company. Still, the first two rounds plus the roar of the cannon caused the Indians to abandon the cabin. With the whites unable to take the cabin and the cannon itself destroyed, the Indians would eventually re-occupy the log redoubt.

The situation was now that the Indians held the high ground, and occupied rifle pits across the valley. The volunteers had cleared their right flank, but were suffering from the sharp Indian defense. The La Roche cabin was both field headquarters and a hospital. Colonel Kelly rode from one flank to the other attempting to control the battle.

Still taking fire from the hills, Company H, with Captain Davis Layton leading, charged up the slope to give the volunteers some breathing room. But at the crest, the Indians counter-attacked and cut off Layton with a half a dozen of his men. Private Frank Crabtree (one of four Crabtree brothers fighting in H Company), came down the hill, wounded in the shoulder and reported the cut off troops to Colonel Kelly. Kelly needed more troops.

Until now, Peo-peo-mox-mox and the five other captives had been left unbound, guarded by a squad of soldiers. The sergeant of the guard was directed to bind the prisoners and to rejoin his unit. Peo-peo-mox-mox objected, yelling, "No tie men! Tie dogs or horses!"[46] When the guards started to tie the Indians, Wolfskin pulled a concealed knife and stabbed a volunteer and five of the six captives made a break for it. Peo-peo-mox-mox lunged for a guard's rifle. The chief was knocked down, and hit in the head with the rifle (with sufficient force to break the stock and bend the barrel four inches). Nathan Olney ran up to great chief of the Walla Walla, cried out, "Peo-peo-mox-mox, you old rascal, there, I'm satisfied now," and shot him in the head.[47] Of the six Indians, five had attempted to escape and were killed while the sixth, making no move to escape was unharmed and tied up.

But now the pent-up rage of the whites revealed itself, for the soldier mutilated the great chief's dead body, cutting off Peo-peo-mox-

mox's ears as well as most of the skin from his head, just as Private Williams had been mutilated.

The second part of the tragedy at the cabin was that it distracted the command, and Company H lost three killed (including Lieutenant J. M. Burrows), and seven wounded, including its captain, Davis Layton. Still, the trapped men made good their escape, coming down the hill with their wounded.

While the Indians were effectively cutting up the volunteers, they lacked the leadership of central command. One element of the Indians, led by the Deschutes Chief Stockwhitley, later recalled how many of the Indians were reluctant to close with the whites, instead relying on long-range rifle fire. Still, with their horses not spent (as were the whites'), the Indians moved more easily from one side of the battlefield to another, reinforcing where needed.

But the day's action had tired both sides. With the gloom of the winter evening settling across the valley, the situation stabilized. December 7 ended with the Indians holding a portion of the hills to the north, occupied rifle pits across the valley, and their entire line was anchored by their reoccupation of the Tellier cabin. Facing them were the volunteers, who dug rifle pits to protect themselves against the Indians.

The morning of December 8 broke cold and frosty, but as the men started to warm themselves in front of the breakfast fires, the battle started afresh, with Indian rifle fire causing the whites to dive back into their rifle pits for cover. Before them were even more Indians than the day before, as Indians had come when told of the battle against the invading whites.

Time had given Colonel Kelly better control of the battlefield. He gave his right flank (resting on the Walla Walla River) to Major Chinn. Holding the scrub brush along the river were the severely tested companies of A and H. They were now commanded by Lieutenants Charles Pillow and Archimedes Hannon, respectively, since both the companies' captains were wounded. Protecting his left flank at the base of the hills, was Company F, commanded by Lieutenant A. M. Fellows since the death of Captain Bennett. The plan was to have the major portion of the command clear the Indian rifle pits and trenches before the Oregon Volunteers. The problem was an unsupported advance with the hills still held by the Indians could not be sustained. Thus, Captain Cornoyer (of Company K) would lead a short squadron comprised of Company B (Lieutenant John Jeffires) and Company I (Lieutenant Charles Hand) to move along the crest of the hills, and clear the Indians off the high ground. Company K was noted for being the "Metis" company, or those of mixed blood from French-Canadian fathers and Indian mothers. Their war cries were as chilling as those of their enemies and their ponies better than the grain-fed mounts of the whites. The assaults started.

Edward S. Curtis Collection, Library of Congress
Nez Perce in fur cap.

Throughout the day, the whites would attack, gain success, and then be counter-attacked by the Indians. Each side gained, lost, and regained advantage, but by the end of the day, all that had occurred was the heavy expenditure of ammunition, with no appreciable gain of ground by either side. Facing the growing numbers of Indians, Colonel Kelly sent a rider for reinforcements. If the overall campaign had gone as planned, two more companies of the First Oregon Mounted Volunteers should have arrived at Fort Henrietta on December 7, and should have marched toward Kelly's location that day. If Companies D and E (Captains Thomas Cornelius and Andrew Hembree, respectively) were nearing the battle, their fresh troops could sway the field in the volunteers' favor.

The rider, an experienced mountain-man named Robinson, mounted Peo-peo-mox-mox's horse, and used its superior speed to out-race any pursuers. With him was Kelly's description of the situation. "The animals have become so poor and jaded that it is impossible to make a successful charge against the Indians who are mounted on fleet horses and can easily escape. We are therefore compelled to act in the defense of our present position which we are now fortifying by making a stockade fort. Our ammunition will be exhausted, I fear, with another day's fighting, and unless we can procure a supply from Fort Henrietta our position will be critical indeed."[48]

Fort Henrietta had the men and supplies Robinson sought. The two companies had reached the fort on December 7, and used the following day to round up stray cattle and horses (run off in the earlier raid when Private Williams was killed). Sometime after midnight, Robinson woke the fort as he rode in, his horse completely blown. Not wasting any time, the two companies immediately ordered a forced march to move to the relief of Kelly's beleaguered command.

For the soldiers in the rifle pits, fear further chilled the day. Most men were reporting their powder horns nearly empty. Indians rode before the command, dangling scalps, including one scalp they claimed was from Fort Henrietta (Private Williams?), implying that the outpost had been annihilated. Aggressive braves had moved down river enough to outflank the companies along the Walla Walla, and were firing into the volunteers' rear. The command was surrounded and close to its end.

The two company relief squadron pushed hard. They rode forty-plus miles before sunrise. After feeding their mounts and themselves, taking some rest, the squadron remounted and pushed hard again. By evening of December 9, the relief force made the Kelly camp, bringing the urgently needed men and ammunition.

The Indians had placed scouts out to warn them if whites were coming. When Cornelius and Hembree's troops were seen, signal fires were lit. While not defeated, the Indians gave word to their villages that it was time for the women and children to pack and leave. Fleeing before the unknown number of white reinforcements, many Indians died in crossing the winter-swollen Snake River.

On the morning of December 10, the command of Colonel Kelly awoke to find the Indians gone. A scouting party moved through the now empty Indian area and counted 196 fires, still warm and smoking. The largest and longest battle of the war to date had ended. Whites commanded the battlefield and claimed victory, but at an extreme cost, and it had been a very near thing.

By December 15, word (Colonel Kelly's message sent with Robinson when the situation was still in doubt) had reached Portland, and *The Oregonian* reported the battle, with the names of the white dead and wounded. These were the names of friends, family, and neighbors. For example, every one of the men in Captain Bennett's Company F had been enlisted from Portland. This was not an impersonal war, but one taking well-known and respected men.

Moving further east, just beyond the site of the old Whitman Mission, the volunteers started to plan for their extended stay in the area. Additional supplies reached the camp on the December 19, but so did word that Colonel Nesmith had resigned. Lieutenant Colonel Kelly called for new regimental elections, and the result was that Thomas Cornelius was elected the new colonel. Kelly returned to the Willamette Valley with a report on his actions up to and including the Battle of Frenchtown, as his four-day fight was now being referred to (on account of the scattered French-Canadian homesteads located throughout the battlefield).

On December 20, Governor Stevens rode into the Oregon camp to be greeted by celebratory rifle fire, and yells of "huzzahs." Hearing of the Oregon troops' "victory," Stevens warned them that there were 600-800 warriors now gathering to attack, and that they were facing a winter campaign.[49] Stevens remained with the Oregon troops until January 1, 1856, hoping to join them in a renewal of an attack on the Indians. Instead, the weather turned bitterly cold. As Waman Hembree (nephew of Absalom Hembree who fought in the company raised from Yamhill County) wrote, "On Christmas Day, we had eight inches of ice on the Walla Walla River and temperatures of 20 to 26 degrees below zero."[50] Giving up hope of martial glory himself, Governor Stevens headed west to Fort Dalles and his capitol, Olympia.

Politics entered the territorial army once more. When Cornelius was elected, it was noted he was a Whig, and Major Chinn protested that he should be in command (being a loyal Democrat, as was Governor Curry). However, within a month, the Governor confirmed Cornelius' appointment, not wishing to override the desires of the troops in the field. Major Chinn would resign because of ill-health, which in his case was not a canard. Chinn would be dead before the end of 1856.

The new colonel of the First Oregon announced his intentions to his men by saying, "I intend to follow the Indians as long as there is ten of them together unless called back by orders from headquarters."[51]

Winter campaigns are hard and this cold winter made any movements painful to the poorly equipped volunteer forces. Supplies were hard to move up the ice-choked Columbia River, and fodder was not to be had in the snow-covered valley. Further, Indian raids on supply trains threatened the command. For example, on February 15, 1856, Fort Henrietta was raided and had 300 horses run off. To supplement their meager supplies, Indian caches were hunted out, and gladly raided when discovered.

Despite their cold and lack of supplies, the volunteers remained in good spirits. Thus, the command continued to send out scouting patrols. On patrol on February 14, 1856, the whites received word that as many as 2,000 Indians had gathered near Priest Rapids, on the Snake River. The patrol, under Captain Hembree, was told that Kamiakin, Stockwhitely, and Five Crows were readying this large body to attack. As they searched further, the report appeared to be false, part of a campaign of fear.

Another patrol found an Indian village on the Snake River and attacked. Four warriors were killed, but much needed supplies were taken in the mid-March raid. None of these attacks amounted to battles, but provided a nuisance effect for one side when the other prevailed. Late winter came and Colonel Cornelius described his situation as desperate when he requested more supplies. Besides food, clothing, and ammunition, his command needed horses. He said that as his horses gave out, "We will have to change the name of our forces from OMV to Raged-Dis Mounted Volunteers."[52] To solve that problem, Cornelius sent two officers to the friendly Nez Perce to buy 300 good mounts; they returned with forty-two.

Some reinforcements arrived. Colonel Benjamin Shaw had been directed by Governor Stevens to support the Oregon volunteers, and joined them in the field, leading the Walla Walla Mounted Militia. Additional troops were raised in the Willamette Valley, to relieve those troops who had suffered the most in combat and the weather. By late February and early March, three new companies of troops had arrived, allowing the tired veterans to return to their homes. With spring, came hope.

A Bleak Winter

Chapter 7 notes

[1] O'Donnell, in *An Arrow in the Earth*, page 222.
[2] Ibid, page 223.
[3] Beckham, *Requiem for a People*, page 165.
[4] Douthit, *Uncertain Encounters*, pages 145-146
[5] Schwartz, *The Rogue River War and its Aftermath*, page 111.
[6] Richards, *Isaac Stevens*, page 264.
[7] Beckham, page 164.
[8] Ibid.
[9] Douthit, pages 147-148.
[10] Beckham, *Oregon Indians*, page 222.
[11] Ibid, page 227.
[12] Berg, *The First Oregonians*, page 98.
[13] Beckham, page 174.
[14] Ibid, page 138.
[15] Ibid, page 176.
[16] John Reynolds' fame rests upon his actions as a major general in the Union Army during the Civil War. A sniper's bullet killed him on the first day of the Battle of Gettysburg.
[17] Augur and Ord were both Union generals in the Civil War, and Fort Ord, California was named for the latter.
[18] Ibid, pages 178-179.
[19] Richards, page 256.
[20] Ibid, page 257.
[21] Beckham, page 70.
[22] James Alden was a Navy officer assigned to the Coast Survey. He had prior problems with slighting senior officers, as he had been a member of Charles Wilkes' U.S. Exploration Expedition, with run-ins with that squadron's commander. From his time with the U.S. Exploration Expedition (commonly referred to as the U.S. Ex.Ex.)., he was familiar with the waters of the Puget Sound, charted during that squadron's time in the Pacific Northwest.
[23] Eckrom, *Remembered Drums*, page 112.
[24] Richards, page 258.
[25] The *Decatur* was in Seattle for an extended period of time. It had hit an uncharted reef near Bainbridge Island in November, giving the reef its name, Decatur Reef. The Navy vessel had sailed to Seattle, and beached itself in order to make repairs to its damaged hull. Hence, while being repaired, the Marines were available to man the blockhouse.
[26] Eckrom, page 95
[27] Richards, page 260.
[28] Eckrom, pages 110-111.
[29] Ibid, page 108.
[30] Ibid, pages 115-116.
[31] Ibid, page 119.
[32] Richards, page 265.
[33] Eckrom, page 123.
[34] Josephy, *The Nez Perce Indians*, page 348.
[35] Ibid, page 349.
[36] Richards, page 250.
[37] Ibid, page 251.
[38] Josephy, page 349.
[39] Ibid, pages 353-354.
[40] Ibid, page 354.
[41] Jackson, *Little War of Destiny*, page 119.
[42] Ibid.
[43] Ibid, page 120.
[44] Victor, *Early Indian Wars of Oregon*, page 443.

[45] Jackson, page 132.
[46] Ibid, page 134.
[47] Ibid, page 135.
[48] Ibid, page 137.
[49] Richards, page 253.
[50] Lockett, in *Tales from the Past*, page 112.
[51] Jackson, page 145.

[52] Bischoff, *The Yakima Indian* War, page 225.

Chapter Eight
Spring Offensive

The first of March saw volunteers and regulars ready to go on the offensive on every front. To the whites, finishing the war and bringing peace once more to the Northwest seemed to be a valid hope. However, fighting was not limited to the battlefields.

To Governors Curry and Stevens, the hostile Indians had to be punished, even exterminated (the hostile Indians, not necessarily all Indians, although some whites certainly believed that, too). They had given their word on treaties and then acted in a treacherous manner. Stevens planned to isolate and protect those Indians who had remained peaceful and to pursue and overwhelm the Indians that were fighting. In speaking with one group of Indians, he described his actions as "a father who punishes his children to make them good."[1] Both governors had territorial forces either in the field or about to take the offensive.

General Wool and the professional military forces stood in contrast to the political forces. First and foremost Wool believed white greed and misconduct had started the war. Many of the battles had been started by the whites, and the volunteers' bloodthirsty actions had merely forced the Indians to defend themselves. Wool asked the volunteer forces to retire or at least restrain themselves, and to "avoid vindictive and unnecessary bloodshed."[2] Wool saw an additional role for the Army: The troops must stand as a shield between the settlers and the Indians. Wool created what was in effect, a peace policy: "Repeatedly, Wool argued that if the volunteers stopped provoking the Indians and got out of the interior country, the Indians would again become peaceful. He communicated that view to his field officers and directed them not to fight the Indians."[3] The result was white dissatisfaction and Indian confusion when some soldiers tried to protect them, while others attacked them.

Whether a spring offensive was designed to wipe the Indians out or move them to separated reservations to protect both sides, the forces were ready. It was time to strike.

Puget Sound

Of the three fronts, the northern front had four good reasons for the early restoration of peace. First, it had the fewest hostile Indians; probably no more than 300 Indians remained in the field, and almost a third of those were allies from the eastern side of the Cascade Mountains. With the death of Kanasket, it was probable that many of those hostile forces would fade away to their homes, leaving their allies in the western region on their own.

Second, the winter campaign destroyed much of the Indians' supplies. If the Indians wanted to avoid starvation, they had to return to the reservations to receive the dole supplied by Stevens' territorial Indian agency. While not abundant, the food provided often made the difference between life and death.

Third, the volunteers had created a series of forts and stockades that had provided some effectiveness in interdicting the normal patterns of Indian movement. While not an absolute shield, the strong points did help, not only to stop the Indians, but to provide protection for the whites. Having a place of shelter nearby allowed many farmers to return to their fields, thus fuelling the local economy.

Finally, with the arrival of elements of the Ninth U.S. Infantry, the U.S. Army had actively taken the field in an attempt to prevent volunteer excesses and to attack those Indians still intent on war. Further, Captain Keyes' strategy of moving his forces into the field and then creating small ambush teams to be placed outside the camps had already seen success, such as the death of Kanasket.

To the whites, this combination of factors made it seem that peace was at hand, that the Indians had nothing left with which to strike. It was just a matter of time. The whites were right about everything, except the will of the Indians to be free and to seek justice. The Indians attacked once more.

Leschi mustered all of his warriors as well as the remaining Yakima Indians led by Qualchan, to make a final push to stop the whites from overrunning them. If they could strike hard, perhaps the treaties could be re-opened. They targeted a key transit area, known to the whites as Connell Prairie.

Knowing the prairie was used by the Indians, the territorial volunteers had erected a blockhouse. The nearby ferry crossing over the White River was protected by a fort, and barracks built to house troops. Captain Joseph White's volunteer engineers were doing the work. Territorial troops were assigned to protect them, one company of which was assigned to First Lieutenant Urban Hicks.

Shortly after dawn, Hicks was patrolling toward the ferry crossing to insure that it was clear of Indians, so that engineers a short distance behind him could work. As Hicks neared the river, he marked fresh signs that Indians had been through the area. As he turned to warn Captain White, the ambush was sprung; the Indians opened fire.

White's Pioneer Company (as the engineers were called) had three men hit. Dropping their equipment, the engineers unslung their rifles and fired back. Seeking a better defensive position, they scurried to the top of the ridge on the river's bank. Thinking they had panicked the whites into retreat, the Indians charged out of the brush, which allowed the whites to drop several before the Indians returned to their cover and attempted to flank them.

The main white camp was aroused by the sound of fighting. As Hicks wrote in his account of the battle, "At camp, great confusion prevailed; no one seemed to be in command, but everyone ready to fight on his own hook."[4] Captain Benjamin Henness, who had been preparing to move out with his company on a scouting patrol, quickly moved his men toward the sound of the fighting. The Indians waited until he passed, and then moved behind and opened fire. Fierce rifle fire from both sides was exchanged, but Henness held.

Three more volunteer companies finally formed up and moved out. Lieutenant Matrin, Captain Van Ogle, and Captain Rabbeson all led companies into the battle. For the first few hours, as the whites tried to organize, both sides fired from cover, exchanging volleys of rifle lead, but with few casualties. However, with reinforcements, the whites formed a plan and readied their attack.

Rabbeson's company of Olympia men would move toward their right, at the low point of the prairie. The center would be the responsibility of the newly arrived Captain Calvin Swindal's Mason County (then called Sawamish County) company, fresh and ready to strike. On the left was the high ground of the river's bank, and two units were detailed to move against it: White's pioneers and Captain Henness' volunteers. In Henness's company was Urban Hicks.

On the Indians' left they had arranged themselves "in a crescent along a low hill,"[5] against which Rabbeson struck. Moving through the middle and flanking the Indians was Swindal's Sawamish men. Unable to hold against such an onslaught, the Indians gave way.

On the whites' left, Henness charged. Hicks related "A party of us...started out to charge the Indians along the brush and hillside. In this charge some of my sailor-boys proved valuable in wading the swamp and climbing logs in the advance. We captured one Indian, who was quickly dispatched."[6] It was to this high ground that many of the Indians from the low point had retreated, and Rabbeson and Swindal started their forces forward in a flanking movement. Heard on the hill were drums and Indian women chanting encouragement to their warriors. With all three white companies now charging toward the Indians, they retreated. "As it was, however, when they heard our yells and knew we had commenced to charge, they quickly began to retreat, dragging their dead and wounded with them."[7] By three o'clock in the afternoon, the seven-hour battle had ended. Evidence and statements from the Indians years later indicated that in addition to the Nisqually and Yakima Indians had been a few other tribes, such as the Chehalis. This defeat saw the collapse of the tribal coalition.

News of this volunteer victory brought the white community joy. If Seattle had been a low point, this was the remedy to the depression of winter. The newspaper in Olympia said it all with its headlines:

Pioneer and Democrat
Olympia, WT
Friday, March 14, 1856

The Indian War!
Battle on Connell's Prairie!
Volunteers Victorious!!

For Leschi, he had fought against the regulars and lost. He had fought against Indian mercenaries led by Patkanim and lost, and now he had fought against the volunteers and lost. It was clear that the war was lost. He started to move his people deep into the mountains, as far as possible from the whites. With Qualchan's assistance, Leschi retreated all the way over the mountains, where he was welcomed by Kamiakin. There, Kamiakin recognized that his ally was beaten, and so suggested that Leschi seek surrender, but not to the hated volunteers. Leschi was told to go to Colonel Wright to seek protection. This was the course of action decided upon by Leschi.

However, for his people still on the western side of the Cascade Mountains, war was still real. On March 14, Captain White's men were fired upon by some Indians. The return fire scattered the Indians, but one white lay dead. This was the last white reported killed in the Indian war fought by the Nisquallies.

It was not the last of the Indians killed. Captain Gilmore Hayes marched his force into an Indian village on the Carbon River. In the opening shots, several were killed and the village captured. A quick tribunal declared that three of the Indians were guilty of having been involved in earlier battles, and so they were found guilty—and shot.

On the Nisqually River, Calvin Swindal's company attacked a longhouse filled with Indians. Four Indians were killed covering the escape of the rest. Urban Hicks found another group of Indians, and reported "As the savages came out…they were shot down, big and little, squaws and all."[8] The final attacks were ordered by now Major Hamilton Maxon. In April, Maxon's troops found a small Nisqually village on the Ohop Creek, and killed everyone in it. Moving on, the volunteers encountered another village at the confluence of the Mashel and Nisqually Rivers (Now the Nisqually-Mashel Washington State Park). One witness, Robert Thompson saw but two men in the village. An Indian who survived, who took the white name of Billy Frank, related what happened:

> Those Indians at the massacre, they were….up on the hill look-
> ing down at the place where the Mashel runs into the Nisqually.
> They said the soldiers came on them and the Indians all ran down
> the hill and swam across the [Nisqually] and ran up the other
> side. And the soldiers were shooting them from the top of the

hill. There was a woman carrying a baby on her back and they shot her. She and the baby fell into the river and floated down....I don't know how many they killed, but there were a lot of them.[9]

These were the last acts of revenge. By mid-March, Colonel Casey was able to report to General Wool that the war in Puget Sound was over. However, the drama was not.

The next act was political. Seeking to assign blame for the Indian uprising (and the volunteer failures), Governor Stevens became convinced he knew who had supplied the Indians. Stevens believed it must have been the French-Canadian trappers, married to Indian women, who lived in the area. He pointed to the evidence that Leschi had stayed with some of the trappers that winter and they were not harmed. Another party of Indians, after killing settlers on the White family farm, had stopped at the home of former Hudson's Bay trapper named Wren on Muck Prairie. Giving aid and comfort to the enemy could not be tolerated. As Stevens said it, "There is no such thing... as neutrality in an Indian war, and whoever can remain on his claim unmolested is an ally of the enemy and must be dealt with as such."[10]

The governor's first order was the arrest and removal of the French-Canadians from their farms so as to prevent their aiding the Indians. When the "half-breeds" refused to stay away from their farms, and were discovered there again at the end of March, Major Hamilton J. G. Maxon arrested them. The territory having no jail, Stevens ordered the men to the custody of the Army at Fort Steilacoom. As Stevens' biographer explained, "his temperament, training and professional career best prepared him to operate as a monarch....he portrayed himself as the territory's only hope for salvation."[11]

The general response to Stevens acting as dictator was strong, and completely opposed to the governor's actions. Many opposed him out of concern for their own freedom. However, the governor continued to order the removal of the Métis[12] farmers. Some of the French-Canadians, now "paroled" at Fort Steilacoom and wanted to return to their farms for spring planting. Colonel Casey could see no basis for the Army holding these men, but was warned by Stevens that "We have reason to believe, from their immunity from danger, [that they] have been giving aid and comfort to the enemy."[13] Casey did not agree and after a short time, said he would release them.

Stevens was faced with the fact that he had no evidence of the men's guilt, and fearing what a civilian court might do, ordered the men tried by military tribunals, staffed with men of his own selection. However, those opposed to the governor's action sought a writ of habeas corpus to gain their freedom. Territorial Judge Francis Chenoweth issued the writ, demanding the Métis' release. The governor responded on April 3 by ordering martial law in Pierce County. Stevens told Casey that the prisoners were to be kept, in total disregard of any writ. Casey replied, "I doubt whether your proclamation can relieve me from the obligation to obey the requisition of civil authority."[14] Stevens ordered men loyal to him to seize the recalcitrant and remove them to a volunteer outpost.

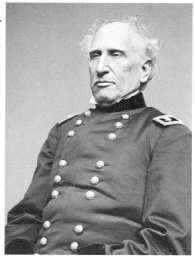

Coloney Silas Casey

The crisis came to a head when the territorial courts opened on May 5. Judge Chenoweth was ill, so the court opened with Judge Frederick West Lander presiding. Lander had been a lieutenant colonel in the territorial forces (and had fought at the Battle of Seattle), but tendered his resignation in the Territorial Army in order to serve the court. Stevens refused the resignation in order to keep Lander under his authority, telling him that he must obey Stevens. When Lander appeared at the court, Stevens was ready. Present was one of Stevens' most loyal officers, Colonel Benjamin Shaw, who was ordered to arrest Lander. Instead, Shaw persuaded Lander to delay court (for two days, not the three days Shaw had wanted). Lander made a personal appeal to Stevens, but the crisis remained.

As May 7 dawned, Lander was prepared to open court. The governor told Shaw that "martial law must be enforced." Ranged against Shaw was the sheriff of Pierce County who, with his posse, was prepared to defend the court. As Lander opened court, two companies of troops under Shaw burst into the courtroom as well as surrounding the building itself. With Lander trying to proceed, Shaw declared the court closed by order of the governor and Judge Lander under arrest. Lander told the sheriff's posse to do nothing to precipitate violence and Shaw took the judge, court clerk, and the court records off to Olympia. Seeking to calm the situation, Stevens had Lander released at Olympia.

Reaction was swift. Many influential leaders sent protests to Congress and the President demanding Stevens' recall. Meetings were called and citizens protested. Stevens' own Democratic Party and many of his former close associates protested his action. This was not mere party politics, but a general outrage at the usurpation of power and suspension of civil liberties.

Stevens defended his actions. He claimed that he needed martial law as the men who he had charged were guilty of treason and that "they were the main original cause of the war." And if the writ of habeas corpus had been allowed, the effect "would have been to paralyze the military in their exertions to tend the war, and to send into their midst a band of Indian spies."[15]

The political crisis grew. Reviewing the organic act which created the territory, lawyers found that the governor had no authority to declare martial law: that power rested solely with the legislature. Others wrote to Washington, D.C., that Steven's "arrogant and unbridled love of power that unfits him for any trust in which life and liberty is concerned."[16]

On May 12, Judge Lander opened District Court in Olympia. His first act was to issue a writ of habeas corpus for all the trappers Stevens had arrested. In reaction, the governor declared martial law in Thurston County, the county in which Olympia is located. On May 14, Landers issued a citation of contempt against Stevens, ordering him to appear before the court explaining his defiance at the writ of habeas corpus. Stevens was going to ignore the court's order until the Territorial Marshal George Corliss appeared at Stevens' office to arrest him. That was prevented when volunteer troops under Captain Bulford Miller stopped the arrest and escorted the Marshal back to the court. There, Captain Miller demanded the surrender of Judge Lander, who had bolted his door. Miller's troops then kicked the door in and led Lander, under arrest again to Governor Stevens' office. When offered parole if he merely refused to open court, Lander refused, and was taken to a military camp to be guarded by troops loyal to the governor.

To settle the issue, which was quickly turning public opinion and support away from him, Stevens ordered a military tribunal to meet and decide the fate of the French-Canadians. The panel was carefully selected to be men of unquestioned loyalty to Stevens: Lieutenant Colonel J. S. Hurd, Major H. Maxon (the arresting officer of the men accused), Captains Calvin Swindal and W.W. Delacy, and Lieutenant A. Shepherd. The tribunal opened on May 20. The first few days were taken up with challenges to the court's authority by the Métis' lawyers, volunteers from the legal community.

Critics of Stevens now feared violence. The former secretary to the governor, George Gibbs, told Stevens that he was wrong and that he was one of those who had written to Washington, D.C. Another longtime supporter turned foe was Elwood Evans, warning the governor, "Military despotism is as hard to bear now as it was in 1776."[17]

Meanwhile, Judge Chenoweth having recovered his health returned to Steilacoom. On May 24, without the governor's knowledge, civil court was reopened. Once more, Governor Stevens ordered Colonel Shaw to maintain martial law by arresting the judge. The crisis deepened, as the judge issued new writs of habeas corpus.

The towns people crowded around the courthouse to defend the court while territorial forces, commanded by Lieutenant Samuel Curtis, threatened to move in. Fearing violence, Colonel Casey ordered his troops to remain in their barracks, but he personally went to the courthouse to intervene. He spoke to Lieutenant Curtis as a soldier, and convinced the young officer to retire rather than use force on his fellow settlers.

Shaw arrived in time to be served with the new writs issued by Judge Chenoweth, ordering the release of the prisoners before the military tribunal. Shaw refused. Judge Chenoweth then told Shaw that he recognized that the colonel was obeying the orders of his superiors, but when the orders were illegal, Shaw had a duty to disobey or be found guilty of breaking the criminal law. The next day, the judge ordered Shaw arrested for contempt of court for failure to execute the writs.

With the crisis at a head, faced with the real possibility of his troops firing on citizens, Stevens relented. On May 25, he ordered

Library of Congress
Captain Christopher Augur

Lander and the other prisoners freed, and returned all proceedings back to civil courts.[18] He requested the release of Shaw, who was needed to head an army mission to the Yakima area, and "suggested" the military tribunal be dismissed. Stevens' attempt at dictatorship ended with the removal of all martial law decrees.[19] And with the end of martial law, so ended the war in Puget Sound. The final acts were not done, but those would be seen in court, not combat.

War on the Southern Front

Lifting the siege at Gold Beach had not only lifted the settlers' hopes, it had positioned the Regular Army on the coast, ready to carry the war to the Indians. Unlike the regular forces on the northern and eastern fronts, the U.S. Army saw a need and was going on the offensive. As always, so were the volunteers, but they were largely confined to the interior valleys.

Lieutenant Colonel Robert C. Buchanan commanded the regulars on the coast. As soon as Gold Beach was relieved, he ordered his troops onto the offensive. With General Wool's blessing, the plan was to move from many different directions to trap the Indians between the forces and compel them to surrender. If they did not surrender, then force of arms would make the alternative plain. To execute the plan, Buchanan ordered Captain Andrew Smith to ride with his dragoons from Fort Lane toward the coast. From Fort Orford, Captain Christopher Augur would move toward the Indian strongholds near the confluence of the Rogue and Illinois Rivers, while finally Buchanan would move his men from Gold Beach, through the mountains, and have his forces converge at the confluence where Augur would have secured a site.

While a sound plan, it failed to account for the two factors beyond Buchanan's control: terrain and weather. Moreover, it failed to account for the activities of the volunteers. Of course, General Wool wanted no collaboration between the regular and volunteer forces, but as Volunteer Brigadier General John Lamerick noted, "I have reason to believe that General Wool has issued orders to the United States troops not to cooperate with the volunteers. But the officers of Fort Lane told me they would, whenever they met me, most cordially cooperate with any volunteers under my command."[20]

The terrain was more difficult than either General Wool or Colonel Buchanan appreciated. Moreover, it was late winter and early spring. Snow was still falling at higher elevations and rain fed the swollen rivers making crossings difficult, at best. Nevertheless, the offensive started.

The opening movement went to Christopher Augur's troops from Fort Orford. Moving to the upper reaches of Euchre Creek, Augur trekked to a Shasta Costa Indian Village on March 19. There, Augur started to burn the cedar houses, destroying not only the Indians' shelter, but much of the remaining food intended to carry them through winter. When the Indians ventured from the woods to contest the destruction, the soldiers killed five.

On March 21 Captain Smith led his dragoons toward the coast. Indians ambushed his command, wounding two men, but the dragoons reached Fort Orford by March 22, much the worse for wear after the hardships endured traveling through the mountain snows. The post's surgeon described them as "totally without provisions and nearly naked."[21]

Meanwhile, the volunteers were stirring. In the main valley near Cow Creek the Rogue Indians attacked Captain Laban Buoy's Company B, Second Regiment of the Oregon Mounted Volunteers (Second Oregon), on March 23. The raid made off with thirty much needed horses of the volunteers, but fearful of ambush, the volunteers did not charge into the thick brush along the creek. The next morning the same company was attacked at dawn and the discouraged and dismounted volunteers retreated to Roseburg.

Preparing to take the offensive, volunteers were moving supplies when, on March 25, a supply train was pounced upon by the hostiles. Elements of Company D, Second Oregon, Major James Bruce commanding, were attacked along the Illinois Valley. The lead point party was set upon by what they estimated were 100 Rogue Indians, but the hostiles quickly faded into the brush when Major Bruce rode up with the main body of troops. It was another successful attack as four volunteers were killed and forty horses captured, as well as twenty-eight mules, with their cargo still on their pack frames. Included in the supplies captured was much needed (by both sides) ammunition.

March 26 saw another foray by the Regular Army. Captain E. O. C. Ord marched from Gold Beach up the Rogue River. They reached a vacant village of thirteen houses, on the Skookum House Prairie. Made apprehensive by the soldiers' approach, the Indians fled to the hills. Ord described the village as being located "in a pretty little river bottom," and immediately ordered it torched.[22] Seeing their homes burning, the Rogue Indians moved back into the river bottom to attack the pillagers. A fierce fight ensued, with five Indians shot and three more drowned as they retreated to their canoes.[23] While the fighting raged, "One old woman kept up a terrible screeching. The guides said it was because we had killed her baby."[24]

The war and its politics continued. In Salem, opposition grew to Joel Palmer's continued efforts to bring the Indians to the Coast Reservation, the eastern edge of which rested against the fertile Willamette Valley. The Territorial Speaker of the House, Fred Waymire, spoke of how Palmer's plan would "create a war where peace has so long prevailed."[25] Even Palmer's friends and neighbors were concerned. The town of Lafayette, near Palmer's home in Dayton, unanimously submitted a petition demanding to know why the coast reservation had been created when it threatened the "personal safety, and of the safety of their property."[26] The protests would continue for days, threatening Palmer's ability to sustain his political support.

Meanwhile, On March 28, in Washington, D.C., Oregon Territorial Representative Joseph Lane introduced a bill to appropriate $300,000 to pay for the wars raging throughout the two territories. Pennsylvania Representative John Allison opposed the bill, quoting General Wool's assertion that the war was started by the whites to gain federal monies.

Writing to a Washington, D.C. newspaper (the *National Intelligencer*), unaware of the bill before Congress, General Wool said the volunteers had done nothing positive for the territory and that the their actions were done in a "most signally barbarous and savage manner," and that if but for their "indiscriminate warfare carried on against them, and the massacre of several parties of friendly Indians by the troops of Gov. Curry, the war would have long since been brought to a close in Oregon."[27]

Whatever the politics, the battles continued. And, as if to demonstrate that General Wool's description was accurate, the volunteers descended upon Indians who had already surrendered to Major John Reynolds at Fort Orford. The ambush, appropriately launched on April Fool's Day, was a surprise assault against a village at the mouth of the Coquille River, in which almost all of the Indians were massacred.

Library of Congress

Captain Andrew Jackson Smith in his later years.

Meanwhile, the regular army was also pursuing an offensive policy. Captain A. J. Smith had returned to Fort Lane to re-equip his dragoons and having done so, took to the field once again on April 13. Once more heading to Fort Orford, Smith encountered a few Indians, wounding two.

Moving in a loosely coordinated advance with Smith were two volunteer forces. The first of these were 300 men of the Southern Battalion, Second Oregon, under the command of Lieutenant Colonel W. W. Chapman. Instead of heading toward Fort Orford as Smith was, Chapman's command broke off and moved toward the lower Rogue River. The two volunteer forces were searching for the band of hostile Indians under Tecumtum, known to the whites as Elk Killer, or Chief John.

Colonel Chapman had two worries. Indian reports had led him to believe that Tecumtum had been reinforced by other tribes, some from as far away as the Klamath Indians, so that the volunteers now faced a force of up to 600 warriors. But, most of the volunteers in the Southern Battalion had their enlistments expiring within thirty days. Without a federal authorization to pay them, Chapman feared that most would just walk away. Nevertheless, Chapman was determined to close with

147

Tecumtum and destroy his band. On April 15, the volunteers moved out along the southern shore of the Rogue River. While Chapman's force did not find the Indians, it did force them to flee, and right into the movement of other troops.

The second part of the volunteers' spring offensive was lead by the Second Oregon's Colonel John Kelsay and the Northern Battalion's 200 men. On April 18, Kelsay's command moved out. As they marched into the mountains, they were ambushed on April 19, and again on April 22. This forced Kelsay to retreat, and on April 23, the two battalions joined together so as to be able to attack the 600 Indian warriors they believed were facing them.

The two battalions now combined, Kelsay commanded they move out on April 27. The Northern Battalion would move down the northern bank of the river to act as a blocking force, while the rest of the troops moved along the southern bank. Finding the camp of Chief Lympe, Kelsay launched a surprise attack. However, the surprise was on Kelsay. As the Northern Battalion pressed the Indians, expecting the southern bank troops to snap close the trap, but those troops commanded by Major James Bruce had not been able to find a suitable ford, and so arrived on the wrong, or northern bank of the river. All the volunteers could do was keep up long-distance fire into the Indian camp, something they continued the next day. Finally, on the day the volunteers crossed the river, they found the Indian camp abandoned.

To deny the Indians the river, a fort was established in the meadow. Four companies of troops manned the location, all under Major Bruce. The fort honored the brigadier general in charge of the Oregon troops fighting the Rogue Indians, John Lamerick. Fort Lamerick blocked Indian movement east and west along the river.

While the volunteers were moving down river from the interior valley, the regulars were preparing to move up river from the coast. The Rogue River's rugged terrain would no longer allow the Indians sanctuary with the forces acting in an unplanned pincer[28] attack. Lieutenant Colonel Buchanan moved his forces to the mouth of the Rogue by May 7, with five companies of Army regulars ready to march.

On May 9, they swept both sides of the Rogue. Buchanan took the larger force, three companies, and worked east up river along the south bank. Captain Smith, with two companies, marched along the north shore. Smith reached the confluence of the Rogue and Illinois

Rivers on May 12, and camped near the present-day community of Agness. Lacking the commonly used trail of Smith's march, Buchanan reached the Illinois on May 13, selecting Oak Flats as his bivouac.

Smith had encountered Rogue Indians along his march who had professed a willingness to seek peace, and the captain had sent the leaders to Buchanan. So, when the main body of troops entered Oak Flat, the Indians were waiting to parley with the head of the U.S. Army in the area.

On May 16, an informal council took place at Oak Flats. While the chiefs asked for peace, Buchanan was not ready to negotiate. Instead, his terms were simple and clear: unconditional surrender trusting to the protection of the U.S. Army. Buchanan recorded in his report that the Indians agreed.

As Captain E. O. C. Ord marched up river with more men and re-supply for the troops in the field, he reported he saw "almost the entire force of the upper Indians" at the Illinois (between Buchanan and Smith's camps).[29] These were even more tribes than Buchanan had already parlayed with, and so sent word for them to come to his camp to speak of peace.

Meanwhile, on May 16, Joel Palmer steamed into Port Orford. In addition to the six tons of supplies he brought for the Indians (about 365 men, women, and children) already gathered in temporary reservations (pending their movement to the Siletz Reservation), he was met by the replacement Indian agent (vice the loss of Ben Wright) for the area: Nathan Olney. Palmer was worried as he had heard reports of Oregon troops attacking friendly Indians, and without word from Buchanan, he decided to move to the Rogue and hike up river to find the army.

As Palmer was heading for Buchanan, so were the Indians. Several chiefs, including such major leaders as Cholcultah (known as George by the whites) and Lympe, had walked into Buchanan's camp professing peace. Asking them to request other leaders to join them in talks (on May 19), more chiefs came, and the talks opened on May 20 when the chiefs arrived, including the main war chief, Tecumtum.

The main points of Buchanan's presentation were unconditional surrender, Army protection, and removal to the new reservation further north along the coast. Without exception, the chiefs stated their willingness to stop fighting, but all wanted to remain in their homelands. The Indians even said they would allow the whites access to their lands to dig for gold. This compromise was not acceptable to the whites; the Indians had to leave their traditional homes. The uncompromising whites forced some chiefs to accept surrender and removal, but not all. Tecumtum told Buchanan,

> You are a great chief. So am I. This is my country. I was in it when those large trees were very small, not higher than my head. My heart is sick with fighting, but I want to live in my own country. If the white people are willing, I will go back to Deer Creek and live among them as I used to do. They can visit my camp, and I will visit theirs; but I will not lay down my arms and go with you on the reserve. I will fight. Goodby.[30]

Cholcultah and Lympe indicated that they did not want war, but neither did they want to leave. Buchanan wielded his stick by presenting a stark choice: Either "peace and kind treatment if they should yield, or, war and all its evils should they refuse."[31] It was later reported by the Indians that Buchanan offered a compromise (Buchanan recorded no such statement). If the Indians would agree to go to the new reservation, after four years, they would be allowed to return and create a reservation in their traditional lands. Whether it was the threat, or an unrecorded promise, Cholcultah and Lympe agreed to bring their people to Big Bend on May 26, and surrender (Tecumtum refused, and readied his people for war). Buchanan also reported that other chiefs had agreed, and that left a single band still hostile: Tecumtum's.

To receive the Indians' surrender, Captain Smith moved his company of dragoons and a company of infantry to Big Bend, a meadow on the Rogue River, arriving just as the sun was dipping into the west, on the evening of May 24. The next day was cold with a heavy rain falling on the troops as they awaited the arrival of the Indians, scheduled for the next day.

Word reached Smith on the May 26 that the Indians were delayed by rivers swollen from the heavy rain, and they would hope to be into Big Bend by the afternoon. As Smith waited, other Indians started to come in, with word that Tecumtum was going to come in with the other Indians, using them as a screen, and attack the soldiers. When no Indians arrived by the evening, Smith ordered his camp moved to high ground and fortified the position.

Meanwhile, Buchanan, believing peace was the order of the day, moved his camp toward the coast, and away from Smith. His movement was leisurely, and on May 26, made camp near present-day Agness.

The next day, the Indians started to appear at Big Bend in numbers. Some started to move down the hill toward the rear of Smith's camp, while others were landing by canoe toward Smith's front. By 10 a.m., Smith noted that among the Indians were some he recognized as belonging to Tecumtum's tribe. He then ordered his men to arms. As he watched, Smith saw the Indians

Edward S. Curtis Collection, Library of Congress
Inashah, Yakima

carefully move to surround his hill position, until at 11 a.m. when the Indians opened fire and charged from three different sides at once.

Smith's forces were both better armed and less well armed than the Indians. The small howitzer Smith had, using canister, drove back the Indian charge. The Infantry had muskets, similar to those the Indians possessed. However, the dragoons had musketoons,[32] short barreled guns with such limited range that the guns were worthless until the Indians were almost on the barricades. After the charge, the Indians retired to the two slopes flanking Smith's camp and poured in a cross fire.

As Smith's battle started to rage, Palmer and his escort of six men finally reached part of Buchanan's command, and learned that the Indians were even then surrendering to Smith at Big Bend. While Palmer was conferring with the Army at Buchanan's camp, they saw that many canoes full of men were paddling up river, saying that they were going to Big Bend. Buchanan sent runners to Smith's command and to Major Reynold's forces which were supposed to be heading to join Buchanan's forces. From Smith he wanted a status report, and from Reynolds, to bring his force up.

The evening of the May 27 found Smith cut-off and surrounded. In the dark, Smith had his men strengthen the breastwork made of such items as fallen trees, saddles, and supplies, by digging rifle pits deep enough to hold up to five men. Hearing the noise, the Rogues moved forward to investigate and seeing the strengthening position, lit signal fires and renewed their attack by 4 a.m.

Buchanan's messenger, hearing the battle as he approached in the evening of the May 27, returned to Buchanan's camp by traveling all night. On the morning of May 28, the messenger reported he could not get close enough to determine numbers, but that Smith was surrounded and in an intense battle. Buchanan immediately ordered Captain Christopher Augur to take his company and march to the relief of Smith's beleaguered command. Asking to accompany the relief force were Palmer, Olney, and W. H. Wright (brother of the slain Ben Wright).

Meanwhile, the Indians pressed their relentless attack. Cut off from water, surrounded by as many as 400 warriors, and with a third of his command killed or wounded, Smith was seemingly doomed. The Indians knew it, too. At one point Tecumtum crawled close enough to the surrounded command and threw them a rope. Then calling out to Smith, the Indian chief suggested that Smith hang himself.[33]

Despite the short distance, the heavily timbered and steep terrain kept the relief column from reaching Smith until almost 4 p.m. on May 28. To break the siege, Augur had his men fix bayonets and attack, "in double quick time."[34] Storming into the surrounded command, the troops broke the Indian stranglehold. As reported in *The Oregonian*, "first and foremost" in the charge was "General Palmer" using his "pistol with good effect, till he obtained a musket as it fell from the hand of a dying soldier."[35] Fighting with Palmer were Wright and Olney.[36]

Augur reported that the hills surrounding Smith were swarming with Indians, and thus ordered another charge to clear the high ground. As Augur's soldiers reached the crest, the Indians simply retreated to the next hill. "Many of my men had been marching all day in a very hot sun and had come the last mile at a run, and were nearly exhausted."[37] Unable to catch the energized Indians, Augur ordered his men to halt for rest. Ordering some of his men to move to trap the Indians, Augur charged again, but watched as the Indians just slipped away into the steep countryside. On the other side of the meadow that formed Big Bend, Smith ordered his remaining men to charge, too. The dual charge finally broke the Indian resistance, and the hostiles moved into the mountains and refuge.

The soldiers came back to Big Bend and the two commands joined. Smith's men had been without warm food since the morning of May 27, and Palmer wrote, "the men proceeded to cook a meal, a luxury which they had been denied for nearly 36 hours. No Indians were seen during the night, and the camp rested quiet." [38]

The Battle of Big Bend was the last major engagement of the war in the south, but not the last skirmish. Moving down river from Fort Lamerick, Major Latshaw led several companies of the Second Oregon Mounted Volunteers toward Big Bend. On May 28, as the other battle raged, the volunteers encountered several bands of Indians (apparently desiring to avoid the fight at Big Bend and wanting to surrender). Moving to trap the Indians between two forces, the volunteers attacked. The Indians quickly faded into the woods, leaving one warrior killed, one wounded (and captured), and seven women and five children taken into captivity. Eventually, these captives would be reluctantly turned over to Palmer for movement to the coast Indian reserve.

Still searching for the hostiles who attacked Smith, Captain Augur led two companies of regulars and one of volunteers in a sweep of the area. The command came upon a village along the Rogue River on June 2. The troops killed three men and one woman. Still searching, on the next day the volunteers fired on canoes moving along the river. These were Indians headed to the coast to turn themselves in and the canoes were loaded with women and children. Fourteen Indians were killed, plus an undetermined number drowned as they fled the firing soldiers. On June 5, Major Reynolds' Third Artillery men found a village of Indians fishing, using the traditional weir (or dam-like structure) method to trap salmon. They opened fire, killing four men, and then burned the village.

By this time, the volunteers were running out of supplies, not having been provisioned by the regulars. Consequently, by June 5, the Second Oregon was leaving the field and most had retired to Fort Lamerick. This was fortunate, as the volunteers were loathe to attempt to distinguish between hostile Indians and those wishing to surrender.

The last foray by volunteers was on June 13, as General Lamerick's own command destroyed abandoned Indian villages and took forty canoes as war booty.

By June 10, Lieutenant Colonel Buchanan had managed to gather 277 peaceful Indians and started for the Port Orford temporary reserve. Palmer meanwhile was trying to bring in more Indians, even sending messengers to Tecumtum, asking for him to surrender. By June 14, Palmer (with Augur) had led more than 700 Indians to Port Orford.

The last of the Indians, Tecumtum's band, finally surrendered and Major Reynolds escorted the Indians to Port Orford for transport, reaching it by July 2. From the port, Major Reynolds would form an escort and start marching the Indians north to the Siletz Reservation. The war in the south appeared to be at an end.

War in the East

Spring saw the two armies of whites prepared for different and uncoordinated offensives. For the volunteers, both territories planned to take the offensive to smite the Indians. From Washington, Governor Stevens called for Colonel Shaw's militia to cross the Cascades and march through the Yakima country, joining the First Oregon Mounted Volunteers in Walla Walla. As noted earlier, Shaw, distracted by the habeas corpus crisis, delayed the spring offensive.

The First Oregon Mounted Volunteers had been in the field constantly since fall. However, the extreme cold had limited all activities and resupply. Nevertheless, the unit was determined to take to the field with the improving weather.

The regulars were the second white armed force. With the arrival of the Ninth U.S. Infantry, General Wool now believed he had sufficient forces to compel peace and keep the Indians safe from white outrages. The Pacific or Third Division of the U.S. Army had a total of thirty-three companies, and of those, twenty-seven were in the Pacific Northwest. Wool's entire command had been stripped, creating a force large enough to separate the whites and the Indians. Wool had three fronts with which to contend, but Puget Sound seemed on the verge of success, and Lieutenant Colonel Buchanan was confident that he could subdue the Rogue River Indians. Now, all that remained was for Colonel Wright to bring peace to the eastern portion of the territories.

In Wool's plan, Wright would display an overwhelming force, so that combat could be avoided, and the Indians would return in peace. Wool ordered Wright to prepare for his campaign, cautioning, "beware of the whites in your rear from whom you have as much to apprehend as the Indians in your front."[39] Wool was referring to Governors Stevens and Curry's plans to renew war in the east. Wool cautioned Wright, "you have no authority to call for volunteers, to employ them or furnish them with supplies. Therefore the less you have to do with them, unless in extreme cases which I do not anticipate, the better it will be for the service. Many of them as well as most Oregonians are for exterminating the Indians and accordingly do not discriminate between friends and foes. The course thus far pursued by Gov. Curry and the Volunteers has only tended to increase our Indian enemies whilst it has subjected the regular service to greater inconvenience or expense." Wool was pointedly referring to the First Oregon's winter efforts in the Walla Walla Valley.

Edward S. Curtis Collection, Library of Congress
Umatilla woman in holiday dress.

The want of support for First Oregon Mounted Volunteers from federal depots as well as the difficulty in bringing supplies up river against the winter's ice had limited the Oregonians from taking the field. But, melting snows changed that.

Early March found the First Oregon stirring from their Walla Walla compound named Fort Bennett[40]. The late winter had the men building canoes to facilitate the crossing of the swollen rivers. Prepared, the first offensive move was to patrol west, and by March 15 they were along the Snake River, about twenty-five miles up river from its mouth. The troops moving out under the command of Colonel Cornealius were elements of Companies A, B, C, D, E, and K. On the north side was the Indian village named Tasawicks, and as the

Edward S. Curtis Colliectio, Library of Congress
Cayuse man.

troopers neared, the Indians hurried to gather their wealth, women, and children, and flee before the whites could attack. The warriors opened fire as the volunteers put into the river. Unable to prevent the crossing, the Indians were now attacked by elements of the First Oregon. Twenty men jumped out of the canoes (which quickly went back for more soldiers) and they moved into the village. Four Indians were killed, and promptly scalped by the whites. But the Indians whose lives had been spent resisting the whites' advance had bought time and most of their tribesmen were able to flee without being captured by the first wave of troops.

The second wave of troops who crossed had their mounts swim next to the boats. Remounting, they rode to try and cut off the Indian wealth, that is, the horse herd. While the Indians escaped, not all of their horses did and the whites, always in need of remounts, viewed the attack as a success. To celebrate, that night in the captured camp a scalp dance was performed by the members of Company K, mixed blood members of the French-Canadian descendants from the area of Oregon known as the French Prairie.

The next day, the colonel divided his command into two wings, leading one and assigning another under Major Narcisse Cornoyer. In coordination, they swept the area to the confluence of the Columbia and beyond. As they did so, only small bands of Indians were found, and four were killed. The colonel attributed the poor success from the forewarning given by the Indians fleeing from Tasawicks. He reported that, "These [Indians] had fled with great precipitancy towards the north. We returned to camp by different routes, having traveled this day some seventy-five miles over a country presenting no indications of having been occupied by a force of the war party of our enemy."[41] While such sweeps did much to keep the Indians always on the move, it was at a cost the poorly equipped Oregonians could ill-afford to pay. Horses and men were wearing out.

Still in the field, Cornealius ordered Company A, Lieutenant Pillow commanding, to re-occupy the abandoned Hudson's Bay post of Fort Walla Walla. This was in an effort to protect his waterborne supply route. Having secured its supply base, the First Oregon turned back up river to march on a suspected Indian village fifty miles away, at the mouth of the Palouse River.

The force moved under constant observation, not always obvious to the tired Oregonians. The troopers crossing the Palouse lands threatened to seize the wealth of the Indians, that is, horses. Making camp, each company around its fires, the Palouse sprang an ambush, firing muskets and arrows into the firelight. An exchange of gunfire ended the raid, but not before Private Harvey Robbins had an arrow in his thigh.[42]

Crossing the scablands proved taxing and as the command reached the area, it was nearing the limits of its supplies. Once more, the critical feature of the First Oregon's actions was the dearth of supplies and support. One patrol did capture about fifty Indian ponies, killing eleven to feed the hungry troopers. Extending their stay with horse meat, two more patrols scouted for as far as fifty miles in several directions, but without finding anyone to fight.

With hunger very real, a crisis of confidence and command occurred on the first day of spring, March 21. As true in all volunteer units of the time, leadership was by election and a mutiny of sorts now occurred. Several units expressed dissatisfaction with horse meat and Cornealius' leadership. The call was for new leadership and then a march home. The Ides of March may have passed, but treason was in the air. Many men spoke of their dissatisfaction until a lowly private, who was also a respected lawyer rose to speak. The anticipation was that George Shields, too, would voice his unhappiness. Instead, he spoke in support of the colonel, asking the men if they thought they had joined to protect their homes or to have fun on a fishing trip. Shields' support of Cornealius combined with calling on their patriotism ended the mutiny.

It had been close, but on March 22 a supply train arrived filling the empty stomachs of troops. When the empty train headed back to

Fort Walla Walla, it took not only the sick and wounded, but forty-five malcontents and their leaders. With fewer discontented bodies to feed, this simplified Cornealius' command problems, as well as his re-supply needs.

Now supported, on March 23 the First Oregon moved into the field once again. The volunteers marched through the high desert of the Columbia Plateau region until the first of April. They never saw the hostile Indians they knew monitored their movement. Even if there was no combat, the Indians felt the presence of the Oregonians moving through their country. Even if there was no combat, the First Oregon felt the presence of loss. The over-burdened Indian horse used for re-mounts were not prepared for the heavy loads of men and supplies and started to die off. Continuing its sweep, the First Oregon "left a trail of dead horses, discarded equipment, and oddest of all, a boat moored in the sagebrush."[43] One company reported every horse dead except sixteen, but they also reported that not a single saddle was left behind.

Seeking the enemy, First Oregon marched as far as Priest Rapids where they encountered neutral Indians who said that Kamiakin was further north. If so, the great Yakima chief was out of the command's reach. With supplies once more running low and many of the troops' limited enlistment set to expire, Cornealius moved his command to the mouth of the Yakima River, the more easily to be replenished by river boat. The First Oregon had to remain in the field until the much anticipated arrival of regular forces. As the colonel prepared his situation report for Governor Curry, he received word on April 2 that the regulars would be delayed (see below). The First Oregon needed re-supply, remount, and re-enlistments if it was to remain a force. It was time to head home for all three of their needs.

The most recently enlisted troops, those with time remaining, were made into a four company battalion and ordered back to the Walla Walla Valley and Fort Bennett. This command was under one of the officers who had help to foment the mutiny, Major James Curl and was to stay in the valley to protect Cornealius' rear until the regulars arrived.

The remaining five companies, Cornealius commanding, would march for Fort Dalles. These were the five most experienced and loyal forces Cornealius had in the First Oregon. Thus, companies C

(Lieutenant Colonel James K. Kelly commanding), D (Cornealius still commanding), E (Hembree), F (Lieutenant Revais now in charge of it), and K (Cornoyer) started to move through the Yakima country in a sweeping action that would ultimately end at Fort Dalles. However, within days of the start, word was received that the regulars were delayed. Cornealius immediately sent James Kelly to assume command of the Walla Walla battalion, which caused Major Curl to resign.

The command had marched as far into Yakima country as Satus Creek by April 7, and could look up the entire valley from atop Horseheaven Hills. In Captain Absalom Hembree's last letter home he described the experience.

> Dear brother, I take this opportunity to let you know what we are doing in this god-forsaken country. We have been living for the past 15 days on horse beef. Our horses are all very weak, many of them giving out right and left.....We have been across the Snake River and all through the Palouse Country. The Indians have fled. We have run them all out of their country. We came down the Columbia to the mouth of the Yakima River. Five companies swam their horses across the Columbia to get down to the Yakima Country.[44]

Unfortunately, Hembree was wrong; the Indians had not been run out of their country.

The morning of April 7 Hembree led a small patrol out, and thinking he saw some stray cattle, he took his nine-man patrol up into the hills. Leading from the front, Hembree was surprised when about sixty Indian warriors burst out of a ravine and charged. Hembree was dropped in the opening volley, but pulling both of his pistols out he opened fire. His first shots took Indian riders off their mounts, dead. Hembree then yelled to his patrol, "My God boys, don't leave me!"[45] This caused five of his fellow Yamhill county friends to try and stem the Indian charge by regrouping, and opening fire. More Indians fell, but the small squad was in danger of being overrun, and so were forced to flee for their lives. As they rode back, one of the Yamhill boys, William Stillwell (a lieutenant in company C of the recruiting battalion) recalled for Hembree's loved ones how they saw the gallant captain still firing his Navy colt revolvers at the Indians on the verge of overwhelming him.

The sound of gunfire roused the rest of the command, quickly mounting in a rush back up the hill. The troopers rode hard in an effort to reach Hembree's last stand, but the Indian resistance was fierce. An all day exchange of rifle fire plus horses charging, each side pursuing, marked a long day with little accomplished, except the recovering of Absalom Hembree's body. The Indians had scalped and skinned his head.

Seeking to smite the Indians who had mutilated the popular officer's body, Cornoyer chased the Indians with seventy-five men, but his spent horses were no match for fresh Indian ponies. Dejected, the troopers returned to the camp. That night, the Indians crawled back into the hills, letting off sporadic rifle fire, deepening the camp's sense of depression.

The next day, the column resumed its march toward Fort Dalles. As they did so, they stumbled upon two Indians, and gave chase. As the two fled into a ravine, Colonel Cornealius fired and dropped one out of the saddle. Seeking revenge, the colonel himself stopped to bend over the fallen Indian to scalp him. As he made his first cut across the hairline, the Indian jumped up, and Cornealius fired again, this time at such close range as to kill the bloody Indian and was able to finish the grisly task. As final insult, the troopers killed the young pony the Indian had been riding, and cooked it for their noon meal.[46]

The command had finally moved to within fifteen miles of Fort Dalles and supplies by April 13. From what they were calling Camp Klickitat, Cornealius learned of the regulars plan to take to the field within two weeks, thus negating the need for the First Oregon to re-supply and resume field operations. The colonel reported to Governor Curry, and prepared for the disbanding of the proud but exhausted Oregonians. But, two more actions were to be added to the regiment's history.

While Lieutenant Colonel Kelly was preparing to abandon Fort Bennett, the Indians attacked the soldiers of the First Oregon on April 20. One soldier guarding the horses was killed. The volunteers' pursuit only succeeded in wearing out more horse flesh. Fort Henrietta was ordered dismantled and abandoned.

The final skirmish of the First Oregon Mounted Volunteers occurred on April 28. In a dawn attack, the Indians raided the horse corrals of the exhausted troopers. Ineffective rifle fire marked a half-hearted

Edward S. Curtis Cikkection, Library of Congress
Nez Perce Warrior.

defense which allowed the Indians to make off with three hundred horses, many of which were too weak to be run for long. And with that last engagement, the volunteers were through. The official discharge date was May 5, 1856. The need for the volunteers had gone with the regular army forces resumption of the field.

U.S. Army in the field, Eastern Front

At the beginning of March, Colonel George Wright was getting ready to take to the field. Prior to any action, a command council met at Vancouver Barracks. General Wool had conferred with Lieutenant Colonel Casey on Puget Sound, with Lieutenant Colonel Buchanan on the Rogue River front (at an earlier council), and he had given explicit instructions to Colonel Wright. He was to proceed up the Columbia, establishing posts to protect the Indians and exclude the whites, and bring the Indians to peace. Included in his orders was the admonishment to fight only as a last resort.

By mid-march Wright was heading up river, pausing at Fort Rains to assess the choke point for his supplies. The area was known as the Cascades of the Columbia. The lower, or western point was called Lower Cascades. Here, steamboats from Portland unloaded cargo which was trans-shipped on a wooden, mule drawn railroad past the Middle Cascades (which was where Fort Rains was built), to the Upper Cascades, also known as Bradford's Landing. There, cargo was re-loaded onto steamboats for the run to The Dalles.

As Wright inspected the area, he found a sergeant's squad of ten men (from Company H, Fourth U.S. Infantry) manning Fort Rains. Believing this point was far too strategic to be so lightly guarded, Wright ordered a full company brought up from Vancouver Barracks. From Fort Rains, Wright proceeded to Fort Dalles, where nine companies of Ninth U.S. Infantry, two of the Fourth U.S. Infantry, and one each from the Third U.S. Artillery and First U.S. Dragoons were to assemble for his expedition. Wright wanted to be heading up river as early as March 24.

Unaware that General Wool had countermanded the orders directing an additional company of Fourth Infantry to Fort Rains, Wright gathered his forces. The Battle of Connell Prairie had occurred and with other tensions in the north, Wool ordered the "extra" company to Fort Steilacoom.

Wright enlisted Indians to act as scouts and as it turned out, some of these scouts had loyalties to their nation, and reported back to Kamiakin of Wright's intentions.

To the Indians, raiding the Willamette was a traditional way of gaining wealth. They knew the volunteers were busy fighting in far away Rogue River, in Puget Sound, and in Walla Walla. The regulars were there, too, and now the remaining Army was going to march away to the north and east. To Kamiakin, this was an opportunity to strike. If he attacked through the Cascades and then rode on to the Willamette Valley, the whites would surely be forced to recall their troops, both volunteer and regular. If the threat were big enough, then perhaps the treaties could be re-opened. All Kamiakin had to do was wait for Wright's departure and when the whites had moved too far east, attack. From Kamiakin's spies, word came that Wright would leave Fort Dalles on March 24. The chief planned his attack for March 26.[47]

Kamiakin had a combined force of 600 Yakima, Klickitat, and Cascade Indians. The dawn attack was divided into three attack groups, one for each part of the portage. One major objective had to be the steamboats tied up at the landings. The Indians slipped into position to attack.

Wright had delayed his departure until March 25. He was only five miles up river from The Dalles when Kamiakin struck.

The attack started well. Each of the three elements struck at nearly the same time, maximizing the surprise. It was a rare example of excellent Indian coordination in attack. Starting from the west, the attack unfolded as follows:

At the west end of the portage, or Lower Cascades, George Johnson was busy loading freight onto the wooden railway when a mixed-blood resident named Indian Jack ran into the clearing yelling that the Yakimas were attacking. This warning was timely as the sailing schooner from which Johnson was unloading was quickly made ready to be unmoored. With the critical warning given, almost all of the settlers had time to climb on board and shove off. Only one person was wounded by an Indian shot, but even as the boat moved with the current, the settlers could see the Indians setting fire to their homes and to the freight. The schooner started to raise sails as two steamboats came into sight. The *Belle* and the *Fashion* quickly came about, built up more steam, and went as fast as both could to alert Vancouver Barracks and Portland. One other survivor of the attack escaped by canoe and he, too, headed for Vancouver Barracks.

Indian Jack had been able to provide a warning when he heard the opening attacks at the Blockhouse, which was Fort Rains.

Sergeant Matthew Kelley had a nine-man detachment of Company H, Fourth Infantry assigned to man Fort Rains. The troopers had spent the evening of March 25 drinking and listening to the martial tales of Herman Kyle, a veteran of Blucher's troops at the Battle of Waterloo. All of the soldiers were moving a bit slowly on the morning of March 26.

Library of Congress
Lieutenant Phillip Sheridan went on to become Army Commander-In-Chief.

Inside the blockhouse, or immediately outside it was the cook Sheridan McManus and his assistant, Robert Williams. Lawrence Rooney was the farthest from the blockhouse, cutting wood up the hill from the fort. One trooper had left to go to the upper landing, and the rest were in the general vicinity.

Rooney died first. His own axe was used to beat in his face. McManus was shot in the groin as he stood in the doorway, a wound that eventually killed him. Another soldier, Jake Kyle, was about 150 yards from safety when he was shot. No longer a threat, he was left by the Indians to cry out in agony as he slowly died from his wounds. A settler named George Griswold was shot down while in open ground, mistakenly relying on his friendship with local Indians.

The rest of the soldiers made it to the safety of the blockhouse and quickly brought the six-pound cannon into play. Fourteen rounds of canister effectively stopped the Indian charges against the fort, and solid shot into the trees caused the Indians to retreat further out of range of the one weapon they could not match. One soldier used the gained space to run to Griswold's home and grab a pan full of donuts and a ham to help sustain the hungry troops.

Now besieged, the pressing need of the troops was for liquids. The soldiers' limited water supply ran out in tending the wounded. That night, two men volunteered to move downhill to the river. Instead of filling their canteens, they moved to the now empty Palmer Brothers' Saloon, used to sustain the mule drivers normally moving back and forth along the wooden railway. In the oldest tradition of the army, the two soldiers grabbed sufficient liquids to sustain them until help arrived: 12 bottles of English porter, one bottle of brandy, some whiskey and wine, as well as some oyster crackers. The two heroes returned to the blockhouse. Now the soldiers just buttoned up and waited for relief.

The most action took place at the more populous Upper Cascades or Bradford's Landing. Here, too, the attack was a complete surprise. James Sinclair[48] was shot down in the first wave. The settlers ran for the fort-like structures of Bradford's and Bishop's stores. Fortunately, inside Bradford's was a supply of rifles and ammunition destined for the Army. This supply would prove critical in the fight.

On each of the three floors of Bradford's, gun holes were cut and settlers started their defense. The Indians were burning other buildings, but as they neared the two redoubts, rifle fire kept them at bay. Instead, the Indians started to roll boulders down the hill, letting them smash into the sturdy walls.

Tied up at the dock, with little or no steam, was the steamboat *Mary*. Moored on the Oregon shore was the steamboat *Wasco*. The *Mary* was a prize the Indians very much wanted to capture, to deny its use to the whites. As the engineer worked to build steam, the crew held off the Indians as they charged. One Indian was killed on the gangplank, and another on the hurricane deck. Finally with just enough steam to move, the *Mary* took off for The Dalles, a little behind the *Wasco*, already en route to summon help.

Inside Bradford's were now forty men, women, and children, eighteen of whom were wounded. One man lay outside the store, wounded, but out of reach of succor from the storehouse. He slowly died from his wounds, with his cries reaching those inside Bradford's. Another man, on the river's edge, was wounded severely enough that he would pass out from the pain and then fall into the river, which revived him so he crawled back up into a seated position. As his wife and children gazed from Bradford's, the man bobbed up and down, repeating the drama, his wife suffered to watch until relief arrived. He died from his wounds on March 30. Two other men had been shot while driving their ox teams. A man and his wife had been killed in their cabin. One man burned to death while seeking shelter in another cabin. Four men were killed at the saw mill, not immediately hearing the attack over the spinning blades. And then the siege started.

The Indians had failed to wipe out the whites in one quick, coordinated attack. Instead, they were now engaged in a siege, with gunfire from keeping each side at bay.

Meanwhile, word was being received both east and west of the crisis at the Cascades. The steamboats took word to Vancouver Barracks and Portland in the west and to The Dalles in the East. Word was obtained by local newspapers. As one paper reported the first word of the attack, it used the biggest headline type it had:

The Oregonian
Portland, OT
Saturday, March 29, 1856

STARTLING NEWS!
CASCADES IN POSSESSION OF INDIANS!!
The town in ashes
The Steamer Mary Burned
Twenty Whites Reported Killed
Arrival of the Troops
Their Inability to Render aid to the Block House
Continued Fighting

Another newspaper would see the attack as the work of an Indian general.

Pioneer and Democrat
Olympia, WT
Friday, April 4, 1856

"…And yet, Cascade city has been attacked, taken, sacked, given to flames, and a large number of its citizens murdered.

Gen Kamiakin versus Gen. Wool—
The attack of the Indians upon the Cascades shows that Kamiakin is a better general than Wool.

Indian rumor has it the next hostile demonstration will be made against Cowlitz landing.

The Oregon volunteers who took the field last September, and who have been in the Indian country ever since, were about to cross the Snake River and give the Indians battle. At this juncture it seems, the Indians have divided their force, and by a military *ruse*, have placed a large war party between both the regulars, volunteers, and settlements, and have re-commenced the war near our doors."

Not content with covering the story, the papers prompted the communities to raise a relief force of volunteers.

The Dalles sent riders to overtake Colonel Wright and the steamboats moved as far east as possible to expedite Wright's relief of the Cascades.

Reaching the two steamboats, Wright embarked with Ninth Infantry companies A, E, F, and I, a detachment of mounted troops from company E, First Dragoons, and company L, of the Third Artillery. The last unit manned four howitzers, two mounted on each of the steamboats.

With the shoal ridden river being too dangerous to run at night, Wright and his 250 soldiers used the daylight to steam west, reaching the eastern beleaguered area on the morning of March 28. *Mary* hit a rock as the two boats headed for the landing, causing it to hang up fifty yards from the beach. The Indians again poured rifle fire into the hapless steamboat once more. Finally freed, the two steamboats made landfall and in a classic amphibious assault, troops fanned out across the hostile shore, being covered by artillery fire. Captain James J. Archer wrote of the action in a letter:

> We returned....arriving before sunrise on the 28th, Friday. The Indians were taken completely by surprise. They fired a few shots as we landed and then took cover in the woods and continued to fire until my company [Company I, Ninth U.S. Infantry] and Winders [Charles S. Winder, E Company] deployed forward at skirmish and drove them off.[49]

The large force quickly relieved the siege of Bradford's store without any further loss of life. Wright then ordered Lt. Col. Edward Steptoe to take two companies of infantry, the dragoons, and one howitzer and gun crew, and march for the relief of the blockhouse and then the lower landing.

When Wright ordered the relief of these two locations, he was unaware that another relief force had come from the west.

Word had reached Vancouver Barracks just after midnight, and the first relief column had moved from Vancouver Barracks by 2 a.m. on the morning of the March 27.

Lieutenant Phillip Sheridan mustered forty dragoons and sailed east on the steamer *Belle*. His troops stormed ashore at the lower landing at 9 a.m. All of the buildings were in the last stages of burning to the ground. The dragoons were quickly attacked by 150 to 200 Indians. One trooper was killed, as were two Indians. In his memoirs, Sheridan recalled how this man was struck down:

> After getting well in hand everything connected with my little command, I advanced with five or six men to the edge of a growth of underbrush to make a reconnaissance. We stole along under cover of this underbrush until we reached the open ground leading over the causeway … when the enemy opened fired and killed a soldier near my side by a shot, which just grazing the bridge of my nose, struck him in the neck, opening an artery and breaking the spinal cord. He died instantly.[50]

Clearly, Sheridan knew it would be impossible to push his meager force through the Indians to reach the blockhouse three and one-half miles up river. Sheridan called for his troops to re-embark, and the steamer moved to the middle of the channel, anchored, and allowed the now exhausted soldiers to gain rest and sleep.

On the morning of March 28, reinforced with ten volunteers, Sheridan took part of his command to the island in the middle of the channel, now called Bradford's Island, part of the Bonneville Dam complex.

Using the island as a screen, Sheridan moved his force up the south side of Bradford, while the rest of his force crossed to the Oregon side and moved up river as well.

Unable to find a crossing point from the east end of the island, Sheridan reunited his command on the Oregon side and then had it ferried across the river to land directly below the blockhouse. At about this time, the steamer *Fashion* had arrived with a company of volunteers from Portland. They stormed from the boat at the lower landing, putting more pressure on the Indians now confronting three forces moving against them.

Singing of deeds of valor.

Below the blockhouse Sheridan readied his troops, attacking to relieve the fort. Now, the Indians were contending with a force from the east, another from the west, and Sheridan charging up from the river. They fled into the woods ending the siege. Sporadic fighting continued for a while, as Captain Archer related his troops' actions against the Indians' as,

> This gave them a lesson and they took to the woods and opened a spotted fire from behind trees till we dashed in after them and drove them off as we had done at the Upper Landing. Only one of our men was killed in this day's work.[51]

Wright hunted for and captured some of the Indians involved in the attack. After an informal trial, Chief Chenoweth of the Cascade Indians plus eight others were ordered hanged. Sheridan helped to conduct the investigation.

> The chief and head-men said they had had nothing to do with the capture of the Cascades, with the murder of men at the upper landing, nor with the massacre of men, women, and children near

169

the block-house, and put all the blame on the Yakimas and their allies. I did not believe this, however, and to test the truth of their statements formed them all in line with their muskets in hand. Going up to the first man on the right I accused him of having engaged in the massacre, but was met by a vigorous denial. Putting my forefinger into the muzzle of his gun, I found unmistakable signs of its having been recently discharged. My finger was black with the stains of burnt powder, and holding it up to the Indian, he had nothing more to say in the face of such positive evidence of his guilt. A further examination proved that all the guns were in the same condition. [52]

Indians hated to be hanged and Chenoweth offered wealth if he would not have to die that way....which he did not. As he was hanged, the noose did not do its job, and the chief was dangling, gagging and choking, until a soldier shot him in the head to end his suffering.

One other group of Indians was found and killed. A Chinook Indian named Chief Spencer, acting as translator for Colonel Wright, was moving his family from the east end to the west of the Cascade for transport to Vancouver Barracks. When they did not report for transport, a search was initiated. Joseph Meek, famed mountain man and a member of the Oregon Militia told Sheridan he had seen Spencer head west, but also saw six men from Bradford's storehouse take after the Indian family. The translator, his wife, his father, and six children were found dead, garroted. The evidence pointed to the settlers from Bradford's storehouse, seeking revenge by killing any Indians they could find. As Sheridan wrote,

> They had all been killed by white men, who had probably met the innocent creatures somewhere near the block-house, driven them from the road into the timber, where the cruel murders were committed without provocation, and for no other purpose than the gratification of the inordinate hatred of Indians...The perpetrators were citizens living near the middle block-house, whose wives and children had been killed a few days before by the hostiles, but who well knew that these unoffending creatures had had nothing to do with those murders....In my experience I have been obliged to look upon many cruel scenes in connection with Indian warfare on the Plains since that day, but the effect of

this dastardly and revolting crime has never been effaced from my memory.[53]

While the attack at the Cascades of the Columbia had failed in its ultimate goal, it had forced the recall of Wright, delaying his march through Indian country. However, as the Indians fled north and east seeking shelter in allies' homelands such as the Spokanes, they encountered the returning First Oregon Volunteer troops, related above, which must have increased their sense of being hounded.

Preparing to resume his march into Indian country, Wright ordered his stores replaced. He needed ammunition and food consumed in the week's actions of movement and combat. However, Wright took one other action. Making sure his supply lines were protected, he ordered Captain Winder to built better protection for the Cascades. The captain and his company erected Fort Cascades, a bit further to the west than old Fort Rains. Now protected by a full company, the choke point of the Columbia River would not be attacked again.

With the newspapers screaming of the tragic and treacherous Indian attack at the Cascades, Governor Stevens used the battle as political fodder. The governor attacked General Wool and the Army, "by citing it [the Battle of the Cascades] as proof of army incompetence."[54] Stevens ordered Colonel Shaw to raise a force of Washington Territorial Volunteers to march into the Yakima country in support of the Oregonians still fighting there. If proof of incompetence was needed, Shaw's movement was delayed by the political crisis caused by Stevens' suspension of habeas corpus.

With the delay of Shaw and the return of the First Oregon Mounted Volunteers, Wright's was the only force left to move against the Indians east of the Cascade Mountains. He gathered his forces and moved out on April 28. Here was the start, if early, of the summer campaign season. The war continued.

Treaties and Treachery

Chapter 8 notes

[1] Richards, *Isaac I Stevens*, page 271.
[2] Ibid.
[3] Josephy, *The Nez Perce Indians,* page 362.
[4] Hicks, *Battle of Connell's Prairie*, page 11
[5] Eckrom, *Remembered Drums*, page 136.
[6] Hicks.
[7] Ibid.
[8] Eckrom, page 142.
[9] http://stories.washingtonhistory.org/treatytrail/aftermath/massacres2.htm, August 27, 2008.
[10] Eckrom, page 143.
[11] Richards, page 275.
[12] Métis were the product of Indian mothers and French-Canadian fathers, and thus were not really of either side.
[13] Ibid, page 276.
[14] Ibid, page 277.
[15] Ibid, page 280.
[16] Ibid, page 281.
[17] Ibid, page 284.
[18] The Métis were given a hearing in District Court, and after a week's testimony, all charges were dismissed as there was insufficient evidence to proceed.
[19] Stevens would be found guilty of contempt of court by Judge Landers, and was fined $50. In typical Stevens' fashion, as territorial governor, he issued a pardon for himself, but allowed friends to pay the court fine for him.
[20] Carey, *General History of Oregon*, page 598.
[21] Beckham, *Requiem for a People*, page 181.
[22] Schwartz, *The Rogue Indian War*, page 120.
[23] Carey, page 598.
[24] Beckham, page 181.
[25] Ibid, page 119.
[26] Ibid, page 121
[27] Ibid, page 123.
[28] A pincer movement is to have two elements of an attacking force come together with the enemy in between.
[29] Ibid, page 135.
[30] Richards, page 284.
[31] Beckham, page 136.
[32] The guns were designed to be fired from horseback, and thus, had to be short to allow for re-loading while still mounted.
[33] O'Donnell, *An Arrow in the Earth*, page 271.
[34] Beckham, page 139.
[35] Carey, page 598.
[36] Olney managed to fight in several of the largest fights of the era, and was not wounded. However, he would eventually die from an arrowhead. While traveling west in a wagon train, Olney had been wounded in an Indian attack, receiving an arrowhead in the head. The doctors were unable to remove it, and thus it remained in Olney's head. About a decade later, Olney tripped, falling on his head, which caused the arrowhead to go deeper into his brain, and finally killing him.
[37] Beckham, page 140.
[38] Ibid.
[39] Guie, *Bugles in the Valley*, page 30.
[40] Named for the popular captain killed at the Battle of Frenchtown
[41] Jackson, *Little War of Destiny*, page 161.
[42] Trafzer and Scheueman, *Renegade Tribe*, page 70.
[43] Guie, page 164.
[44] Lockett, *Tales from the Past*, pages 112-113.
[45] Guie, page 168.
[46] Ibid, page 169.
[47] March 23 was the full moon, and the Indians wanted as much of the waning moon as possible.

Hearing of Wright's movement, Kamiakin timed his dawn attack with light enough to find their way through the dark woods.

[48] The former Chief Factor of the now abandoned Hudson's Bay Fort Walla Walla.

[49] Beckham, page 35.

[50] Sheridan, *Indian Fighting in the Fifties*, page 55.

[51] Beckham, page 35.

[52] Guie, page 59.

[53] Ibid, pages 62-63.

[54] Schlicke, *General George Wright*, page 123.

Chapter Nine

Summer Campaigning

T he summer of 1856 was going to see the end of the regional wars if General Wool's plan came to fruition. On May 15, Lieutenant Colonel Casey declared war in the north finished. In the south, with the end of May nearing, Lieutenant Colonel Buchanan reported that his front was under control. Now, all that had to be done was for Colonel Wright to subdue the eastern front, hopefully without further bloodshed. The end could be seen.

War in the south

June saw the war, particularly for the Regular Army, change. By June 15, Buchanan brought an additional 700 Indians to the Port Orford temporary reservation, joining more than 400 who were already there. No longer was it a war against the Indians, but now a war to protect the Indians. As Fort Orford's surgeon wrote in his diary, Buchanan "issued orders to shoot any man who attempts to kill an Indian."[1]

Two steamboats moved Indians north to Portland, and from there transported to the western reservation. They suffered disease, culture shock, seasickness, homesickness, and depression. Other Indians were forced to move by land, trudging north along the rugged Oregon coast. But the choices for the Indians were stark.

The tribes of Northern California, who suffered from the same type of warfare, were not removed to a reservation and their fate was extinction. The tribes ceased to exist. Even for the Rogue River tribes, fighting was not a real option. Not counting women and children killed, the Indian warriors suffered a thirty-two percent fatality rate[2] in the combat just concluded, and probably a similarly high number of injured, a total casualty rate well over fifty-percent. This choice for the Indians was unsustainable. If they stayed off the reservation, the Rogue Indians faced the same fate as their Northern Californian brethren.

But a simple declaration of peace could not end this war. Many tribes or bands remained out in the woods. Most Indians wanted to live in their homeland so they stayed hidden in the hills. Local authorities hired men such as William Tichenor[3] to hunt down and capture the recalcitrant. Certainly one notorious Indian remaining at large was Enos. For Enos, the war did not end until July 26, 1856, when he surrendered. He was the only Rogue Indian to be held accountable for his conduct during the war. He was ordered held for trail, an event that would stretch on into the future.

The Army was charged with protecting the whites from the Indians, and the Indians from the whites. For that reason, three army posts were created to guard the Siletz Indian Reservation. The main post was the Indian agency associated with Fort Yamhill, which had been constructed as the first of the Indians reached the reservation (March 26, 1856). Another post guarded the western portion of the Willamette Valley and the Coast Mountain range: Fort Hoskins. This fort and the third fort guarding the reservation, Fort Umpqua, were both established July 26, 1856. Fort Umpqua had a slightly different mission. Located along the eponymous coastal river, this fort's mission was to prevent the Indians from returning to their homelands, thwarting any attempt to walk along the coast from the Siletz reservation.

While the U.S. Army saw the war as done, the settlers of Southern Oregon did not. First, any actions by Indians still hiding in the woods, such as stealing food to survive was evidence of continued hostile resistance. Second, many saw any actions by other tribes, such as the Modoc on the east side of the Cascade Mountains, as being part of a coordinated effort by the Indians to resist the whites. Thus, the Jacksonville *Table Rock Sentinel* reported of "The War with the Modocs," on August 9, 1856. Three engagements were noted and seen as a continuation of the hostile Indians' war on whites.

The newspaper reported on a July 30 engagement, the volunteers were moving from Natural Bridge (near Merrill, Oregon) to Tule Lake (then extending into Oregon) and, "chased them [Modoc] to an island some 500 yards from shore. The guard charged on foot through the water which was only three feet deep. The Indians escaped in canoes. Their village and provisions were burnt. One Indian was killed."

"On the same day, another body of Indians were chased…and one killed. At night it was found that John Allen of Co. B was missing. After three days' search his body was found horribly mutilated."

The paper reported a third battle that occurred on August 2. A detachment of twenty-three men were "surrounded near Bloody Point [just south of the Oregon-California border] by nearly two hundred Indians. The savages immediately opened a heavy fire" and the command was forced "to cut their way through them." The whites reported one trooper killed and two wounded. As was typical of white reports, they reported more Indians killed and wounded.

These were characteristic of the southern Oregonian settlers' views that the war continued, their lives were threatened, and those Indians remaining behind from the deportation to Siletz needed to be exterminated. The war would not be over until the last Indian was killed.

War in the North

Once more, to the regulars, the war was over. The U.S. Army had triumphed. But the clarity with which the Army viewed the situation was not shared by the settlers' point of view: Indians threatened the white way of life.

Leschi was still at large, as were other Indians. The Yakima Indians who had crossed the Cascade Mountains in winter to join the Nisqually fight were hiding in the foothills, waiting for the passes to clear to ease their journey back to their homeland. The injustices that caused the fighting remained. As Qualchan said, "The sufferings of these people, caused by the whites, has determined me never to surrender or quit fighting them so long as I live."[4]

And if the war was a real threat, as many believed, then Governor Stevens as both chief executive as well as the Indian Commissioner, viewed his responsibilities to include ending the war. He was convinced the war in the west was unresolved as long as Leschi remained free, and he viewed the war, east and west, as one and the same. Stevens received word that Leschi had fled (with Qualchan) to the east side of the mountains. He sent emissaries to the Yakima seeking a council. On May 15, their chief Te-i-as went to meet with the Governor in Olympia, escorted by the Puyallup Indian mercenary Patkanim. Using a Catholic priest as a translator, the two talked on May 16. Stevens offered to meet with the other Yakima chiefs, particularly Kamiakin, to discuss the treaties, and he also offered money as a reward for the capture of such chiefs as Leschi. For the Nisqually chief, the blood money was $400. This was the insult that broke the talks, as once more Isaac Stevens demonstrated his complete failure to understand Indian culture. Te-i-as told the governor,

> I did not come here to get a reward for the blood of my friends. When I want blood, I take it from my enemies on my race I came at your request, for the benefit of my people only. Rather than see those three men you mentioned captured and hung by you and your people, we will fight until the last man of us is killed. Give us honorable peace and we will accept it, not otherwise.[5]

Stevens' efforts to end the war had failed, but that did not mean the fighting on the west side would continue. Washington volunteers persisted in their activities, despite Casey's declaration of war's end. Patrols rode throughout the summer and new blockhouses were constructed, such as at Tokel Creek (near the critical Snoqualmie Falls crossing point), to interfere with Indian movement. Of course, with the political crisis created by the furor of habeas corpus, Stevens needed a distraction, and war provided the needed side show. Without a war in the Puget Sound area, Stevens turned his focus to the east. Stevens called on his trusted colonel, Benjamin Shaw, and ordered Washington Territorial Troops to ride east to war and glory.

War in the East

The eastern portions of the territories had remained the domain of the two territory's troops until spring of 1856. As the First Oregon Mounted Volunteers were returning from a winter in Walla Walla, the governors of both territories were raising more troops to send out in the summer campaign season. Until then, the force remaining in the field was the U.S. Army, under command of Colonel George Wright.

On April 28, the combined forces under Wright headed north from Fort Dalles, following the same trail Granville Haller had the prior fall. Among the objectives of his mission were to establish new forts to protect and control the Indians. As the army moved, its first run-in with the Indians seemed to presage a repeat of the Haller expedition. Wright moved into the Yakima Valley and as he approached the old Catholic mission, he met Indians. On May 11, Wright described a skirmish with over a thousand warriors. It was a show of force by the Indians demonstrating their ability to resist invasion, but nothing resulted from this first, impressive show by the Yakima.

Wright continued north with his force finding difficulty in crossing rivers swollen with spring snow melt. Finally, at the Natches River, the current proved too much, so Wright ordered the command into camp, and put his engineers to work to bridge the river (and the swampy shores).

Across the water were the Indians. Within the Indian camp, divisions had occurred between those such as Kamiakin who wanted war, and those who had tired of the war and wanted peace. The peace camp comprised of Te-i-as, fresh from meeting with Stevens in Olympia, Owhi, and the Sinkiuses chiefs Quil-ten-e-nock and Moses. Unable to bring the two sides together, the Kamiakin's war party would eventually ride east to the Palouse country. Behind, with the peace party were about 200 warriors. Those seeking peace would make tentative approaches to Wright. Knowing of Peo-peo-mox-mox's fate when captured under a flag of truce, the Indians were wary of Wright.

Meanwhile, Stevens was preparing his own "war party." He had written to Wright[6] suggesting that the regulars and the volunteers join in an "energetic and united" effort against the warring tribes. Wright responded by describing his mission as one of peace (in accordance with his orders from General Wool). Thus, the two commands would act separately.

Stevens ordered Colonel Shaw to prepare a force to campaign east. On June 12, the Washington Territorial Volunteers rode out with a column of 175 mounted troops, thirty-six mule skinners, and a supply train of eighty-two pack mules and twenty cattle. Shaw went looking for war, and that is what he would find.

Once more the Indians decried two foreign forces within their country. One, the regular army, was professing peace. The other, the volunteers, was demanding war. A historian has suggested, "The Indians in the Yakima camp were confused because the governor and Army followed different courses."[7] While some confusion did result, the Indians could and did distinguish between the regular Army and volunteers. Many of the Indians had already experienced the settlers' desire for extreme war and while they viewed the Army more favorably, they were reluctant to trust them completely. Still, the Indians would prefer to deal with Wright than Stevens' forces.

Thus, the peace-party Indians made an initial offer to come to Wright, which they did not keep. When Wright was reinforced by Lieutenant Colonel Steptoe on May 27 and did not strike out, the Indians saw an opportunity for peace. With Wright staying put along the Natches River (as his engineers continued to work on a bridge), it seemed as if he intended to stay. In addition to the bridge, the engineers created earthworks of wicker baskets filled with dirt (called gabions).

Individual Indians would peacefully visit the army camp. Enough contact had occurred for Wright to report his observations back to Wool. In his May 30 report Wright wrote, "They seem to think and say that they had strong and good reason for the murders they committed, both of the miners and the Indian agent [Bolon]; the outrages of the former [alleged molestations of Indian women] and the injudicious and intemperate threats of the latter, if true, as they say, I doubt not, maddened the Indians to murder them"[8] But, still the chiefs had not come into Wright's camp.

One reason for their delay was that they had sent a messenger to Father Charles Pandosy. After his mission was destroyed, Pandosy had been forced out of the Yakima Valley, and was now in Northern Washington near Colville (where the gold strike had brought the miners the previous year). The messenger told Pandosy that the Yakima needed his advice, and showed what Wright had sent them. Here, with a man they trusted, the difference between the Regular Army and Governor Stevens' policy became clear, and any confusion the Indians had was resolved.

> "Are these proposals sincere or not?" the chief asked him. Pandosy recognized that the peace proposals had come from the President of the United States. "If the proposals had been offered by the chiefs of this country [Stevens and the Territory], I would not trust them too much; but I saw…their great Chief is speaking and the Americans who are here must do what he wants; he has sent soldiers to make peace, you have nothing to fear."[9]

Here was the reassurance the Indians needed. When the Indian chief returned with Pandosy's words, he also brought a letter for Wright, who immediately accepted Pandosy's offer to act as an interpreter and intermediary.

The opening round of talks with the chiefs started on June 9. The Yakima leaders camped on the far side of the river, keeping the barrier as protection and sent word to Wright. The initial entreaty from the Indians led Wright to say, "All of them sent the most friendly messages, declaring they would fight no more and they were all of one mind, for peace."[10] Wright even noted that Kamiakin had "sent the strongest assurance of friendship and of his determination to fight no more." [11] With Kamiakin staying across the river, eventually Te-i-as and Owhi entered the army camp.

Edward S. Curtis Collection, Library of Congress
A Nez Perce chief.

The history of the war was laid out at this meeting. Wright's account stated, "Owhi related the whole history of the Walla Walla treaty and concluded by saying that the war commenced from that moment; that the treaty was the cause of all the deaths by fighting since that time."[12] While Wright believed what the Indians said, he also told them that they must submit, return what they had stolen, and if they continued to fight, his army was "large enough to wipe them off of the earth."[13] The Indians promised to comply with Wright's orders, and to return with their people in five days.

Wright's initial report was good news for Wool. As always, in Wool's mind, the sole source of the conflict was white greed and hatred. With such good news from Wright, Wool wrote to the Assistant Adjutant General, "the gratifying intelligence that the Indian wars have ceased in the Department of the Pacific. We have no enemies to contend with but the exterminators of the Indian race."[14] Of course, Wool was referring to white settlers.

But instead, the Indians vanished. Kamiakin, unable to trust the whites, took his warriors to the Palouse country. The others simply ignored Wright and went about their typical summer gathering activities.

Wright ordered Steptoe to remain at the Natches River, establishing Fort Na-chess. Then the main command marched north across the finished bridge, and into the Indian country.

With Father Pandosy's help, Wright convinced Te-i-as and his family to surrender as hostages. Sweeping the valley, the Army would eventually gather more than five hundred men, women, and children and herd them to Fort Dalles. Wright's campaign had resulted in the round-up of the peace party Yakima, but Owhi had fled and Kamiakin was still hostile. Still, there had been no bloodshed.

But Wright had one more impact on the war during his march through Yakima country. Moving to the site of Father Pandosy's mission on Ahtanum Creek, Wright met with the fugitives from the west, the Nisquallies. Here, Leschi and his fellow chiefs told Wright of their plight, their side of the war. They explained that they wanted to return to their homes, but feared what would happen to them. Stevens had earlier warned Wright that in case he met Leschi, Wright was to do nothing that would "save their necks from the executioner."[15] Wright provided Leschi and the other Nisqually letters of free passage to return, but Wright's letters could only guarantee Army reaction. It seemed as if Wright was ensuring peace in the Puget Sound as well as the Yakima Valley. The colonel met with many Indians who reported that the reason they had fought was because they had been coerced by Kamiakin (such as the Klickitat Indians under Towatax). Wright reported that to all of the Indians, he had "dispelled their fears of Kamiakin, who has oppressed and robbed them for many years, and should he ever return to this country, these Indians will all unite against him."[16]

Wright stayed in the field until early August. He ordered Major Robert Garnett to establish Fort Simcoe, in the heart of Yakima Country (August 8, 1856). With that, Wright returned to Fort Dalles, seeming to have ended the war.

Colonel Shaw arrived in the Yakima Valley expecting, as did Stevens, to find Wright's infantry out-matched by the mounted Indians and in need of the mounted volunteers to hunt down the warring tribes. Instead, he found Wright peacefully dealing not only with the Yakima, but even the Nisqually. There was no war for Shaw in the Yakima Valley.

However, there was conflict. One of his company commanders, the experienced Major H. J. G. Maxon, let his men clear their rifles by firing them, which was in direct violation of Shaw's orders. Seeking to punish Maxon, a "mutiny" resulted. Both parties wrote to Stevens for support. The outcome was that the governor supported Shaw, but Maxon's company was unwilling to cooperate, and so rode miles apart from the main column. The Maxon Mutiny would have unforeseen consequences for the Washington Territorial forces.

Adhering to his orders, Shaw then marched for the Walla Walla Valley to take over operations left undone by the retiring First Oregon. The reason for Shaw's orders to move to the Walla Walla stemmed from two letters Stevens had received from Bill Craig. Craig was married to a Nez Perce woman, had lived at Lapwai for years, had acted as a translator at the Walla Walla council of 1855, and was the Indian agent to the Nez Perce. On May 27, Craig had written to Stevens (his boss, as the Superintendent of Indians for Washington Territory) that he had heard "the Indians say they had made the whites run out of their country and will now make all the friendly Indians do the same."[17] The whites referenced were the First Oregon Mounted Volunteers. In a follow-up letter written on June 8, Craig reinforced the belief that there were still hostile Indians in the Walla Walla Valley. Craig even stated that he might have to leave the area or be killed.

But Shaw was not acting as the only territorial force in the east. First, believing Craig, Governor Stevens went to Fort Dalles himself. Stevens organized another company of Washington volunteers, under Captain Goff, with William Craig and some Nez Perce scouts in another company. These troops would head for the Walla Walla area, too.

In addition to Washington troops, Oregon's Governor Curry had ordered the creation of the Oregon Rangers, a three company battalion under the command of Major Davis Layton. Many of these men were veterans of the First Oregon Mounted Volunteers. Company A was commanded by Captain Alfred Wilson (former First Oregon captain), Company B by Captain Hiram Wilbur, and Captain William Haley had Company C. The Rangers were ordered to patrol the Oregon Trail to safeguard the pioneers during the wagon train season.

The first movement of the Rangers was a mid-June scout of the upper John Day River in central Oregon. Word was received that a hostile band was preparing to attack in coordination with Kamiakin's efforts in Washington. Instead, Layton found nothing but peaceful Indians. Over 900 Tygh, Deschutes, Wasco, and John Day Indians were heading for the Warm Springs Reservation created for them in 1855. Layton returned to Fort Dalles to prepare his Rangers for patrolling the Oregon Trail.

Re-fitted, the Rangers headed east. Near the old Catholic mission on the Umatilla, Layton came across an armed and ready band of Indians. Seeking reinforcements, he intercepted Captain Goff's Washington troops en route to Walla Walla, and followed the hostiles. Overtaking them on the upper portions of the Burnt River, the Oregon Rangers attacked on July 15. The day-long battle, between the Rangers and Indian warriors (this was a war party, not a village), resulted in an unknown number of Indians killed, as well as two Rangers. Among the items recovered from the defeated Indians was what was believed to be the scalp of Absalom Hembree, of the First Oregon.[18]

As the Oregon Rangers were patrolling the Oregon Trail, Colonel Shaw reached the Walla Walla Valley on July 9. There, he conferred with the faithful Lawyer of the Nez Perce and William Craig. Lawyer once more pledged the great tribe's loyalty, and Craig, now a lieutenant colonel of the Washington territorial forces, gathered together seventy-five Nez Perce warriors under Spotted Eagle (part of Lawyer's band). If there was any danger, reported Lawyer, it was from a small group of malcontents.

Well reinforced, Shaw searched for Indians to fight. Using a Nez Perce Indian scout named Captain John,[19] Shaw's command headed south, up into the Blue Mountains of Oregon. Crossing into the mountains, Shaw reached the traditional Indian grounds in the valley of the Grand Ronde.[20] As the Washington Territorial troops rode into the valley, on July 17, they came upon a village. Shaw reported,

> After proceeding about five miles, we ascended a knoll in the valley, from which we discovered dust arising along the timber of the river. I immediately sent Major Maxon and Captain John forward to reconnoiter...[21]

Shaw then returned to his command and arranged his six companies of troops for battle.

At this moment, a large body of warriors came forward, singing and whooping, and one of them waving a white man's scalp on a pole. One of them signified a desire to speak. Whereupon, I sent Captain John to meet him, and formed the Command in line of battle. When Captain John came up to the Indians, they cried out to one another to shoot him, whereupon he retreated to the Command, and I ordered the four companies to charge.[22]

This was the official version of how the battle started: Captain John was threatened. The unofficial version is that the village was comprised of Cayuse and Walla Walla Indians, most of whom were old men, women, and children. When the village was surprised by the sudden appearance of troops, the inhabitants immediately started to prepare to flee with their belongings. The historian Josephy notes that a few warriors did ride out to screen the camp, but it was Shaw who sent Captain John out to initiate a parley.[23] Richards notes that the whole camp was thrown into panic when they discovered that the troops were not Colonel Wright's regulars, but the feared volunteer forces. "A Cayuse messenger approached to report that the camp contained mostly women, old men, children, and a few young men."[24]

In any version, Shaw's rode into the village, scattering the Indians, with many seeking refuge in the timber along the river's bank. Dividing his command into wings, each attacked with vigor. The troopers closed to use their six-shot pistols. The Washington troops chased the Indians for fifteen miles until their spent horses caused the command to halt. In addition to capturing nearly 300 horses (and thus allowing the command to have re-mounts), Shaw was able to report many Indians killed, and their supplies destroyed. Shaw reported a great victory.

He did not mention in the official reports that the majority of those killed were women and children. "Men, women, and children ran in terror, and Shaw's men, inflamed with racial hatred, chased them and cut them down."[25]

During the melee, Maxon and a group of about sixteen men had crossed the river. Thinking he was cut off and in need of help, Shaw sent a party to search for him. At the close of the day, Maxon was still not found, and had not shown up at camp. The next day, Shaw sent out another party to search for Maxon. The searchers were ambushed by the Indians, and one man was killed, but Maxon was not found. Shaw had no choice but to head back to his base.

As they returned, Shaw prepared his report for Stevens. In it, he wrote of a glorious victory. If there had not been a lot of Indian warriors, it was assumed that they were gone from the camp to attack the Oregon Rangers, who that day were fighting fewer than forty miles away. To Stevens, it was the news he had been waiting for, and the news he needed to distract the angry populace from his lingering political problems of the spring. Stevens immediately rushed the news to the local press, claiming credit for the Oregon Ranger's victory at Burnt River:

Pioneer and Democrat
Olympia, WT
Friday, August 8, 1856

The Commander-in-Chief [Gov. Stevens]. . . appreciation of their late brilliant and successful achievement at the Battles of Grand Ronde and Burnt River.

"There were present on the ground about 300 warriors of the Cayuse, Walla-walla, Umatilla, Tygh, John Day and Des Chutes tribes, commanded by the following chiefs: Stock Whitley, Simmis-tas-tas…"

The Oregon press used the reports to chastise the regular army and to make unfavorable comparisons with the volunteers' efforts:

The Oregonian
Portland, OT
Saturday, August 2, 1856

FROM THE SEAT OF WAR NORTH
Two Battles With the Indians!
Oregon and Washington Volunteers Victorious !!!

"It may appear strange that, notwithstanding the whole regular force of the United States army have been in the field for months, they have done nothing, except to follow and *feed* the Indians, while the volunteers have followed, fought and whipped them

every where when ever they have been enabled to find them…..
The people of Oregon and Washington Territories have ample
cause to complain of Gen. Wool….”

With such victories, Shaw seemed to fulfill Stevens' trust in him.
Shaw returned to the Walla Walla Valley as a conqueror. But, upon his
return to the valley, several events cast a shadow on his triumph. First,
the missing Maxon and his men were already waiting for Shaw at
Walla Walla. Maxon's explanation of having been cut off, and riding
back to camp to wait struck everyone as ludicrous, and Shaw dismissed Maxon (and his company of loyal men) for cowardice.

Next, the man Shaw had detailed to bring goods promised to the
Nez Perce had arrived with the pack train, only to find the Nez Perce
hostile. First, the Nez Perce had discovered that during Shaw's last
visit, several of his men, seeking to test their courage, had selected
Indians at random and had killed them as if for target practice. Some
of those they selected were Nez Perce.

Second, the Indians had a real apprehension over more volunteers
in their valley. The volunteers made problems. Even William Craig,
married to a Nez Perce, feared remaining in the valley.

Shaw was ready. He sent Captain John with a letter to Lawyer
promising peace. But within the letter, Shaw said if the Nez Perce
"beat their drums for war, he would parade his men for battle."[26] Then
Shaw received a report from Craig saying that word of Shaw's victory
had had a subduing effect on the Nez Perce. The news of the white
victory allowed Lawyer to once more gain ascendancy in political
control within the tribe. To Shaw (and ultimately Stevens), the victory
at Grand Ronde was the force that kept the Nez Perce out of the war
with the whites.

But, the other effect of the Battle of Grand Ronde and the troubles
with the Nez Perce was to bring Governor Stevens to a decision. Stevens declared he would return to the valley of the Walla Walla and
hold a council with the Indians to address their grievances. Stevens
felt he could dictate terms to the Indians after Shaw's victory. But, in
addition to gaining advantage over the Indians, Stevens saw an opportunity to undercut General Wool's constant criticism that Stevens'
real desire was to prolong the war. If Stevens met with the Indians,

he would be able to undermine Wool's comments with the Army and within Washington, D.C.

Stevens dispatched runners with word to the Indians of his intent to meet with them again at Walla Walla. Prepared for the council, he left Olympia on August 11. Arriving at Vancouver Barracks, Stevens conferred with Colonel Wright, and invited Wright to join him in a territorial-Army joint council. Wright acted duplicitously. He said he was unable to go with him personally, but would direct Lieutenant Colonel Steptoe to accompany Stevens, and toward that end the two men journeyed to Steptoe at Fort Dalles. Wright extracted a promise from Stevens that with regular army protection, Stevens would send the Washington volunteers home. Actually, Wright had received orders from Wool to direct Steptoe to the Walla Walla Valley, establish a new army post and evict the volunteers, even if it meant arresting and disarming Shaw's command. None of this was conveyed to Stevens, and so Stevens' promise was given under a false promise of Army cooperation.

And, yet, Stevens was aware of General Wool's August 2 proclamation:

> No emigrants or other white, except Hudson's Bay Company, or persons having ceded rights from the Indians, will be permitted to settle or remain in the Indian country, or on land not ceded by treaty, confirmed by the Senate and approved by the President of the United States.

Wool made the White Salmon River of Washington and the Deschutes River of Oregon as the line east of which whites were not to settle. Wool's authority to do so, in light of the Oregon Land Donation Act, was of dubious legal right, but in the shadow of the proclamation, Wright's telling Stevens that Steptoe was 'accompanying" Stevens was pure fabrication.

Operating under a false impression of Regular Army cooperation, Stevens headed east from Fort Dalles on August 19, with Steptoe to follow. On August 23, Stevens reached Shaw's camp in the Walla Walla, ahead of the slow moving pack train of supplies and gifts for the Indians. In conferring with Shaw, Stevens noted that most of Shaw's men's enlistments were ending soon, but they decided that they would not be needed, since Steptoe was headed toward the Valley with his Regular Army forces.

The tenor of the council was set before any Indian arrived. As one historian noted, "The idea of another council with Stevens, especially at ill-omened Walla Walla, seems to have been repugnant to almost all the Indians."[27] As the slow moving pack train was nearing the Walla Walla River, on August 28, it was raided by Indians who made off with some of the valuable stores. More than 100 Indian warriors of the Cayuse, Walla Walla, and Palouse tribes celebrated their good fortune in plundering the pack mules.[28]

Stevens called upon Shaw's men to be vigorous in their actions against the Indians, even if outnumbered. If they were bold, they could defeat any Indians, and thus, "In this way only can the superiority of our race be established."[29]

The events in the Walla Walla Valley were still seen by the public as part of a regional war. The press refused to accept the Army's assurance that everything was under control. In Portland, the newspaper reported the events with bold headlines:

**The Oregonian
Portland, OT
Saturday, Sept 6, 1856**

**Another Fight with the Indians, North
A Supply Train Lost!**

Affairs North

**More Depredations in Southern Oregon
Seven Whites Killed!!**

With the end of August, the Indians started to arrive. All were tense and many hostile. Some tribes had refused to attend. The Spokane and the Coeur d'Alenes had not come, but Stevens had already heard from them, through their Catholic priest, Father Ravalli that they were holding Stevens to his word that no white soldiers would travel north of the Spokane River.

The Walla Walla, Cayuse, and Umatilla were angry and threatening: it was their village Shaw had destroyed on the Grand Ronde, on Stevens' orders. The Nez Perce came, but only in limited numbers, with such influential leaders such as Looking Glass staying away. Oregon Indians, such as the John Day and Deschutes Indians came, and so did the Yakima and Sinkiuse (with rumors that Kamiakin was coming with warriors).

With the opening of the meeting near, Steptoe and the Ninth Infantry arrived, and moved on. They did not stay with Stevens, but moved on to a point eight miles further up river to establish a new army base, Fort Walla Walla. Army "protection" let Stevens send all but one company of volunteers home. The sixty-nine men of the Washington Territorial Volunteers would form Stevens' honor guard company, rather than act as a defense force against such overwhelming numbers of Indians.

Stevens opened the council in his old style. He spent the first two days lecturing the Indians on their treachery, on the virtues of the treaties signed, and their requirement to honor the accord. His listeners sat in angry silence. Finally, they replied.

A Cayuse chief, Tum-neh-how-lish told the governor,

> Why are you talking to us? I have a head to think, a heart to feel, and breath in my body; I am equal to you. For that reason, as we are equal, I do not know why you are to tell me what to do.[30]

More Indians spoke. They spoke of their need for their homelands, and their willingness to fight for them. The great Nez Perce Eagle From the Light recalled how members of the First Oregon had hanged a Nez Perce, who was guilty of nothing more than being an Indian. He asked, would the Oregon volunteers be treated the same as the killers of Bolon?[31] None of the Indians spoke as a friend of Stevens. The council was not going as Stevens had envisioned.

Alarmed, Stevens sent a rider to Steptoe asking for help.

> One half of the Nez Perces and all the other tribes, except a very few persons, are unmistakably hostile in feeling. I particularly desire you to be present today, if your duties will permit, and I will also state that I think a company of your troops is essential to the security of my camp.[32]

Steptoe, in keeping with his orders from Colonel Wright, declined to attend. For once, the treachery had been done against Stevens. However, Steptoe did offer to send his company of dragoons to Stevens, but only to escort the governor to the Army camp, not for protection.

Stevens had courage. Even without the Army, the governor continued the council. He replied to the Nez Perce chief Eagle from the Light that the reason the Nez Perce had been hanged by the Oregonians was because he had been a spy for the hostile forces in the area. Without waiting to counter this statement, the Nez Perce chief Speaking Owl demanded, "Will you give us back our lands? That is what we all want to hear about; that is what troubles us. I ask you plainly to have a plain answer."[33]

Ignoring Speaking Owl, Stevens called upon Lawyer to aid him. The old chief rose to remind the others that they had agreed to the treaty, but other Nez Perce shouted him down. Many Nez Perce chiefs said that they had not understood the treaty, they did not want to give up their lands, and Stevens and Lawyer had tricked them into selling.

As things grew heated, rumors arrived that Kamiakin and Owhi were near with Yakima warriors. Then Steptoe sent Stevens another blow. Steptoe's command, "in execution of certain orders received from General Wool," would not be available to assist Stevens.[34] Stevens was now without any meaningful Indian help, and he could expect no help from the Army. He had no choice now; he moved his camp to the Army fort.

As Stevens and Shaw led their camp toward the soldiers at Fort Walla Walla (now under construction), the whites were in for another shock. Encamped between the council grounds and the army were the Yakima, including Kamiakin, Owhi, and Qulachan. Stevens feared the powerful Indians, but this time, Kamiakin had come in peace.

After the treaty of 1855, other Indians accused Kamiakin of treachery in that he signed for fifteen other tribes, and not the two he had said to Stevens he had authority to sign for as chief. He had protested his innocence to the other chiefs. Among those most angry with Kamiakin had been the Sinkiuse chief, Quil-ten-e-nock. In the June meetings with Wright, Quil-ten-e-nock had presented his case, and the colonel had given him a letter acknowledging the Sinkiuse role in bringing peace to the Columbia Basin. The chief of the Sinkiuse had come to the council grounds of Walla Walla to meet with Stevens and have the injustice righted. To act as his supporters and witnesses,

Kamiakin, Owhi, and Qualchan had agreed to come to support the Sinkiuse claims.

Quil-ten-e-nock approached Stevens but the governor declined to discuss the issue. The council ended with the Sinkiuse denied justice again.

When the council resumed at Steptoe's camp, the Indians remained enraged. With the exception of the Lawyer faction within the Nez Perce, a decided minority within the Nez Perce, the Indians were arrayed against Stevens. There was no point in going farther. Stevens closed by saying, "Follow your hearts; those who wish to go into the war go." To add further insult to Stevens, the next day Steptoe met with the still gathered tribes and pronounced, "My mission is pacific. I have not come to fight you, but to live among you....I trust we shall live together as friends."[35]

On September 19, Stevens headed for home escorted by his single company of volunteers and one band of Nez Perce led by Spotted Eagle. Having gone three miles from Steptoe's camp, the Stevens' party was attacked at one in the afternoon. In the lead was Quil-ten-e-nock, and Qualchan. Among the tribes attacking were 120 Nez Perce. Stevens estimated as many as 450 Indian warriors attacked him. To prevent Steptoe from doing anything, another group of Indians set fire to the dry grasses near Fort Walla Walla.

Stevens moved his party into the classic circle, using the wagons as cover. Andrew Pambrun was with the party as a translator. He recalled the opening attack,

> ...Just as we finished making a pen with the wagons chained together and the animals secured therein we were surrounded. An Indian rode up at full speed to one of our herders, who was in the rear with some loose animals, within ten feet and fired aiming at his head but missed. This was the signal for a general attack...[36]

The attacking Indians called out to the Nez Perce escort to flee, and Stevens, fearing they would be shot at in the confusion, or possibly fearing treachery, released Spotted Eagle and his warriors. Twice the volunteers charged a threatening group of Indians. Seeing an opportunity, Benjamin Shaw charged. The party of soldiers rushed after some Indians who were apparently fleeing, but actually they led the troopers into a trap. As the trap was about to be sprung, an Indian ignorant of the plan yelled out, "You band of squaws, what are you running from white men for? Turn on them and kill them all!"[37] Stevens sent a rider to Steptoe for help. He replied that he was too busy finding fresh grass for the mounts to ride to Stevens, and suggested Stevens retreat to the Army camp. This prompted Stevens somewhat sarcastically to reply that the retreat to the army was a good idea, "but it is impossible for me to move back without assistance. We have around us about 300 Indians."[38]

Steptoe received the last message at around 11 p.m. This finally made clear to Steptoe the governor's plight, and he ordered dragoons, infantry, and a howitzer to go to the relief of the governor's party. Further, the army was ordered to attack, if necessary. Once at Stevens' camp, the Army was able to march the entire party back to Steptoe's camp by 4 a.m.

The Indians felt betrayed. The Army had remained aloof from Stevens, had made it clear that they were not part of Stevens' efforts, most particularly in war. Seeing a distinction, the Indians felt as if Steptoe had gone back on the words he had just spoken, of being friends. Still angry, the Indians attacked Steptoe's position. Quil-ten-e-nock led one charge at Steptoe's camp, but was hit in the hip by a rifle shot, and knocked from the saddle.[39] Discouraged at their leader's wounding, warriors rode in and picked him up, but howitzer fire ended any further attack without loss of life.

The attack led by Quil-ten-en-ock had two dramatic impacts. First, it was the death knell of Stevens' last peace initiative. With the exception of Lawyer's faction, Stevens had no Indian allies.

Second, the attack seemed, at least in Steptoe's mind, to vindicate Stevens whole approach to handling the Indians. Lieutenant Colonel Steptoe would report to Colonel Wright on the actions during September, and conclude, "In general terms, I may say that in my judgment we are reduced to the necessity of waging a vigorous war, striking the Cayuses at the Grande Ronde and Kami-ak-kan wherever he may be found."[40]

This report to Wright was unacceptable. General Wool had given explicit orders, and Wright was hopeful of executing those orders, particularly now with all of the volunteers out of the field. On October 5, he returned to the Walla Walla Valley with Steptoe, and more regular troops. Hoping to succeed where Stevens had failed, Wright called for a council, but only five Indian chiefs came: Three Cayuse and two Nez Perce. While Wright made a favorable impression, it was made upon too few. Wright acknowledged the Indians' legitimate objections to the treaties of 1855, and knew they only wanted to be left alone. With the treaties still not ratified, Wright promised to keep whites out of Indian lands until the treaties became law. He offered that "The bloody shirt shall now be washed and not a spot left on it… all past differences must be thrown behind us….let peace and friendship remain forever."[41] One historian suggests that the Indians took Wright's words to mean the land was theirs, forever.[42]

These statements helped to defuse the situation in the Walla Walla Valley. Steptoe was able to complete the construction of Fort Walla Walla. By November, General Wool was reporting that the war was over in the Pacific Northwest. The summer campaign season had succeeded in establishing the illusion of peace, if not actual justice.

Summer Campaigning

Chapter 9 notes

1 Douthit, *Uncertain Encounters*, page 157.

2 Ibid, page 161.

3 Tichenor was a sea captain who plied the Oregon Coast. His greatest fame came from his efforts to establish a port of refuge at Port Orford (the later site of the town and Army post with a similar name, Fort Orford) in 1851. His first attempt resulted in the small group of men being besieged at the rock formation now called Battle Rock. He continued to be a strong advocate for coastal development.

4 Splawn, *Ka-mi-akin*, page 58.

5 Ibid, pages 58-59.

6 Wright and Stevens had an acquaintance that went back as far as their time in Mexico during the Mexican War. In fact, it had been Wright who had helped to carry the wounded Stevens from the field during the Battle of Molino del Rey.

7 Richards, *Isaac I. Stevens*, page 294.

8 Guie, *Bugles in the Valley*, page 37.

9 Kowrach, *Missionary of the Northwest*, pages 106-107

10 Guie, page 38

11 Kowrach, page 107.

12 Guie, page 38.

13 Josephy, *The Nez Perce Indians*, page 365.

14 Jackson, *A Little War of Destiny*, page 173.

15 Schlicke, *General George Wright*, page 128.

16 Guie, page 42.

17 Jackson, page 172.

18 Ibid, page 174.

19 Captain John had been active with Stevens going to the council with the Blackfeet, and was part of the Stevens Guard when Stevens returned the previous December. Further, Captain John had been a scout for the First Oregon as well.

20 In theory, the Walla Walla treaties of 1855 had awarded part of the valley to Joseph's Nez Perce, and the rest of the valley was reserved for the Cayuse and Umatilla Indians.

21 Bischoff, *The Yakima War*, pages 284-285.

22 Ibid, page 285.

23 Josephy, page 369.

24 Richards, page 297.

25 Josephy, page 369.

26 Ibid, page 371.

27 Burns, *The Jesuits and the Indian Wars of the Northwest*, page 150.

28 Trafzer and Scheueman, *Renegade Tribe*, page 74.

29 Guie, page 373.

30 Buschoff, page 293.

31 Richards page 304.

32 Bischoff, page 294.

33 Josephy, page 374.

34 Ibid.

35 Ibid, page 375.

36 Pambrun, *Sixty Years on the Frontier in the Pacific Northwest*, page 106.

37 Ruby and Brown, *The Cayuse Indians*, page 250.

38 Bischoff, page 296.

39 Ruby and Brown, page 252.

40 Josephy, page 376.

41 Ibid, page 377.

42 Pambrun, page 253.

Chapter Ten
A Calm

It was official: the war was over and on December 18, 1856, General Wool declared that peace had been restored throughout the region. Certainly, the combat had stopped. But, the political fighting continued and so did the killing on the frontier. For the next twenty months "calm" officially reigned over the Pacific Northwest.

The Northern War

In the Puget Sound region, the Indian leaders were still on the loose and Governor Stevens was reeling from the political ramifications of his martial law declaration. Both of these problems, the Indians and the Governor, would be resolved during this period.

For Leschi, he had Colonel Wright's letter giving him a good conduct pass, and what he sought was peace. But, Stevens still had a $500 bounty on Leschi's head. During October 1856, Leschi went to the Hudson's Bay post of Fort Nisqually and spoke with the post's chief trader, Doctor William Tolmie. Leschi told Tolmie that he wanted to remain on his land and hunt. To show his good faith, he offered to cut off his right hand. The trader declined the offer and Leschi faded into the hills.

Meanwhile, Leschi's brother, Quiemuth, sought peace, too. Voluntarily, Quiemuth surrendered and was taken to Governor Stevens' office in Olympia, quietly slipping into town with his white escorts around 2 a.m. to avoid detection by the sure to be aroused populace. Meeting them at his office, Isaac Stevens told Quiemuth's escort to keep the chief in the office until morning, when a sufficient escort could take the party to Fort Steilacoom for trial. But, the effort to go to the governor's office undetected failed. Settlers, some of whom had lost relatives in the fighting, broke into the governor's office at dawn and a fight ensued. During the melee, Quiemuth was shot, and then stabbed, dying in a pool of blood on Stevens' floor.

The governor, without a sense of irony, was outraged that citizens would take the law into their own hands. He had the murder suspect arrested, but at trial, no one could or would identify him as the man who fatally stabbed the chief, and thus the culprit was freed.

In was also in November 1856 that Leschi was captured for the bounty on his head. On November 13, a nephew of Leschi, Sluggia, and another accomplice, Elikuka, captured the great Nisqually chief as he fished on the upper Nisqually River. The two Indians turned Leschi over to the Indian agent Sidney Ford for the bounty. In keeping with the tradition of white promises to Indians, the $500 was not paid, but instead the two Indians received some blankets.[1] Agent Ford brought the chief to stand before Stevens in Olympia, on almost the same spot Leschi's brother had died shortly before. It was their first face-to-face meeting since the Christmas 1854 treaty council, but their conversation was unrecorded.

Wishing to avoid a repeat of Quiemuth, the governor had Leschi quickly removed to a safe location and requested a special session of the territorial court to convene: Judge Chenoweth presided. The charge was for the murder of the white Abram Moses, an officer in the Washington Volunteers, killed in combat on October 31, 1856, on Connell's Prairie.

The one day trial brought eighteen witnesses forward, including Sluggia,[2] who in apparent atonement for betraying his uncle, declared that Leschi had not killed Moses. Another witness, white, said he had seen the Indian kill the officer. The defense argued that Leschi had not killed the lieutenant, and if he had, the act had occurred during a period of declared war, and thus fell under the legal defense of an act of war.

After the first five hours of deliberation, the jury was divided eight to four for conviction. Moving away from a hung jury, two members cast their votes for guilty, but after another five hours, the jury remained, ten to two for conviction, with no hope for changing the two hold-outs' minds. Stalemated, the trial ended in a hung jury.[3]

A second trial began on March 20, 1857. That day ended with the jury bringing back the desired verdict of guilty, and it was left to translator Colonel Benjamin Shaw to tell the great chief his sentence: hanging.

The territorial Supreme Court allowed Leschi to make a personal appeal. His words were recorded.

> I do not see that there is any use in saying anything...I do not know anything about your laws. I have supposed that the killing of armed men in time of war was not murder; if it was, the soldiers who killed Indians are guilty of murder, too....I could not gain anything by going to war with the United States, but would be beaten and humbled and would have to hide like a wild beast...but I nursed my anger until it became a furious passion which led me like a false Ta-man-u-ous[4]....I went to war because I believed that the Indians had been wronged by the white men, and did everything in my power to beat the Boston[5] soldiers, but for lack of numbers, supplies and ammunition I have failed. I deny that I had any part in the killing of ....Moses. As God sees me, this is the truth.[6]

Unsurprising, the court upheld the verdict and the sentence. Some Indians responded to the verdict with criminal acts, but nothing would dissuade the Territory of Washington from the execution of the sentence. On January 22, 1858, the Sheriff of Pierce County escorted Leschi to the gallows. But as he arrived, white supporters of Leschi (or political enemies of Governor Stevens) intervened by arresting the sheriff on a charge of selling whiskey to Indians. The tactic was shorted-lived. The court merely ordered another date of execution, and on February 19, 1858, the great Nisqually chief died at the end of a rope.

As for Leschi's nemesis, Isaac Stevens, he was not governor when the Nisqually was hanged, nor was he even in the Washington Territory. In the spring of 1857, Stevens' term as superintendent of Indian affairs had expired, and he was not re-nominated for the position.[7] Undoubtedly, this was political fallout from the martial law debacle of the previous spring. Further, it was obvious that his hope for another political appointment as governor of the territory was doomed, so Stevens ran for Territorial delegate to the House of Representatives. He ran as a Democrat, and his opposition was from the newly created Republican Party. Created from the former Whig Party, plus those who were opponents of Stevens' high-handed ways,[8] the Washington Territory Republican Party had little time from its creation in January 1857 to field an effective opponent[9] to Stevens, who was still popular with the general Washington Territory population. When the election was held, Stevens won with sixty-five percent of the vote. Certainly one reason Stevens gained such a huge margin was that the Indian war veterans believed that Stevens would be most effective in getting the U.S. Congress to enact legislation to pay the territory's war debt, including salaries owed the volunteer soldiers.

Thus with much time elapsed for politics, Leschi's appeal for clemency was heard by the new Washington territorial governor, Fayette McMullin who refused to save Leschi's life.[10] Isaac Stevens was in Washington D.C. when his Indian enemy was executed.[11]

The Southern War

In Southern Oregon the battles were over and the remaining Indians were hunted down. As in the north, one Indian was singled out for special attention: Enos (the killer of Ben Wright). After he had surrendered in July 1856, the Army transferred him from Fort Orford to Vancouver Barracks for trial by "civil tribunal."[12] Ultimately returned to Port Orford for trial, Enos was charged with murder and desertion (from the Gold Beach Guards). Among the witnesses listed to appear against him were Captain Floyd-Jones (U.S. Army), Joel Palmer, William Tichenor, and several other Indians and whites. However, when the trial was set, one of the principal witnesses, Christina Geisel (wife of slain husband and sons) was not to be found. On April 11, 1857, the justice of the peace ordered the sheriff to release the prisoner, who had a blacksmith strike the chains off of Enos. Immediately, a mob grabbed the mixed-blood Enos and hauled him away for a more informal judicial proceeding. The sheriff reported what happened next:

"Whiskey was given him and he partly confessed to having assisted in the killing of his three companions…[Enos] was hanged on historical Battle Rock,[13] where his body was buried."[14]

Enos was not the only southern Indian to die during this period. As part of a special investigation of the wars (see below), J. Ross Browne visited the new Coast Indian Reservation. His tour brought him to the reservation where he listened to the Indians councils as they told him of their reasons for war, and the results—death.

A Calm

At Grand Ronde, Chief Sam (the white name for Toquahear) spoke of broken promises.

> The Government—Uncle Sam—has not complied with these promises. We have waited and waited because the Agents told us to be patient, that it would be all right bye-and-bye. We are tired of this. We believe Uncle Sam intends to cheat us…..Who are we to believe? …. [Captain Smith, Joel Palmer and others] promised us that as soon as the war was over we would be permitted to return to our country. Now the war is over. Why are we kept here still? This is a bad country. It is cold and sickly. There is no game on the hills. My people are all dying. There will soon be none left. The graves of my people cover the valleys. We are told if we go back, we will be killed. Let us go, then, for we might as well be killed as die here. [15]

This lament was repeated over and over again. At Siletz, Browne heard more cries for justice. Chiefs identified by their white names all stepped forward. Chief Joshua declared, "I want to say for my people that we have not been dealt with in good faith."[16] Chief John (Tecumtum) declared,

> For my own part, my heart is sick. Many of my people have died, since they came here; many are still dying. There will soon be none of us left….My heart is for peace. When there was war we fought like brave men. But there were many of us then. Now there are few. I saw after we had fought for our country that it was no use, that we could not stand it for long. I was the first to make peace. My people were dwindling away before the white man.[17]

Chief George decried being cheated of his home land.

> I also want to tell you what my heart is….That portion [Evans Creek and Table rock] was reserved for own use. We did not sell it; and such was the understanding when we signed the treaty. I would ask am I and my people the only ones who have fought against the whites that we should be removed so far from our native country? …But to us it is a great evil….I am told the President is our Great Father. Why then should he compel us to suffer

here. Does he not know that it is against our will? If he cannot fulfill the promises made to us through his agents, why does he not let us go back to our homes. Does he like to see his children unhappy? We are told that if we go back, the white people will kill us all—that their hearts are bad toward us. But the President is powerful. Let him send a paper to the whites and tell them not to trouble us. If he is powerful they will obey him. We are sad now. We pine for our native country. Let us go back to our homes, and our hearts will be bright again like the sun.[18]

Browne would report that as many as 900 of the Indians on the coastal Reservation were ill when he visited; many would die. As one historian has written, "The reservations were death camps for the displaced and dispirited natives of western Oregon."[19]

The Eastern War

To the east, an uneasy truce existed. The perceived cause of the war—to the Indians, the treaties, and to the whites, the murder of Bolon—was unresolved. The treaties had been sent to the Senate, but they remained unratified. Bolon's murderers remained at large as did the foremost Indian war leader, Kamiakin.

However, the volunteers had been pulled from the field. Left in their place was the regular U.S. Army. Colonel Wright had his headquarters at Fort Dalles, and two of his three major field commanders (the third being Lieutenant Colonel Casey at Fort Steilacoom) were guarding the Indian lands. Major Robert Garnett had established Fort Simcoe in the heart of the Yakima Nation country, and Lieutenant Colonel Edward Steptoe[20] was building Fort Walla Walla near the "war" tribes of the Cayuse, Walla Walla, and Umatilla lands. Not only did these forts help to pacify and protect the Indians, but they helped to keep whites out of the area, in accordance with General Wool's directive.

There were occasional murders—whites (usually miners) by Indians, and Indians by whites, but no large actions as in the recent conflict. It did seem as though the war was over, and peace prevailed. Of course, there were reports of war about to commence which put the troops on alert. For example, on December 27, 1856, Father Pandosy sent word to Fort Simcoe that he had heard that Kamiakin planned an attack. The war chief was leading a raiding party of not just Yakimas, but Walla Wallas, Palouse, Spokanes, and even Nez Perce Indians. Post commander Captain Dickenson Woodruff (Garnett was on leave) did not think the priest was lying, but believed he had been duped. The post was too well manned, so the captain believed the report a ruse to keep troops from protecting the livestock. He did send a patrol to reinforce the herd, but arrived to find that a mere fourteen Indians, led by Chief Skloom, had raided the cattle and horses in order to feed his hungry people. However, the Indians also captured the herder, Frederick White.[21]

This captive provided a unique opportunity for insight into the Indians. On December 31, the Indians allowed him to write a letter, which was delivered to Fort Simcoe. In the letter, White described how the young, angry warriors wanted to kill the whites, but it was Chief Skloom who had prevented bloodshed. White indicated that Skloom wanted peace. Captain Woodruff wrote back to Skloom, informing him that only Colonel Wright had the power to grant Skloom's request, but if the Indian released his captive, Woodruff would tell his colonel that "Skilloom, chief of the Yakimas, is a true man, and has but one heart and one tongue."[22]

What ensued was an exchange of letters and information. White was able to write he had found out who the murderers of Bolon were, and supplied their names. Notably, the names provided the Army were not the names the Army thought or sought, such as Qualchan or Kamiakin. Finally, Skloom gave White a horse and released him, apparently through a desire for peace. The intelligence exchanged would be of use in the up-coming episodes.

Still, the signs for peace were good. In the spring of 1857, came word from Steptoe at Walla Walla that Kamiakin was on his way to the valley—not at the head of a war party, but to offer peace. While the chief did not show, Steptoe was heartened, but by the fall of 1857 Steptoe was reporting that if the treaties were enforced, he feared the Indians would once more take to the warpath. The Cayuse were particularly troubled by many disreputable whites intruding into their country. "The intruders appropriated spots on which Indians' lodges stood, ordering their occupants to move out."[23] If a proper act of justice could prevail (a new set of treaties), then war might be avoided. If not, then 1858 promised to be bloody.

Regional Events and Politics

But other dynamics were in play throughout the region. General Wool asked to be relieved of his command on December 4, 1856. This request was granted, and a new commander of the Division of the Pacific, Brigadier General Newman S. Clarke, was appointed. He arrived at Vancouver Barracks in June 1857, to confer with his primary subordinate in the field, Colonel Wright. Once more, new reports were recounted of miners killed, and livestock runoff (even a recent raid on Fort Walla Walla's cattle), but overall, the peace declared six months prior was holding. With Governor Stevens' election to the House of Representatives in July 1857, one of the Army's harshest critics would be plucked from the Northwest. And, Clarke met with James Nesmith at Fort Dalles to coordinate Army policy with the new Superintendent for Indian Affairs for both Washington and Oregon Territories.

The meeting with Nesmith was critical for the region's future. Nesmith and Clarke agreed on many issues, such as keeping the whites from intruding onto Indian lands. Furthermore, they foresaw future difficulties on two issues. First, the information provided through Frederick White's captivity now identified the murderers of Andrew Bolon, and both agreed that these Indians must pay for their criminal acts (with their lives). Second, when the Walla Walla treaties were ratified by the Senate, the enforcement of the provisions could provoke an outbreak of hostilities again. Recognizing the injustices of the treaties, Clarke promised to use his influence against the treaties' ratification and to urge new treaties be negotiated with the tribes—this time by men such as Nesmith and Clarke.

Clarke took steps to keep the peace. He continued General Wool's order to prevent white settlers east of the Salmon River of Washington, and the Deschutes River of Oregon. He had Steptoe's command physically remove whites who had moved back to the Walla Walla Valley. And he had his command be honest with the Indians, telling them that there was not a general amnesty; those Indians guilty of crimes would and must be punished. From the Army's point of view, peace could be maintained through a strong, armed presence, and through fair and just treaties.

Another issue lingered throughout the region: payment to the territorial governments for their military expenses from 1855 and 1856. Washington, D.C. had received different accounts of the events.

Certainly the War Department had General Wool's report and belief that the territories had fomented the war as a means of raiding the U.S. Treasury. The Interior Department had reports from Indian agents Stevens and Palmer, and the President had reports from the territorial governors, Curry and Stevens. The territorial delegates, Oregon's Joseph Lane (a noted Indian fighter) and Washington's new delegate Isaac Stevens, both wanted money for their territories. What was fair?

Three different commissions or reviews were ordered to investigate the war. As a result of congressional legislation (August 18, 1856), Secretary of War John B. Floyd ordered

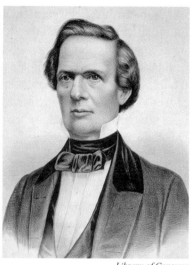

Library of Congress

Joseph Lane was a noted Indian fighter and later served as Oregon Territorial Governor and U. S. Representative.

one commission, which was comprised of three men. The first was a Willamette Valley resident, Lafayette Grover, a respected member of the territory, a future Oregon governor, U.S. representative and senator, and a future chief justice of the Oregon Supreme Court. The second member was Army Captain Rufus Ingalls. A third cousin and good friend of Isaac Stevens, he would be sympathetic to the territorial claims, as would Grover. The third member of the panel was less certain to be as understanding and agreeable to claims made by Washington and Oregon territories: Captain Andrew Jackson Smith of the First U.S. Dragoons.

The Floyd commission's charge was to determine the number of volunteers who served, the length of their service, and the expenses that were proper and necessary to be paid to the territories. After examination of the records, the commission decided that $1,409,644.53 was due to payroll for the volunteers while $3,040,304.80 was appropriate for supplies. Of these approximately $6,000,000, $4,500,000 was to be paid to Oregon and $1,500,000 to Washington.

A second examination, resulting from the same legislative directive, was an Interior Department examination as to the causes of the war, how the Indians were treated, and the expenditures by the Bureau of Indian Affairs (principally Stevens and Palmer or their agents). The Secretary of the Interior assigned J. Ross Browne to undertake the examination for the Interior. Browne's 1857 report determined that the treaties were not the cause of the war, no missteps were taken by Stevens, and the two territories had no choice but to call out volunteers. Browne's report supported territorial claims as legitimate war expenditures. It was during this investigation that Browne met with the Indians at the Coast Reservation, noted above.

After receiving these reports, Congress directed a third audit on February 8, 1859, conducted by R. J. Atkinson of the Treasury Department. Not surprisingly, the Treasury decided that the claims by the two territories were excessive, and reached a conclusion that cut the Floyd Commission's findings by fifty-five percent. It would be this figure of $2,714,808.55 that would ultimately find its way to the two territories.[24]

The final political movement of the time was the drive to make Oregon a state. One of the first steps was to draft a constitution and in June 1857 an election for a constitutional convention was held. Once the drafters were elected, the convention convened on August 17, 1857. They wrote a constitution and submitted it to the voters who approved it on November 9, of the same year.[25] The territory was ready for the Congress to make Oregon a state.

The constitution was a remarkable document that reflected the people and the times. While the issue that loomed largest at the constitutional convention, as well as nationally, was slavery, other racial matters were included in the document. For example, Chinese arriving after the adoption of the constitution could not file mining claims, and Chinese, negroes, and mulattos could not vote. By a separate vote in November, free blacks and mulattos were excluded from entering the territory, and subsequently the state.[26] The Indians were not thought of as potential citizens.

Here, finally, the elements were brought together for the final stages of the war. Politically, Oregon was moving toward statehood, and while only a territory, both it and Washington were flexing their political strength. The two territorial delegates were requesting monies from Congress as well as pushing for Senate ratification of the treaties. The two territories had had a hand in a change in Army leadership (even the willing cooperation of General Wool, who could not wait for transfer to a post back east), and the U.S. Army had the strength and men in position to deal with Indian issues.

While the period of calm had lasted from the fall of 1856 to the spring of 1858, it was truly the calm before the last storm. The battles of 1858 would doom Indians to the treaties they hated. With the war's resumption, the era was moving toward its final treachery.

Chapter 10 notes

[1] Richards, *Isaac I Stevens*, page 309.

[2] Sluggia would not live to see his uncle hanged. In October 1857, another Indian killed Sluggia in revenge for his betrayal of Leschi.

[3] Eckrom, *Remembered Drums*, pages 153-156.

[4] An Indian spirit.

[5] From fur trading days, the British were called "King George men", and Americans "Bostons."

[6] Ibid, pages 156-157.

[7] The two superintendent positions for Oregon and Washington were combined into one office, and James Nesmith, late colonel of the 1st Oregon Mounted Volunteers was appointed to the office.

[8] Another political issue was the charge of Stevens' intemperance. The Republicans basically charged that Stevens was staying sober only long enough to win the election.

[9] The Republican Party's candidate was Alexander Abernathy, brother of former Territorial Governor of Oregon George Abernathy.

[10] Richards, page 311.

[11] There was one other battle in the Puget Sound area in November 1856, but it was not really part of the war by American Indians. A raiding party of British Columbia Indians attacked into Puget Sound, and was ultimately stopped by the U.S. Navy near Port Gamble, Washington. The *U.S.S. Massachusetts* confronted the Indians and ordered them to surrender. When they did not, the Navy boxed the raiders in between the *Massachusetts*, a merchant ship named the *Traveller* (armed with cannon transferred from the Navy ship), and Marines and sailors ashore, also armed with cannon. On November 21, 1856, after refusing to surrender, the combined power of both ships and the land force opened fire, and the Marines charged. Finally, on the 22nd, after having suffered twenty-seven killed, and twenty-one wounded, the Indians surrendered, and were taken back to Vancouver Island.

[12] Douthit, *Uncertain Encounters*, page 165.

[13] Battle Rock was named for an Indian-white battle that occurred on June 9, 1851, and not during the period covered in this work.

[14] Ibid, page 166.

[15] Beckham, *Oregon Indians*, page 235.

[16] Ibid, page 238.

[17] Ibid, pages 238-239

[18] Ibid.

[19] Ibid, page 234.

[20] Both of these officers held "brevet" rank awarded for bravery during the Mexican War, and are often referred to by those ranks, such as Lieutenant Colonel Steptoe.

[21] Guie, *Bugles in the Valley*, page 59.

[22] Ibid, page 62.

[23] Ruby and Brown, *The Cayuse Indians*, page 255.

[24] Carey, *General History of Oregon*, page 621.

[25] Joseph Lane was returned to the Congress as Oregon's territorial delegate in the same election.

[26] Ibid, pages 510-511

The War Resumes

1 858 would herald the real end of the war, but not until the final battles had been waged. It seemed as if all the efforts from the end of 1856 until the new year of 1858 were unraveling, that once more the whispers of war were growing into the cries of combat.

With the New Year, rumors and warnings of war were heard. In January, the commander of Fort Walla Walla, Edward Steptoe, was writing to his chain of command of the dangers posed by the Indians surrounding him. He warned, "There has never been a doubt in my mind that very slight encouragement would at any time suffice to revive their late hostile feelings."[1] Certainly one reason for the unease was that despite General Wool's order (endorsed by the new Pacific Division commander, General Clarke), whites were moving back into the Walla Walla Valley. The Indians ordered the whites to leave (in accordance with their treaty rights), but instead, the whites appealed for protection.

One Indian agent (of the Flatheads of western Montana) visited Oregon City and spoke of "The state of the Indians is alarming, or at least uncertain all around." Richard Lansdale went on to note the Indians "*wish* to be friendly," but if the whites were to move on building the military roads planned, the Indians "*will kill them* [italics Lansdale's]."[2]

Father Joseph Joset of the Jesuits ministered to the Coeur d'Alenes and wrote how Kamiakin had "particularly tried to gain over" that tribe, and the Yakima chief, with the Palouse chief Tilcoax was counseling war.[3] While Father Joset believed he was keeping the Coeur d'Alenes and the Spokanes out of the war coalition, Father Peter De Smet (also of the Society of Jesus) wrote of an alliance of nine tribes, able to quickly bring warriors against the whites: "In a few days a body of 800 to 1000 warriors was organized."[4]

The actions of white miners gave a constant stimulus to war. As the avarice driven whites went through Indian lands to Colville in Northern Washington or further north, into British Columbia, seeking gold, they often attacked Indian women for pleasure or killed Indian men for sport. This prompted Indian attacks, which in turn called for white protection from the Army.

One white outrage stimulated the Sinkiuse chief Quil-ten-e-nock to seek revenge. He spoke to his fellow Indians of their plight:

> Colonel Wright is now far away and those who are in charge are not keeping faith. We have made peace, but our enemies still hound us…We are now so poor that we cannot move our camps. Our squaws are wailing, our old men discouraged and our papooses no longer play around our wigwams. Everything seems dead….I have now enough. The word of a pale face shall pass by my ears as the idle wind. In my poverty and humiliation I blush. I have been a bold man, born of a race of warriors who have never turned their backs on a foe. My father was the bravest of the brave. His name struck terror to his enemies. I have always been a free man, and shall be again. I will disgrace his name no longer by keeping this false peace.[5]

Words such as these were what the Catholic priests were hearing and reporting. And Quil-ten-e-nock was true to his word. After the next white humiliation, the great Sinkiuse chief shot the man, but before the white died, he returned fire, silencing the chief's voice forever.

More pressure was building from the miners, calling for the army to protect them and punish the savages preying on them. Then word came of a new Army plan. What was needed was a military road, connecting the eastern Washington area with western Montana. A road was ordered built starting from Fort Walla Walla. First heading north and then east through many former warring tribes' homelands, the road proceeded to Fort Benton, the head of navigation on the Missouri River. Assigned to survey and then build it was Lieutenant John Mullan.

To the Indians, particularly the Spokane, Palouse, and Coeur d'Alenes, this was another white betrayal. The whites, that is Governor Stevens, had promised that they would not move north across the Snake River, at least not without the permission of the tribes. But here were the whites headed for the heart of that country.

By March 1858 miners were killing Indians, white soldiers were still breaking their word, and everywhere it seemed the whites were taking Indian lands. More and more Indians were calling for war. In Yakima country, many who favored war wanted to follow Kamiakin, while others such as Owhi had agreed to stay peaceful. But, the outrages, the humiliations, and then the death of Quil-ten-e-nock were pushing many to fight. Owhi's son, Qualchan had tried to keep his father's peace pledge, but speaking of the dead Sinkiuse chief, Qualchan now vowed war, too. "Had I refused my father and stayed to help Quil-ten-e-nock fight, doing my duty as a warrior, he would not now be dead. I will take up his fight where he left off."[6] The arena was set to explode.

Sensing the pressures, General Clarke directed his personnel in the Columbia Department (the Pacific Northwest) to prepare for good weather operations. At Steptoe's command, the general ordered Fort Walla Walla to be placed "in a state of full efficiency, at the earliest possible date,"[7] in order to find out what the Indians were up to, whether war or peace. Already Fort Walla Walla had seen threatening signs. Palouse warriors raided horse and cattle herds throughout the fort's valley, including the post's cattle herd on April 12 (by the Palouse)[8] and rancher Walter Davis' on April 17. Steptoe certainly wanted to "stop this thieving."[9] In Portland, *The Oregonian* called the raid an instigation for war by Kamiakin.[10]

Adding to the tensions were the on-going Mormon problems in Utah. Army troops were headed that way to confront the separatist religious refugees. It looked as if another war in the West might compete for troops and supplies. Rumors came with threats. Major Garnett at Fort Simcoe reported that Yakima Chief Skloom said Mormons were working throughout the area urging Indians to attack the whites. While unverified, it was credible that Mormon emissaries might be seeking a "second front" to distract the U.S. Army from the fight in Utah. It was more critical than ever to find out what was happening with the Indians. General Clarke needed information.

Library of Congress
Lieutenant David Gregg

Eastern Washington Territory was the eye of the growing tempest. Numerous pressures added to the increasing barometric intensity swirling about today's Palouse country. The reports added to the swirling storm of war, with word that Kamiakin was in the Spokane—Coeur d'Alene area preaching war, miners in the Colville area crying for protection, the new military road being surveyed from Fort Walla Walla, rumors of eastern Washington Indians at unrest, and finally, that Mormon agitators were working the Indians. Clearly, Major Steptoe's command was the logical one to seek the truth.

On May 6, 1858, Lieutenant Colonel Steptoe set out with three undermanned companies of First Dragoons (Companies C, E, and H) and one part of a company of Ninth Infantry (E Company), mounted. E Company, Ninth Infantry, Captain C. S. Winder commanding, was the best armed unit, carrying the standard infantry weapon, the 1841 rifle. While accurate, the long gun was incapable of being reloaded from horseback. The foot soldiers also freighted two mountain howitzers.[11] Most of the dragoons slung the ineffective musketoons across their saddles. This was true of Captain Taylor's[12] C Company and E Company, led by Second Lieutenant William Gaston. H Company, however, led by Second Lieutenant David Gregg, had ten carbines to field test as a replacement for the short-barreled, limited-range[13] musketoon. The 1841 rifles and the new carbines would be crucial in the unfolding events.

Clearly Steptoe was not leading a major combat campaign. He had left behind at Fort Walla Walla B Company, under the command of Captain Frederick. J. Dent (brother-in-law of U. S. Grant), the rest of E Company, both of the Ninth Infantry, and Captain William Grier's I Company, First Dragoons, acting as the post commanding officer in Steptoe's absence. A typical combat force would have fielded two of the remaining three companies. As further evidence that Steptoe's expedition was not punitive, he ordered his 158 men to carry only routine patrol amounts of ammunition (about forty rounds per man). One other problem would beset the expedition: the troops were mostly raw recruits.

Complicating the situation, three leading officers were ill. The column's commander, Lieutenant Colonel Steptoe, had suffered a stroke in 1855 that had earlier left him unable to ride a horse, at least temporarily.

No less fragile was the health of two other officers. Captain Winder had just finished a two-year medical leave of absence and Lieutenant William Gaston had cancer steadily growing within his neck. Believing it to be fatal, Gaston had often told fellow officers of his desire to die a warrior's death rather than be slowly consumed by the agonizing cancer.[14]

Indian signs increased as the column marched east and north. Kamiakin was reportedly with the Palouse and his friend, Chief Tilcoax. The war chiefs were well informed of the Army's movement by Indians, often feigning friendliness to the Army.

Although this was Palouse country, Steptoe marked other Indians as well. Near the Snake River the column met with friendly Nez Perce, who told of a large gathering of Palouse ahead. Here was the first sign of trouble. At the Snake River, the mixed-blood civilian John McBean hired to scout for Steptoe refused to go farther north, telling Steptoe that he would be attacked. Not heeding the warning, Steptoe hired Nez Perce Indians, led by Chief Tammutsa, also known as Timothy, to scout for his command. This had unforeseen consequences.

Rather than take the direct route toward Colville, the column swung a little further east, and then north, nearly entering the Coeur d'Alene country. Indians, professing peace and friendship made contact with the column as it pushed north. A few Indians warned the troopers that the tribes ahead were listening to agitators such as Kamiakin, who called for the whites to be stopped. Inflaming matters, Steptoe's Nez Perce scouts would taunt these Indians saying, "Coeur d'Alenes, your wives, your horses, your goods shall very soon be ours."[15]

As word spread that whites were marching, more and more Indians gathered in camps ahead of the white line of march. Kamiakin rallied the warriors saying, "We now have the opportunity to kill this whole command, thereby making the white man afraid forever to attempt to pass through our country."[16] "Tilcoax was said to have chided the Coeur d'Alenes into joining the hostiles, saying that they were 'very brave in words' but acted 'like cowards and women.'"[17]

Marching north, on Sunday May 16, 1858, the column was at Pine Creek camp when it stumbled onto a party of Indians, who seemed to be waiting to ambush the troopers. Captain Winder described what he saw, "At first sight with my glass I could count but 70, [but] in a few seconds as if by magic [more Indians] appeared all around us, some 800, and in half an hour from 1,000 to 1,200, the Indians say 1,600 which may be true."[18] The large party of warriors appeared across the rolling hills. A few rode out, as if to parley. Their leaders had heard that Steptoe had come to destroy their nations. If that was his mission, the Indians were prepared to defend themselves. Steptoe proclaimed his peaceful intent and desire to talk, saying he was headed for Colville, but the Indians had no trust. Some chiefs, seeking peace, had sent word for a Jesuit missionary, Father Joset. Arriving on that Sunday, Joset argued for peace, but inadvertently persuaded the Indians not to fight on the Christian Sabbath.

Joset met with many chiefs, always counseling peace. The Jesuit had some Indian chiefs with him, but they were not war-chiefs. But even the peace-inclined Chief Vincent of the Spokane said he had demanded of Steptoe, "what he meant by coming that way upon us."[19] Vincent insinuated the column's swing way to the east was a ruse, rather than a direct march to the Colville mines. Here, quite possibly, Steptoe sealed the fate of his command. He insisted that he was merely marching for the mines, a statement which the Indians saw was false. Father Joset described the statement as like marching "from Paris through Berlin to Turin."[20]

Why had Steptoe swung so far east, into the Palouse country? To the Indians, whites were obviously intending to march through the Coeur d'Alene and Spokane country, and not for the mines. Certainly, there was Steptoe's desire to learn the feelings of the Indians, and he truly did not anticipate war. But also, there was another, less obvious reason. Timothy, his taunting Nez Perce scout chief, was involved in a personal dispute with the Palouse Chief Tilcoax. As Timothy led the Army east and north, he found evidence of his hated enemy Tilcoax heading north. Timothy led the army after the Palouse. Tilcoax now perceived the Army to be chasing him and his Palouse Indians. This unspoken desire, which remained concealed from Steptoe, undoubtedly contributed to the perception that the whites were once more lying.[21]

Attempting to fulfill his mission, Steptoe spoke to the Indians, but found no listeners. Seeing that it would be impossible to complete any talks, Steptoe ordered his command to head back. At this point, Steptoe sent the first of two riders back to Fort Walla Walla. The first messenger took a situation report to Grier at Fort Walla Walla. It was not a call for reinforcements. He

Wikimedia Commons
Lieutenant Colonel Edward Steptoe

reported "the Palouse are in front of us…They say that they will fight; I daresay they will, but I hope we shall be able to give them a good drubbing."[22] Steptoe simply reported the situation with an order to have Grier send troops to guard the Snake River crossing point. This was done, as noted below.

Later, after things became critical, Steptoe would send another messenger. This one carried a different message, and was not a mere situation report. Fearing the Indians' intent, Steptoe had an Indian rider, Wie-cat, take message back to Fort Walla Walla with word of the danger he was in. The plea was never delivered. Believing that the command would be wiped out, Wie-cat did return to the Walla Walla Valley, but not to seek help for Steptoe. Instead, Wie-cat tried to rally the Cayuse and Walla Walla Indians to attack the weakly defended fort.

Steptoe headed south and made camp. As his troops headed south, the Indians were openly threatening. Captain Winder noted that the warriors were all "around us, yelling, whooping, shaking scalps and such things over their heads, looking like so many fiends."[23] As the soldiers set up camp, the dragoons kept to their horses, facing outward, guarding against any attack. For three hours, the horse soldiers eyed the horde riding around them. Even with the belief that help was not needed against the Indians, it must still have been a frightening night as the troopers were enclosed by Indian camps, all singing and dancing around the flames, as the warriors sang their war songs.

Still, there were chiefs urging the Indians not to attack the whites. Within this side of the Indian camp, Father Joset was welcome. He tried to tell the chiefs that they had to control their warriors, "whosoever engages in battle without the order of his chief is guilty of all the evil which flows from it."[24] Joset said to the Indians that tomorrow he would go to the white chief (Steptoe), and then bring the chiefs there—to settle the issues peaceably. It seemed to Joset that maybe he had a chance to prevent war, if the chiefs could control the hot-tempered young warriors. Throughout the night, the warriors danced to the pounding of the drums, clearly audible to the soldiers in their bivouac six miles away. Many Indian warriors prepared for battle, openly defying the peace-inclined chiefs.

The various tribes prepared for war in their own tradition. Among the Indians present were the following tribes: Coeur d'Alenes, Spokane, Kalispel, Walla Walla, Palouse, Nez Perce (who fought on both sides), Kettles, Okanogans, Thompsons, Yakima, Cayuse, Sinkiuse, Flatheads, Kutenais, Pend d'Oreilles, and maybe a few others, in smaller numbers. Some warriors painted their ponies, others themselves. Some tribesmen wore ornately decorated war bonnets, while others stripped to a simple loin cloth, with a single eagle feather attached to a headband. The young men of the tribes were preparing to kill whites.

Before the first light of dawn, the army rolled out and headed south, toward Fort Walla Walla. Monday, May 17 had the sun barely up when Father Joset called for his horse to ride to the whites and prevent the war. Instead, he was met by a Palouse shaman, Tshequyseken, of the militant Tilcoax faction. Yelling to be heard above the war cries, the medicine man asked Joset, "Do you see now the deceit of this people?" Grabbing a horse, Joset headed out to find Steptoe, only to reach the now empty white camp. Many warriors followed the priest out, and seeing the Americans gone, they yelled that the whites were fleeing in fear.

Joset spurred his horse on, and after three miles, he finally overtook the retreating whites. Reaching Steptoe, Joset explained the anger of the Indians, and their intent to stop the whites' road through their country. Further, he spoke of the Indian outrage at Steptoe coming into their country unannounced, and with so many armed men. Steptoe protested his peaceful intent, averring he was marching to the Colville mines to seek answers. Joset noted later that he, too, was suspicious of Steptoe since the army was so far from the main line of march. But, Steptoe told Joset of his meeting with the Indians yesterday, and how he had thought there would be bloodshed, but since the council had ended without killing, he was now hopeful he could march home in peace. Joset said the two of them could talk as Steptoe marched, and Joset would bring the chiefs to Steptoe. However, when Joset went back to the Indians, all he could find was Vincent of the Coeur d'Alenes. Many chiefs were trying to counsel peace, but the hot-heads were preparing to fight.

When Joset returned with Vincent, Steptoe praised the chief for his efforts at peace-making the previous day, but then, perhaps the last hope to avoid war was interrupted. A Nez Perce scout for the Army, Levi, rode up and lashed Vincent across the shoulders with his riding crop. As Levi did so, he taunted Vincent to open fire. The other Nez Perce scouts were openly hostile. Was this the opportunity Timothy's people had been seeking of obtaining revenge on Tilcoax? What better chance for the humiliation of Tilcoax than when Timothy had such strong allies as the U.S. Army? But even then, Vincent held his temper, and merely replied that Levi would be "ashamed" for having struck another Indian.[25]

As Steptoe conferred with Vincent and Joset, another Indian rode up with the news that the chiefs could not restrain their young warriors. With that warning, Steptoe and Vincent shook hands, and the Indian and the priest rode toward the Indians, once more trying to stop a war.

And it seemed that perhaps they had. As the two men counseled peace, many Indians seemed to agree. But then one Coeur d'Alene Indian for war, Melkapsi, slapped a chief for peace, Victor, and the two wrestled. Father Joset physically intervened in this fight, too, and it seemed as if his actions had had an effect. By placing himself between the two, he seemed to shame the aggressor. With peace restored there, the priest rode back to the main Indian camp to tell the young men there would be no war that day. About a half hour after he reached camp, a rider came in to proclaim the war had started, as indeed it had back at the column of troops marching south.

Melkapsi was a disciple of Kamiakin; he wanted war. As the Catholic father rode away, some of Melkapsi relatives now added to his shame, saying to him, "What do you do? You maltreat your own people! If you wish to fight, behold your enemies."[26] And before the group of Coeur d'Alenes were the white troops, in a slight valley, crossing a stream. Down the hill the young warriors charged, opening fire as they rode.

As the Indians charged, the rear guard held their fire, under orders to avoid a fight if at all possible. There had been sporadic rifle fire from the Indians before, seemingly just to make noise. The dragoons hoped that this was another case of just making noise. But then a trooper was shot from his saddle, Lieutenant Gaston had a horse shot out from under him,[27] and the soldiers, thinking their popular officer killed, returned the fire. The officer grabbed a remount, unwounded, and resumed his command.

The situation now was of a column strung out, crossing the stream. The column had covered three miles by 8 a.m., when the Indians opened fire. A company of dragoons guarded each flank. In one of the first charges, the troopers dropped three of the Coeur d'Alenes chiefs, which further enraged the Indians. If there had been any hope for this to remain a rearguard skirmish, the three dead chiefs ended it. As Vincent explained after the conflict, "I had no intention to fight, but at seeing the corpse of my brother-in-law I lost my head."[28] Steptoe ordered his column to keep moving, relying on his dragoons to keep the Indians from breaking his line of march.

Another charge dropped Lieutenant Gaston again (as well as two privates), but this time he was confirmed in his wish to die in combat and not from cancer. On the side of the column protecting the flank, First Sergeant William C. Williams tried to take command with Gaston's death, but he, too, was thrown from his saddle as he was mortally wounded.[29] As more Indians joined, around noon, a coup party made a foray against the column's pack train, and a few of the mules were captured.

In the mountains. Spokane camp.

The dragoons would try to cover the infantry, then surge ahead to a high point, holding it until the column moved up, and then repeat the maneuver. With the column constantly moving and fighting, there had been no time to distribute more ammunition from the pack mules, and the officers were reporting to the head of the column that the men were down to four rounds of ammunition a piece. The fight was becoming critical. While the non-commissioned and commissioned officers had their sabers, none of the dragoons had them, being ordered to leave them at Fort Walla Walla. Once the men exhausted their rifle fire, the dragoons would have their colt revolvers, but after six shots, it would be a massacre as the defenseless men would be down to their fists and knives. Further, as more Indians joined the fight, they were attacking the head of the column, slowing any movement toward the distant and seemingly forlorn hope of safety at the fort.

Pausing once to get water, the howitzers were unlimbered and fired a few rounds each. This checked the Indian advance, but once the watering was completed, the column moved again, using its precious store of ammunition.

Steptoe's command was in dire peril of being cut down piecemeal as they moved. After six hours of continuous fighting, Steptoe ordered the troops to head to the crest of a hill and to circle in defense (near the present day town of Rosalia, Washington). Commanding the dragoons to provide covering fire, Steptoe led the column scrambled to the top of a low hill. In the firefight, Captain Taylor of the Dragoons (on the right flank) was shot through the neck. Now Gaston's E Company (of the Ninth Infantry) and Taylor's C Troop were without their leaders.

Taylor had been a popular officer, and the dragoons wanted to retrieve the obviously wounded officer, writhing on the ground. The struggle became fierce as troopers dismounted to recover the dying Captain Taylor as the Indians swarmed upon them.[30] Fighting hand-to-hand, the Colt revolver of particular use with the Indians upon the soldiers. Another trooper, Victor De Moy, swung his empty rifle as a sword, keeping the Indians at bay and allowing his comrades to carry the wounded officer up the hill. The former French army captain was heard shouting, "My God, for a saber!"[31] De Moy, shot from his horse, shot two of his attackers with his revolver as they came at him, and as the rest of the troop climbed to the top of the hill, leaving him behind, he saved the last bullet for himself.

Steptoe now had his soldiers at the crest of a hill overlooking Pine Creek. The howitzers resumed their fire, but were as ineffective as the musketoons. The two best weapons were the colt revolvers at close range, and the Sharp's carbines at distance. Captain Winder recalled making their stand among "1,000 of those infuriated devils."[32]

Some reports had Kamiakin organizing charges against the whites,[33] and the Indians made two attempts in the afternoon to roll over the badly bloodied command. As the day moved toward dusk, Steptoe's command fought the Indians until nightfall using the long range 1841 rifles and the recently issued carbines. The Spokanes and Coeur d'Alenes attacked Steptoe's back, or from the north. In his front were the Palouse, with the other tribes (in much smaller numbers), filling in where they might. Soaring arrows and musket fire were steadily cutting men down. The desperate troopers fired back, holding the Indians at bay. However, even with the distribution of all the ammunition from the pack mules, the heavy fighting had reduced each man to three rounds of ammunition.

As night fell, the Indians ceased their main efforts, and sporadically fired at the whites. Around the hilltop, the soldiers saw the glowing fires of the Indian camps and listened to the warriors' victory cries and song. The army men did not know that Kamiakin was urging more combat to finish the whites that night, telling the warriors:

> Our work is not finished. Let us keep up the fight. No doubt their ammunition is about exhausted. One more battle and they are ours. The dead and wounded are with them and the sight will make them fear us more. We have them now in anguish. Let them not escape. We can finish them in a short time and then we can lie down to sleep. If we do not get them now, dawn of day will not find them there.[34]

But the Indians argued against a night battle, confident that the soldiers would wait for morning, when they would be more easily killed.

Surrounded by burning campfires and shouting Indians, the troopers were faced with the terror of the dark. Everyone knew that unless a miracle happened, this was their last night on Earth. Steptoe recalled no one "doubted that we would be overwhelmed with the first rush of the enemy."[35] Steptoe called for a heroic final stand. Instead, the officers persuaded him that they must try to escape. If the command was wiped out, the only recourse left for Fort Walla Walla would be to retreat to Fort Dalles, since they were too weak to hold out. The column had to try for Walla Walla. Hastily burying his dead as well as his howitzers, Steptoe, with the lightened force, made a stealthy retreat in the darkness. There was a gap between the Indian lines. Father Joset later reported that the Spokane Indians had gone to get fresh horses, and this left an opening for the whites to move through.[36]

The departure was well timed. Kamiakin finally persuaded the Indians that they could wipe out the whites that night. Shortly after midnight, the Indians made an unusual night attack, only to find the whites gone.

A night march of eighty miles to the Snake River brought the command to Captain Frederick Dent, who met them with a column of sixty-six men as part of the previous plan to protect the river crossing, and helped them cross to relative safety. Steptoe lost eight killed, had eleven wounded, and reported one missing.[37] Indian sources put their casualties at nine killed and forty wounded. The historian Burns credits Steptoe with a remarkable escape: "Steptoe had managed one of the cleverest retreats in Indian-fighting history."[38]

The situation for the Army was serious. The Fort Walla Walla command feared the Indians would attack, and the post was still recovering from the terror of their close scrape. Charles Winder reported his own fears in a letter stating how for days afterward, he relived the battle he had just been through. Steptoe would carry through the rest of his career (which was to be short[39]) the reputation of the "Steptoe Disaster," which was later described as "one of the most sad events that ever befell our cavalry."[40]

After the battle, Father Joset was upset by his failure to halt the war. Commended in Army reports as very helpful, and recognized as a peace-maker, nevertheless, the Catholic priest saw some failure on his part. Wanting to know what had happened, Father Joset went to one of the Coeur d'Alene chiefs he had thought as a force for peace, and asked what the whites had done to cause the fighting. Chief Vincent replied the whites had done nothing, "all the fault is on our side."[41]

In once sense, it did not matter which side had started this round of fighting. Now, once more, war was in the Northwest.

The War Resumes

Chapter 11 notes

[1] Burns, *The Jesuits and the Indian Wars of the Northwest*, pages 168-169.
[2] Ibid, page 169.
[3] Ibid, page 194.
[4] Ibid.
[5] Splawn, *Ka-mi-akin*, page 83.
[6] Ibid, page 86.
[7] Carey, *General History of Oregon*, page 614.
[8] Trafzer and Scheuerman, *Renegade Tribe*, page 76.
[9] Josephy, *The Nez Perce Indians*, pages 379-380.
[10] Burns, page 200.
[11] The mountain howitzer's range was so limited, that Hudson's Bay trade muskets out-ranged the cannon.
[12] Taylor was a captain by brevet, and a first lieutenant by rank.
[13] The musketoon had an effective range of less than fifty yards.
[14] Schlicke, *General George Wright*, page 146
[15] Burns, page 205.
[16] Splawn, page 90.
[17] Trafzer and Scheuerman, page 78.
[18] Burns, page 204.
[19] Ibid, page 212.
[20] Ibid.
[21] Ibid, page 205.
[22] Ibid, page 211.
[23] Ibid, page 212.
[24] Ibid, page 215.
[25] Ibid, page 218.
[26] Ibid, page 220.
[27] Splawn, page 90.
[28] Burns, page 221.
[29] Schlicke, page 149.
[30] Captain Taylor lived long enough to convey his undying love to his wife and two children. They had recently joined him at Fort Walla Walla.
[31] Burns, page 223.
[32] Ibid, page 225.
[33] Schlicke, page 149.
[34] Splawn, page 93.
[35] Burns, page 227.
[36] Ibid, page. 228.
[37] Missing was First Sergeant Edward Ball, Company H, First U.S. Dragoons. As the column made their escape from the hilltop at night, a small group was left behind to keep the fires lit, and trick the Indians into believing the command was still there. Not wanting to allow the Indians to gain the medicinal alcohol in the pack train, it was ordered destroyed. Ball accomplished his mission in a manner that does credit to the capacity of the frontier soldier to drink. When the rear-guard troops snuck out, Ball was passed out in the bushes. The Indians missed him as he hid, or believed him to be dead, and Ball walked back to Fort Walla Walla, arriving six days late. For his gallantry, his misconduct was overlooked.
[38] Ibid.
[39] By the end of the year, Steptoe would be on sick leave for the rest of his life. In early 1861, Steptoe suffered another stroke, this time a severe one. However, he was appointed a lieutenant colonel and assigned to the 10th U.S. Infantry on September 8, 1861, seemingly as a pension, but would be dead by November 1 of that year.
[40] Ibid, page 230.
[41] Ibid, page 233.

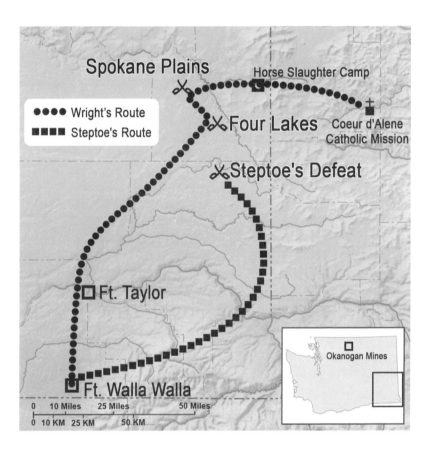

Eastern Front
1858

1. Steptoe's defeat   May 18, 1858
2. Four Lakes   September 1, 1858
3. Spokane Plains   September 5, 1858

Chapter Twelve

Might Makes Wright

Word of the Steptoe Disaster spread up and down the west coast. *The Oregonian* newspaper simply reported it as "Indian War Recommenced." The lull was over, and war had resumed.

Colonel Wright reported to General Clarke (on May 26) that, "All the Indians in that section of the country have combined for a general war, there is not a shadow of a doubt," and the enemy was "numerous, active, and perfectly acquainted with the topography of the country." In an eerie repeat of Major Rains' report after the Haller defeat, Wright recommended a thousand men, as had Rains, in a striking force of "two or three columns."[1] The difference this time rested with the general commanding the Pacific Division. Unlike Wool, General Clarke was bent on crushing the Indians once and for all.

On June 2, Clarke informed the War Department that his new headquarters was Vancouver Barracks so he could assume direct command of the theater. Furthermore, he called upon the War Department for reinforcements to destroy the tribes. From Salt Lake City, General Albert S. Johnston ordered the Sixth U.S. Infantry to move to San Francisco for shipment to the Northwest. General William S. Harney, en route with 3,000 troops to support Johnston in his war against the Mormons, was halted, and prepared to move to New York, from which he would sail with more troops to assume overall command of a war to eliminate the Indians who had dared to attack a U.S. Army command.

Meanwhile, Clarke deboarded at Vancouver, and ordered a council of war, "becoming harsher than [Governor Isaac] Stevens had ever been."[2] The June 23 arrival of Clarke heralded the massing of retributive forces to crush the Indians. He would seek peace, if the Indians surrendered those who had fired on Steptoe, recognized the Army's right to move where it wanted, and built any road it chose through their lands (e.g. the Mullan Military Road from Fort Walla Walla to Fort Benton). As Clarke remarked in a letter to Father Joset, the Indians "must suffer for their disobedience, and atone for their guilt."[3]

But, if the Indians did not accede to his demands, he was ready, for the Army would force acquiescence. At the council with Wright, Steptoe and Garnett, Clarke gave instructions. Garnett's forces at Fort Simcoe would be added, and then he would march north through the heart of the Yakima and Sinkiuse tribal lands. He would reach the Okanogan River, ensure the safety of the miners at Colville, and coordinate with Wright to envelope hostile forces.

Wright would assume command of the larger strike force and sweep north from Fort Walla Walla. This would be no "showing the flag" march as Wright had done in 1856. Clarke instructed Wright, "You will attack all the hostile Indians you may meet, with vigor; make their punishment severe, and persevere until the submission of all is complete."[4] Additional instructions would be forthcoming as each command neared its departure date. However, the tone had been set: Wright would use his might to make everything right once more.

Life was tense throughout the region. Word came from British Columbia that in June Indians emboldened by Steptoe's defeat had attacked miners along the Fraser River. After miners had been scalped and mutilated, the local forces created three columns, numbering 160 men, and started hunting down and killing any Indian they found.

Even as war flamed north, other actions to the south created fear. A group of seventy-six miners left Fort Simcoe in mid-June, bound for the Fraser River Valley. After they crossed the Wenatchee River, their Indian guide bolted. Led into an ambush, they were attacked by Indians and five of the Californians died: One in the initial rush, two drowned as the miners retreated across the Wenatchee River, one died from his own gun, and one died for no other apparent reason than pure fright. For four days the party ran south, seeking the protection of Fort Simcoe. Finally reaching the post on June 26, seven more of the miners were hospitalized from the wounds they had received in their fight with the Indians.[5]

Garnett told Clarke that 100 Indians attacked the miners, including such war-mongers as Owhi, Qualchan, and Skloom.[6] Furthermore, "the Indians had no just provocation for their conduct toward the miners."[7]

More miners headed north, but they moved in much greater numbers. A July group of 250 miners moved out and were not threatened.

But, it was not only miners who were ambushed. In July, a pack train destined for Fort Walla Walla was attacked. The thirteen men, led by civilian packer W. J. Lindsay and Lieutenant Wickliff, were surrounded and besieged by a force about five times its size. It seemed another massacre would take place along the Touchet River as the Indians charged the whites seven times. Finally, unable to break or stampede their quarry, the Cayuse Indians withdrew.[8]

A Hudson's Bay Brigade headed for Colville left Fort Walla Walla on July 4. The Hudson's Bay usually traveled unchallenged by Indians because of their good relations, but this time George Blenkisop took greater care, and moved in a wide arc to avoid the enraged Indians of the Palouse country. Three times the King George men reported meeting hostile Indians before reaching their Fort Colville. Near the mouth of the Snake River, eight canoes of Yakima Indians, painted for war, were bluffed off by building campfires and yelling, to simulate a larger white camp. Again, surrounding the Hudson's Bay Brigade near the mouth of the Spokane River were painted warriors. It was only the intercession of a mixed-blood employee that persuaded the Indians to move off. Thinking they were safe, the brigade finally reached Fort Colville only to find it surrounded by hundreds of angry Indians. Here, the Indians were dancing their war and scalp dances, preparing themselves for future glory. The fur trading British marched through the painted Indians, but noticed they were displaying their trophies. One mark of their success was the saddle of Captain Taylor, still with his blood on it from the Steptoe defeat. The Indians looked forward to fighting more of the "white women" sent to subdue them.[9]

Indian agent John Owens was trying to avert war. On July 9, he met with some of the agitated Indians at Colville. They resisted any talk of peace. Instead, Owens said he would meet with the Coeur d'Alene, Spokane and San Poils in a few days. He could move into such hostile Indian country only with a personal escort from the peace inclined Spokane Chief Garry. Reaching Spokane Falls on July 12, Owen found the situation worse. If the Indians had been hostile at Colville, they were timid in comparison to the those in the heart of the enemy's land, Spokane country. The agent would report later to his boss, James Nesmith, "I have just returned from one of the blackest councils, I think, that has ever been held on the Pacific slope. Five hundred fighting men were present, elated with their recent success; the dragoon horses were prancing around all day; the scalp and war dances going all night."[10] There would be no peace, and Owens was lucky to escape with his life. He would report that the Hudson's Bay was supplying Indians with arms, a charge denied by the Most Honorable Company.[11]

With peace overtures a failure, the war option was the remaining choice, and Clarke ordered his commands into the field.

First into the field was an element of Wright's command. Captain Erasmus Keyes (Third U.S. Artillery) acted as Wright's second-in-command, but he first had a mission to accomplish. On August 7, Keyes struck north from Fort Walla Walla to create a defensive redoubt at a Snake River crossing. With his artillery men lugging four field pieces, as well as acting as red-leg infantry,[12] Keyes also had a dragoon company acting as flankers and scouts. The command marched toward the river, covering the terrain burned by retreating Indians in an effort to deprive the Army of forage.

The day after Keyes' departure, Fort Walla Walla discovered that Indian raiders had taken three dozen oxen. Dragoons, under Lieutenant Henry B. Davidson, rode after them. Despite the slow-moving oxen, the dragoons did not re-capture the needed livestock.

To protect his rear, Wright met with the Nez Perce Indians. Twenty-one chiefs signed a peace accord with Wright, hoping that the favorable terms of the Stevens' treaty be granted the Nez Perce. Additionally, the Nez Perce provided thirty warriors as auxiliary scouts, assigned to Lieutenant Mullan. They were even given old Army blue jackets, so they would not be confused with other Indians in the heat of battle.[13]

The Keyes column trudged through the burnt land, always observed by hostiles. The flanking dragoons surprised and captured one Walla Walla Indian. He revealed nothing of the Indians' intention and was released. On August 10, the column finally reached the point where

Drawing by Gustav Solon

Colonel Wright makes peace accord with the Nez Perce before 1858 campaign.

the Tucannon River joins the Snake and there, under the direction of Second Artillery Regiment's Lieutenant John Mullan, and Third Artillery's Captain F. Wyse,[14] they built a fort. But even as Keyes scouted for the best location, Indians and sentries opened fire on each other. Two Indians were captured, but jumped into the Snake River to escape. Mullan jumped after them and started to wrestle with one. The Indians hurled rocks at the diminutive officer, who tried to use his pistol, but the river had made the powder useless. As the two struggled, they plunged into deeper water, with the swift current threatening both. Each gave up the fight to save himself, and the Indian swam to his freedom. Mullan, wet but alive, returned to shore to resume building the fort.[15]

The new fort rising amid the volcanic dust and rocks was named Fort Taylor to honor the officer killed during the Steptoe fight. Meanwhile, Keyes sent his dragoons and supply train back to Fort Walla Walla to bring up supplies to be pre-staged for the coming campaign of Wright's column. Rations of 30,000 man-days were placed at Fort Taylor to ensure Wright's men would be amply supplied in the coming campaign.

To further ease Wright's movements, a ferry was established under the protection of Fort Taylor's guns. When Wright reached Fort Taylor on August 18, he found the site well protected with new grass sprouting for the command's mounts, as well as a location that made his river crossing much easier. Wright ordered his supply train back to Fort Walla Walla to bring up more supplies, and the troops rested in relative safety.

Wright recounted to Clarke on his command's status and his mission. In regard to the troops, Wright said, "I have a body of troops, both officers and men, in the highest order, and on whom I feel that I can rely with perfect confidence." The months spent at Walla Walla had included much drill and practice, and even the recruits were better trained than most experienced troops in the west. Still, Wright reported his misgivings.

> Yet, with all these circumstances in my favor, I am greatly apprehensive that the results of the campaign may fall short of what is expected by the general and the country. From all that I have learned, we must not expect the enemy to meet us in pitched battle; although haughty, insolent, and boastful now, when I approach he will resort to guerilla warfare, he will lay waste the country by fire, and endeavor by every means in his power to embarrass and cripple our operations.[16]

Many others who had knowledge and experience with the Indians shared this fear. James Nesmith wrote to Isaac Stevens that "I apprehend that the whole thing will be a failure and that the Indians will keep out of their way."[17] The Jesuit priests also reported their concerns that Wright's march would disperse the Indians into the mountains.

Nevertheless, Wright was ready to lead nearly 600 soldiers into Indian country to smite the hostiles. He had the five companies of Third Artillery (with 310 privates acting as infantry), two companies of the Ninth Infantry, and four companies of First Dragoons. In addition, he had 100 civilian muleskinners to keep the command supplied, caring for 800 animals (including the dragoons' mounts). Two days after he reached Fort Taylor, the army started across the Snake and into Indian country. Wright carried five weeks' worth of supplies, in effect giving him a deadline to complete his mission.

The second arm of Clarke's strike force was to sally forth from Fort Simcoe. Major Robert Garnett would lead his column north. It consisted of a much smaller force of one company of the Fourth

Infantry, and three companies of the Ninth Infantry. The 314 officers and men needed 225 pack animals (and fifty civilian packers) to carry its fifty-day ration of supplies. Not able to get any dragoons, Garnett put thirty men (ten each from the Ninth's companies) on horses to act as a mobile scout and flanker unit. On August 10, the Fort Simcoe striking force marched.

On day four of the march, Indian scouts spotted that the hostiles responsible for attacking the miners were about twenty miles ahead. Garnett ordered half his mounted force to ride ahead and attack the

Library of Congress
James Nesmith

guilty (by presumption) Indians. The attackers were placed under the command of Second Lieutenant Jesse K. Allen.

At dawn of August 15, Allen led his men in an excited attack on the sleeping Indian village. The assault captured twenty-one Indian warriors, about four dozen women and children, and scores of Indian horses and cattle. Five Indians were killed, one while attempting to escape, one later in the bushes, and "Three of the men, having been recognized as participants in the attack on the miners, were shot in compliance with my general instructions on the subject," Major Garnett reported.[18]

The army suffered one killed in action. "It has become my painful duty to communicate. . . the death of 2nd Lieut. Jesse K. Allen....Allen died the death of a soldier. He fell . . .at the moment of accomplishing a successful surprise on a camp of hostile Indians. There is reason however to fear that he was shot accidentally by one of his own men in the darkness of the hour."[19]

Despite sorrow at the loss of a popular young officer, the command moved on. With Allen dead, Garnett appointed another officer to take charge of the mounted men. That officer, George Crook, set off on August 20 for a side trip of sixty miles up the Wenatchee River. Led by two Indian scouts, the men mounted mules for the excursion.

Coming up to the village on August 21, Crook called out the chief and warned him that the army wanted the murderers of the miners, but that if they were not surrendered, Crook would attack, and "in harboring those men, that in a fight we would have to kill many of our friends."[20] The chief promised to surrender them, and the next day, the Indians came into Crook's camp.

> As fast as the chief would point out one of the murderers, I had a non-commissioned officer and two men shadow him, so as not to create an apprehension, and when they were all shadowed in this way, at a given signal they were to grab their man. So, at the signal given by me, four men were captured.[21]

A fifth Indian, not fingered by the chief, was also captured. He was the village's medicine man. Explaining that they were to be executed for their crimes, Crook gave them time to prepare. According to Crook, "they all acknowledged their guilt…except the medicine man, who invoked all kinds of curses against us."[22] Crook ordered them executed. "This whole business was exceedingly distasteful to me, and as my 2nd Lt. Turner rather enjoyed that kind of thing, I detailed him to execute them."[23]

Mission accomplished, Crook returned to Garnett's column. The soldiers marched as far north as the Hudson's Bay Fort Okanogan, where frightened Indians told of Wright's actions further east (see below). No longer needed as Wright's game beaters, Garnett started toward Fort Simcoe on September 15.

As they moved south, they paused at Lake Chelan. Here, George Crook created his "navy." While Garnett marched along the Indians trails, Crook used captured Indian canoes to paddle down the Columbia River. Using the river as a highway, Crook encountered many Indians, but found none that were hostile. His only brush with danger came during one night.

> During the night I thought I would visit the sentinel who was posted in the brush near by. I hadn't more than gotten out of my blankets with my bare feet before a Mr. Rattlesnake struck his rattles. He was evidently coming to get in bed with me. I called the sentinel who killed him with the butt of his musket.[24]

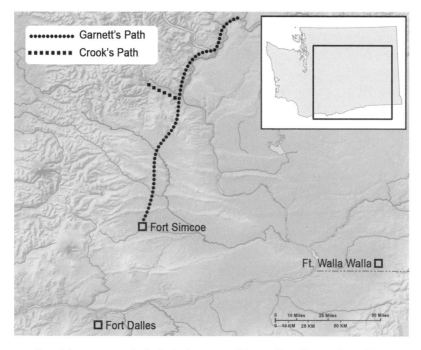

Crook's navy ended their journey fifty miles from Fort Simcoe, noting "I abandoned my fleet at Priest Rapids with many regrets, as I don't know that ever in my life I enjoyed a trip with such keen zest and pleasure."[25]

When both elements of Garnett's command returned to Fort Simcoe, their forty-five days in the field had covered over 500 miles of country, killed the guilty, and captured or forced the surrender of all Indians encountered. Nearing the fort, a runner brought tragic news to Major Garnett. His wife and son were ill with bilious fever. Hurrying ahead of his troops, the major arrived at his post only to find his loved ones dead. Thus ended the Garnett expedition.

While Garnett failed to win battle honors, that was not the case with Colonel Wright's command. As Garnett marched north in parallel movement, Wright's troops crossed the Snake River in what was the most successful campaign of the era.

Before Wright was the largest concentration of Indian forces ever assembled in the Pacific Northwest. They did not fear Wright. With the exception of artillery, the Indians had the same weapons as whites: muskets. The "Indians were well armed,"[26] and as the historian Burns pointed out, the Indians "had never felt anything but irritation for the blundering of the volunteer militia in previous wars, and the Steptoe fiasco convinced them that there was nothing to fear from professional warriors."[27] Finally, the Indians actually had a strategy for defeating Wright's large command.

The Indian plan was twofold. First, they were hoping to draw off the dragoons and deal with them separately. Once the mounted men were eliminated, the hapless infantry could be annihilated at will and at a location of the Indian's choosing.

The means of drawing off the dragoons was the second part of the Indian strategy. Kamiakin and Tilcoax urged an attack on Wright's supply train.[28] Setting the grass afire, an attack would cut off the supply mules, and the dragoons would be forced to fight away from the infantry. For if Wright's precious supplies were lost, he would have to retreat.

The column moved north under constant Indians over watch, who reported back to the tribes. Riding almost as flankers, Indian watchers reported every action of the column.

At camp on August 30, some sentries were fired on. "'*Boots and Saddles* is sounded,' wrote Lieutenant John Mullan, 'and a squadron of dragoons....and foot troops...moved forward to attack.'"[29] Nothing came of this incident, but it heightened the command's tension. On August 31, the Indians saw another opportunity to strike. Setting fire to the grass, they made a diversionary attack against the Nez Perce scouts at the front, and tried to cut out at least some of the mules in the rear pack train. The front troops of dragoons roared ahead to defend the scouts, and while the rearguard dragoon troop came up to defend the pack train, it turned out to be unnecessary. The grass was too green from recent rains to do much more than smolder, and when the wind shifted, it forced the fire back on itself. As Lieutenant Lawrence Kip reported the action, the fighting happened quickly:

> Just before getting into camp, the hostile Indians rode up near our column, set fire to the grass and fired upon our rear guard. Their objective was to make an attack under cover of the smoke, but the grass was too green to burn freely, and the maneuvres [sic] of the troops at once defeated their intentions.....Captain Keyes then ordered Captain Winder's company of rifles to deploy

across the rear of the column, at right angles to Lieutenant Ihrie's deployed on the right and Captain Hardie's on the left, and parallel to the column, thus forming a rectangle about the train.[30]

This was the Indian's last chance to dictate the outcome of the battle. The army set up camp twenty miles south of the Spokane River.

September 1 dawned as it had most of August: hot and arid. While thunderstorms had pelted the grass with heavy rain at times, it had been localized. The majority of the country was parched, making for dusty marching. The Indians expected Wright's column to continue marching north and camp on the banks of the Spokane. They planned to again attack the supply train as it crawled forward, moving into drier grasses along the way. The Indians prepared to do battle as the column moved out.

Kip reported the events as starting this way:

> . . .At daylight, we found the Indians increased in number, still posted on the hills overlooking us. Their manner was defiant and insolent, and they seemed to be inviting an attack.. . .Shortly after, the dragoons, four companies of artillery, the howitzer battery…and the two companies of rifles[31] were ordered to drive the Indians from the hills and engage the main body.[32]

Leaving his camp (and pack train) well guarded, Wright moved his command out in two columns: one of dragoons (about 100 riders), and the other of infantry supported by artillery (about 220). Before him was a hill covered with Indians, now named Battle Butte. He would use the infantry to charge the hill, and have his squadron of dragoons, under William Grier ride around the butte to the right and catch the Indians as they were forced off the hill. As another force to prevent the Indians from escaping, Lieutenant Mullan led the Nez Perce scouts to the left, so the Indians could not ride to the west.

After forcing the Indians off the crest of the hill, Brevet Major Grier reported that they had gathered in large numbers at the back base of the hill. In his official report, Colonel Wright wrote, "On reaching the crest of the hill I saw at once that the Indians were determined to measure their strength with us, showing no disposition to avoid combat."[33] Wright ordered the troops forward, with Captain Ord's company moving before the command as skirmishers.

Before Wright lay four lakes, with prairie and woods between them. But more impressive were the Indians. Kip recalled,

> On the plain below us we saw the enemy. Every spot seemed alive with the wild warriors we had come so far to meet. They were in the pines on the edge of the lakes, in the ravines and gullies, on the opposite hillsides, and swarming over the plains. They seemed to cover the country for some two miles. Mounted on their fleet, hardy horses, the crowd swayed back and forth, brandishing their weapons, shouting their war cries, and keeping up a song of defiance. Most of them were armed with Hudson's Bay muskets, while others had bows and arrows and long lances. They were in all the bravery of their war array, gaudily painted and decorated with their wild trappings. Their plumes fluttered above them, while below skins and trinkets and all kinds of fantastic embellishments flaunted in the sunshine. Their horses, too, were arrayed in the most glaring finery.[34]

One account has the Indians lined up by tribes, as if in military formation:

> According to Chief Stellam of the Coeur d'Alenes, reminiscing perhaps inaccurately thirty years later, the braves had begun their battle in roughly tribal grouping. The prominent figure at their right wing was Kamiakin with his Yakimas and Palouse. The Spokanes and other tribes had gathered particularly on the left. Among those in the center were the Coeur d'Alenes.[35]

The infantry started down the hill, driving the Indians before them. Artillery opened up on the Indians hiding in the trees to the right. Both of these forces were trying to drive the Indians out onto the plains so the dragoons could charge down upon them. The Indians were trying to hit and run, riding forward, firing, and then riding back to where they assumed they were out of range. Here, the new rifled guns took their effect, hitting many.

> But Minnie [sic] balls and long range rifles were things with which now for the first time they were to be made acquainted. As the line advanced, first we saw one Indian reel in his saddle and fall, -- then, two or three, then, half a dozen. Then some horses

would dash madly forward, showing that the balls were telling upon them. The instant, however, that the 'braves' fell, they were seized by their companions and dragged off.[36]

Wright pressed on. With so many Indians being hit, they turned for cover. This was the chance the dragoons had been waiting for, and from behind the infantry line was heard the command to mount, and then Major Grier shouting, "Charge the rascals!" Wright's official report stated, "At a signal, they mount, they rush with lightening speed

Library of Congress
Erasmus Darwin Keyes

through the intervals of skirmishers, and charge the Indians on the plains, overwhelm them entirely, kill many, defeat and disperse them all."[37] Wright declared Grier's dragoons made "the most brilliant, gallant, and successful charge I have ever beheld."[38] The Kalispels chief Xanewa, was killed as the dragoons rode forward, their sabers slashing.[39] Kip related, "We saw the flash of their sabres [sic] as they cut them down. Lieutenant Davidson shot one warrior from his saddle as they charged up, and Lieutenant Gregg clove the skull of another."[40]

With the dragoon horses blown, the infantry advanced once more, driving the now tired Indians before them for two miles, until finally Colonel Wright ordered the buglers to blow recall. "A number of our men had never before been under fire, but begrimed and weary as they were, we could see in their faces how much they enjoyed the excitement of the fight."[41] As well they should, for the Army had not suffered a single casualty, either killed or wounded. It had been a completely one-sided affair. In fact, the troops were able to march back to camp in time for the noon meal. Instead of pressing on with his tired command, Wright ordered three days' rest, situated next to the beautiful lakes he had seen from the crest of the hill.

Wright's report commended the twenty-five officers within his command, including the two surgeons. Of the twenty-four combat officers (including Wright), seventeen would serve as Civil War generals (by rank or brevet). For the Confederacy, three made Brigadier General, while William Pender made Major General, and was a corps commander. Of the Federal generals, eleven were Brigadier Generals (by rank or brevet) and two were Major Generals: Edward Ord and Erasmus Keyes both commanded corps during the Civil War. Never was the percentage of future generals so high as those who fought with Wright in his campaign of 1858.

And the campaign was not over. While it was evident to the Indians that the new rifles, coupled with such strength of arms displayed by Wright foreswore any hope of repeating the Steptoe success, they were not ready to concede defeat. They still had a chance:

> …The war chiefs of the different tribes and factions were…. unanimous in their opinion that the only chance of attaining a measure of success would be in rough timbered country, and fighting in anything like open country was hopeless.[42]

The Indians needed to stampede the pack train. In order to stampede the mules, the Indians needed the army out of its camp and advancing through dry grass. But, after September 1, the weather had turned cool and showery. It would be difficult to fire the damp grass. And yet, chiefs such as Kamiakin advocated that they at least try.

Father Joset later recounted that the first battle had disheartened the Indians. He related that it was not the long range rifle fire, as Army officers claimed, but the relentlessly advancing infantry keeping up a steady fire. And when the Indians paused to regroup, the dragoons charged through the infantry in the true tactic of cavalry, that is, as a shock force. The Indians may have been beaten, but they learned lessons that they planned to apply in their next battle.

On September 5, Wright resumed his advance to the north. As the Indians watched, they noted the wind was from the north, which was perfect. They bided their time until Wright's column left the pine forest and onto the rock strewn prairie. If a fire could be started, the north wind would drive it onto the white army, forcing them back into the pine trees where the dragoons would be less effective, and the Indians could fight from ambush. And if the whites forced a fight on the prairie, the rocks would make it difficult for the dragoons to advance. The terrain was on the Indian side this time.

As the battle started, the Indians poured musket fire into the startled command. Wright was almost struck, but calmly asserted command, directing his forces to repel the Indians.

Lieutenant Kip recalled the opening of the next battle.

> We had just emerged from the rough broken country and entered on a prairie, when they were seen occupying the woods on the right side of us, evidently about to make an attack. We had nearly reached the woods when they advanced in great force, and set fire to the dry grass of the prairie, so that the wind blowing high and against us, we were nearly enveloped by the flames.[43]

Wright ordered the pack mules to the center, to better protect them. And then Wright was forced to respond to a flanking attack by the Indians.

> Then on the hills to our right....were feats of horsemanship which we have never seen equaled. The Indians would dash down a hill five hundred feet high and with a slope of forty-five degrees, at the most headlong speed, apparently with all the rapidity they could have used on level ground.[44]

To protect his flanks, Wright ordered four companies of Third Artillery to advance to his army's sides. The red-leg soldiers advanced, coolly jumping the flames, and pushing the Indians back. When the Indians sought shelter in the pines, the unlimbered howitzers opened fire. And then the infantry charged yet again.

And yet, the Indians tried to reach their target, the pack train. As one officer, George Dandy noted later,

> If the enemy had succeeded in stampeding and capturing this train, we would have been left in a desperate condition...But the packers and troops were quick to obey their officers and saved the train....It was only by the very great coolness and courage of the officers and men that the calamity of a stampede was averted in this case.[45]

When the Indians had been forced out of the pines and into the open, the dragoons attacked. When the ground became rough and dangerous to the horses, the infantry advanced. In every case, the artillery fired shot into any group of Indians trying to gather together to counter-attack. It was a battle of repetition. Each attack seemed similar to the one before: infantry, artillery, dragoon, artillery, infantry, artillery, dragoon, and on and on.

Having the Indians again in the trees, Wright ordered his howitzers once more into action. Shelling the forest, the barrage killed or wounded many of the Indians who had sought shelter. Among the wounded was the great Yakima chief, Kamiakin, "…accompanied by his youngest wife, Colestah, who was known as a medicine woman, psychic, and 'warrior woman.' Armed with a tone war club, Colestah had vowed to fight to the death by her husband's side. For this reason she went into battle wearing her finest buckskin dress with her hair tightly braided around her head. When Kamiakin was wounded, Colestah carried him off and used her skill as an Indian doctor to nurse him back to health."[46]

As the infantry advanced, they drove the Indians ahead of them. Through four miles of timbered country the infantry shouldered forward. The Indians, finally driven back onto the plains, were charged once again by Grier's dragoons. As the dragoons charged, the fighting became fierce.

> Among the incidents of the fight was one which happened to Lieutenant Pender. Firing his pistol as he charged, just as he dashed up to the side of an Indian he discovered that his revolver had caught on the lock and was useless. He had not time to draw his sabre, and was obliged, therefore, to close with his enemy. He grappled the Indian and hurled him from his horse, when a soldier behind him dispatched him.[47]

The chase continued. As Kip noted, "Yet our enemy could not thus leave the field, but groups gathered, and the flying stragglers again united in the woods which surrounded us on every side."[48] Whenever the Indians rallied to a defensive position, the howitzers opened fire and the infantry cleared the position. After a twenty-five mile battle, the Indians fled across the Spokane River.

The assessment of the outcome of the Battle of Spokane Plains came from many sources. The popular press reported it thusly:

Might makes Wright

Pioneer and Democrat
Olympia, WT
Friday, September 17, 1858

Another Indian Fight!!
The Hostiles Completely Routed!

Father Joset wrote after the two battles,

> From the first the colonel knew how to disable them, and it
> was practically no fight, but a complete rout.....the brave Colonel
> Wright so well persuaded them that, by their own admission, they
> cannot even think of war any more.[49]

From one of Wright's officers, the future Major General Erasmus
Keyes, came a professional review.

> I doubt if in the history of our country there has ever been
> an Indian campaign in which as much was accomplished at an
> equal cost. The good result was due to three causes: The proper
> instructions of the soldiers at the commencement, the excellence
> of the quartermaster's department, and the admirable fitness of
> our commander, Colonel George Wright.[50]

The war, at least as far as the battles were concerned, was over.
There was killing left to be done, and the end to be settled, but the
Indian wars of the era were over.

Chapter 12 notes

[1] Burns, *The Jesuits and the Indian Wars of the Northwest*, page 237.
[2] Jospehy, *The Nez Perce Indians*, page 382.
[3] Schlicke, *General George Wright*, page 154,
[4] Ibid, page 155.
[5] Guie, *Bugles in the Valley*, page 113.
[6] Garnett erroneously reported that Quil-ten-e-nock was killed in this fight, but the death of the
  Sinkiues chief, reported to Garnett, was confused with another, earlier attack of miners.
[7] Ibid, page 114.
[8] Ruby and Brown, *The Cayuse Indians*, page 258.
[9] Burns, pages 251-252.
[10] Ibid, page 255.
[11] However, in a subsequent battle, Wright would recover a British musket with an 1857
  manufacture date on it.
[12] The term red-leg infantry comes from the scheme used to designate the various branches of

the Army. The dragoons were market by orange flashings on their uniforms, the mounted rifles green, the recently created cavalry had yellow, infantry were light blue, and artillery had red flashings. With that color system, an artilleryman had a red stripe down the sides of his uniform trousers, and thus, when acting as infantry, they were called red-leg infantry.

[13] The Nez Perce were covering all bets, in that they had warriors fighting on both sides in the coming campaign, although they probably had more fighters against the Army than with them.

[14] Brevet Major Wyse would remain in command of the fort once the Wright command moved out. The fort was manned by Company D, 3rd Artillery.

[15] Schlicke, page 160.

[16] Ibid, page 161.

[17,18] Burns, page 276.

[19] Guie, page 120.

[20] Ibid, pages 119-120.

[21] *Crook, His Autobiography*, page 62.

[22] Ibid, page 63.

[23] Ibid.

[24] Ibid, page 64.

[25] Ibid, page 67.

[26] Ibid, page 68.

[27] Burns, page 273.

[28] Ibid, page 283.

[29] Brown, *The Indian Side of the Story*, page 236.

[30] Trafzer and Scheuerman, *Renegade Tribe*, page 85.

[31] Kip, *Indian Wars in the Pacific Northwest*, page 53.

[32] The rifles were the newly issued rifled guns, the 1855 Springfield .58 caliber rifle, using Minie balls. The old muskets had an effective range of 100 to 200 yards, while the new guns had a maximum range of over 1,000 yards, and effective range of 400 to 600 yards. The long-range rifles gave the whites a chance to stand off and still effectively hit the Indians.

[33] Ibid, pages 53-54.

[34] Schlicke, page 167

[35] Kip, page 55.

[36] Burns, page 293.

[37] Kip, pages 56-57.

[38] Schlicke, page 168.

[39] Burns, page 292.

[40] Ibid.

[41] Kip, page 57.

[42] Ibid, page 58.

[43] Brown, page 235.

[44] Kip, page 63.

[45] Ibid, page 64.

[46] Schlicke, pages 171-172.

[47] Trafzer abd Scheuerman, pages 87-88.

[48] Kip, page 65.

[49] Ibid.

[50] Schlicke, page 174.

[51] Ibid, page 175.

Chapter Thirteen

Checkmate

For the whites the battles had been bloodless victories. All that remained was for Wright to fulfill General Clarke's command "to make their punishment severe, and persevere until the submission of all is complete." Specifically, Clarke wanted every Indian responsible for attacking Steptoe found and punished, and the attack's leaders singled out—that is, hanged.

After the Battle of Spokane Plains, Wright wanted the unconditional surrender of the Indians. If he did not act quickly, the tribes would disperse, and head toward all points of the compass. Chief Garry of the Spokane Tribe, a traditional friend of the whites and peace advocate, approached Wright on September 7, and the two met a couple of miles up river from the Great Falls of the Spokane River. Garry told Wright "that he had always been opposed to fighting, but that the young men and many of the chiefs were against him, and he could not control them."[1] Garry promised peace.

If he thought his statement would be well received, he was mistaken. "Garry was stunned by the reception."[2] Wright told Garry,

> I have met you in two battles; you have been badly whipped; you have had several chiefs and many warriors killed or wounded; I have not lost a man or animal. I have a large force, and you, Spokans, Coeur d'alenes, Pelouzes, and Pend d'Oreilles may unite, and I can defeat you as badly as before. I did not come into the country to ask you to make peace; I came here to fight. Now, when you are tired of war and ask for peace, I will tell you what you must do. You must come to me with your arms, with your women, and children, and everything you have, and lay them at

my feet. You must put your faith in me and trust to my mercy. If you do this, I shall tell you the terms upon which I will give you peace. If you do not do this, war will be made on you this year, and the next, and until your nations shall be exterminated.[3]

Never had so complete a statement of unconditional surrender been given. Was there really any choice? True, some Indians were willing to fight, but how could any tribe hope to defeat the endless stream of white soldiers that replaced every soldier killed? The Indian coalition was once more divided, with chief against chief, and tribe against tribe. Garry left, utterly defeated, and afraid of the whites.

Library of Congress
Spokane Chief Garry

Another Spokane chief went to Wright, this one not of the peace faction. Polatkin had not only fought in the last two battles, but against Steptoe, too. When he and his warriors rode into Wright's camp, they were seized and shackled at the wrist and ankle. One of the warriors with Polatkin was accused of attacking miners, and Wright followed Clarke's instructions: The next day, he hanged the man.

On the morning of the hanging, two of Polatkin's sons rode the river bank opposite the gallows. From the perceived safety of the far bank of the river, they called for their father's freedom. Wright ordered the sentries to open fire. Both sons fell, one mortally. The message delivered by word, bullet and rope was to surrender and hope for mercy, or die.

Wright moved his camp further up the Spokane River on September 9. As he did so, the command encountered a herd of 800 to 1,000 horses. They were quickly seized as a prize of war. What to do with them? The Indians would surely try and stampede them, an action which risked taking the dragoon mounts and pack mules with them. The troops could not move the herd with them, and the herd could not be left to the Indians to recover. Wright ordered a board of officers to decide the course of action.

The decision: keep a few of the best, and kill the rest. For two days the soldiers did as ordered, killing singly and then in volleys the horses. The gore was unimaginable, and the camp was soon called Horse Slaughter Camp. The whites believed that slaughtering the horse herd would strand the Indians in place.

The destruction of their horses shocked the Indians. But, it was not because they were left unable to move, but from the waste of what they used to measure wealth. As Father Joset explained later, the power of a white chief to destroy with such total disregard an enormous amount of wealth, "added not a little to the fright of the Indians."[4]

Wright received a letter from Father Joset on September 10. The priest had returned to his Coeur d'Alene mission, further east. As those tribe members returned to the mission, led by Vincent, they told the priest of the battles, and their desire now to seek peace. The Indians asked Joset to "plead" for them with Wright.

The courier from Joset arrived during the horse slaughter, which dismayed the Indian messenger. Joset's letter reassured Wright that the hostile faction was "down and suing for peace." Immediately Wright had the Indian messenger take his reply to the priest. He repeated much of the instruction given Garry, but added a promise to Joset that no Indians would be executed for acts of war (as distinct from the killing of miners, for example, in peace).[5]

Having killed the horse herd, and not waiting to hear from Father Joset, Wright resumed his march east. He had enough rations to keep in the field until October 5, and he did not want to waste the waning days of late summer. Following the Spokane River, he found and destroyed Indian winter food caches. As the command headed further up river, the terrain became more rugged and timbered. Encumbered by wheeled howitzers and wagons, Wright ordered his column to become more flexible. The wagon loads were shifted to mules, and the axled vehicles left behind. As soon as the column moved again, the Palouse of Tilcoax, still unwilling to concede defeat (and certainly wishing to revenge the destruction of the chief's horse herd), burned the Army's vehicles.

However angry and hostile Tilcoax's warriors were, they were too few to attack. If they had been inclined to do so, September 12 and on would have presented the perfect chance to strike. Wright's column was strung out over six long miles and marching single file through dense forests, choked with Mountain Mahogany, huckleberry bushes, and every kind of underbrush. The trail through the forest was so narrow no flankers could be put out. It was the perfect hit-and-run ground, but the Indians, always lurking, did not have a sufficient force to strike.

On September 13, The Army reached Father Joset's mission. Wright's report to General Clarke summed up the column's actions over the past week-plus:

> The chastisement which these Indians have received has been severe but well merited, and undoubtedly necessary to impress them with our power. For eighty miles our route has been marked by slaughter and destruction.[6]

To add to Wright's spectral slaughter and destruction, the Indians saw an omen appear in the heavens. Donati's comet streaked through the stars, another harbinger of the white man's ascending power.

At the mission Father Joset, his associate Father Joseph Menetrey, and the religious brothers worked to bring the Indians to surrender rather than suffer attack by Wright. The clerics treated the officers and men of the Army with great kindness. By September 17, the Coeur d'Alene's had gathered and Wright held a council in which he dictated his terms.

The terms were to be the same with each tribe: turn over the Indians who attacked Steptoe, return stolen government property, allow the army free passage (that is, the Mullan Military Road), and allow whites unmolested passage throughout the tribe's lands. To further ensure their good conduct, five families were to be given up as hostages and taken to Fort Walla Walla. Chief Vincent of the Spokane's confessed his guilt. "I have committed a great crime. I am fully conscious of it and am deeply sorry for it. I and all my people are rejoiced that you are willing to forgive us."[7]

But here was the crux of the issue for the Indians. To the Indians, they could compromise on any condition set for peace, *except* punishment for their tribal members. Punishment meant death by hanging,

246

and to the Indians, if death was inevitable, then it was preferable to die in battle than to be strung up by a white man's rope.

To Wright, if he were to adhere to Clarke's orders, then he could compromise on every issue, *except* punishment. As Clarke had enjoined Wright, "They must suffer for their disobedience, and atone for the guilt into which their bad acts have brought their people."[8]

Into this stalemate, Father Joset proposed a compromise. The priest would get the Steptoe attackers to surrender, but as a temporary measure, and with the assurance that they would not be executed.

Wright was faced with a quandary. If he accepted the priest's proposal, he would be in conflict with his orders. If he did not, then the chance for ending the war that month, let alone that year, would probably evaporate, as would the Indians into the mountains. Well and good to have Clarke issue the orders, but Wright was in the field, meeting with the Indians when he had the advantage of victory. Here, with a tribe that had traditionally been friendly to the whites, Wright accepted the Catholic Father's proposal. With a tentative and preliminary treaty agreed on, Wright started west and then south to Fort Walla Walla.

On September 21, more Indians came to Wright. While saying they were Coeur d'Alene, they were really Palouse, testing to see if they might gain they same treatment given the Coeur d'Alenes. The next day, the Army arrived at Latah Creek, where Father Joset had told the Spokane Indians to assemble to confer with Wright. Reportedly, hovering nearby were Kamiakin and Tilcoax, too afraid of Wright's "justice" to enter the Army's camp. On September 23, the Spokane council was convened.

Once more, Wright listed the conditions for peace. There was no choice and Father Joset told this to the Indians. The Spokane chiefs spoke: "I am sorry for what has been done, and glad of the opportunity now offered to make peace with our Great Father. We promise to obey and fulfill these terms in every point."[9] Garry, Vincent, Polatkin, and other Spokane chiefs signed. Some lesser tribes also signed, as did the warrior chief of the Coeur d'Alene, Melkapsi, who had missed the previous council. He was berated by Wright, and after speaking (in his language) to a fellow brave, Melkapsi stood up, and addressed Colonel Wright. "I am aware that I have committed a great crime. I

Edward S. Curtis collection, Library of Congress
On the Spokane River.

am very sorry for it. My heart is castdown. . .I am ready to abide by the terms you propose."[10]

To the historian Josephy, "As soon as he [Wright] had the documents, however, he adopted a totally new and savage attitude."[11] Wright started to hang more and more Indians as a warning to the others of what would happen if they did not keep the peace.

As the evening started to fall, Owhi, the Yakima chief, rode into Wright's camp. In a 1908 interview, Sanchow, called Mary Moses by the whites, related the events. Sanchow was Owhi's daughter, and sister of Qualchan. As Garnett moved north from Fort Simcoe, he had met with many chiefs, among them was Owhi. They had promised to adhere to the peace terms dictated by Garnett, but Owhi decide to take his family, including Sanchow and Qualchan, to safety, away from Garnett, to the Spokane country. Accompanying him was the Sinkuise chief, Quetalahkin (brother of Qul-ten-e-nock).

Camping on the Spokane River, Owhi heard of Wright's request that the Indians come to the peace council. Owhi had heard of Father Joset's promise to Indians that they would be under a safe-conduct pass, and so, according to Sanchow, her father and brother believed they could enter Wright's camp without fear.[12] What transpired was just another page in Indian history.

As soon as Owhi rode into camp, the chief was seized. Wright chastised him for breaking his promise to come in with his people when they had met in the early summer of 1856. Now, Wright told Owhi to summon his son, or die. In shackles, Owhi sent word for his son.

The next morning, although not contacted by his father's messenger, Qualchan rode in with his family and two warriors. Captain Keyes was in the camp, and looked in surprise at what was described by Lieutenant Kip as, "one of the most desperate murderers on this coast." Keyes opened Wright's tent flap and called in, "Colonel, we have distinguished visitors here!"[13]

When Wright came out, he greeted Qualchan by telling him that he had his father. The Yakima warrior chief asked where, and Wright indicated the chained Owhi across the camp. Surprised that his father did not have the safe conduct promised, Qualchan started to react, but was quickly overcome by the guards. A trial was held. As Lieutenant Kip wrote,

> In all the battles, forays, and disturbances in Washington territory, Qualchien has been one of the leading spirits. The influence for evil which he exerted was probably greater even than that of either Owhi or Kamiaken. Of the three, he was the most addicted to fighting and bloodshed. He has been directly charged with the murder of nine white men at various times. In the action of March 1st, 1856, on white river, Puget Sound District, in which Captain Keyes commanded, Qualchien was present with fifty Yakima warriors.[14]

The trial was brief. "Fifteen minutes after his capture, the officer of the day received an order from Colonel Wright to have him hung immediately."[15] Fighting until the end, Qualchan was wrestled to the ground, a noose put over his head, and then hauled away to swing, dying in front of his father and his wife. Latah creek now had a new name: Hangman's Creek.

That same evening, Palouse started to come into the camp, seeking peace. As fifteen warriors rode in, they were seized. Six were hanged, and the rest made prisoners. The next day, Wright continued his march toward Fort Walla Walla.

On September 30, Wright camped on the Palouse River, in the heart of the tribe's homeland. More Palouse rode in for a council. Wright set the tone quickly: "Tell them [he instructed the translator] they are a set of rascals and deserve to be hung; that if I should hang them all, I should not to do wrong." Wright gave them instructions on what they must do, and said that if they did as told, he might consider a treaty with them in the spring. "If they do not submit to these terms, I will make war on them; and if I come here again to war, I will hang them all, men women, and children." [16] He then told them they had to turn over the Indians who had attacked miners. One Palouse, and three Indians of either the Yakima or Walla Walla tribes, were immediately hanged. ". . .[W]hile the victims expired, kicking and squirming desperately, he [Wright] made the other Indians continue their council with him."[17]

It was on the same day that Wright composed his report to General Clarke.

> Sir: The war is closed. Peace is restored with the Spokanes, Coeur d'Alenes and Pelouses. After a vigorous campaign the Indians have been entirely subdued, and were most happy to accept such terms of peace as I might dictate."[18]

The next day, lead elements of his column reached the Snake River and Fort Taylor.

The following dawn Wright reached the fort and was greeted by a multi-cannon victory salute. Lieutenant Mullan galloped off with Wright's reports for the general.

On October 3, Fort Taylor was abandoned, and the entire column headed toward Fort Walla Walla. As the troops started across the Tucannon River, Owhi made a break for freedom. Striking Lieutenant Michael Morgan across the face with a riding whip, Owhi rode off with his feet still chained beneath his horse. Morgan fired a pistol, hitting the great Yakima chief once. Then a dragoon Sergeant Edward Ball (of the Steptoe battle) rode up and shot Owhi in the head. Thought fatally wounded, Owhi suffered until dark before he expired from the gunshot.[19]

Reaching Fort Walla Walla the next day in a windy, cold, and wet march, the men welcomed the rest while the officers celebrated that evening. The last act of the Wright foray took place on October 6. Another council of dictation took place with the Cayuse and Walla Walla Indians. Spectators were stalwart Nez Perce allies such as Lawyer and Looking Glass. Once more Wright told the collected Indians that they must abide by his commands, or face his wrath and their tribes' destruction. And as he had before, Wright ordered those he believed guilty hanged. Four Indians swung, including Wie-cat, who had been sent with Steptoe's message. The once great nation of Cayuse had been brought to utter ruin. Cayuse chief Howlish Wampoo noted the tribe's fate.

Edward S. Curtis Collection, Library of Congress
Nez Perce Man

> We had thousands of horses and cattle; the hills and valleys were covered with them; where are they now? Not an animal is to be seen over this wide expanse. . .we are stripped of everything.[20]

But, these were not the last deaths. Garnett had requested bereavement leave after the loss of his wife and son. Prior to departing on his leave (which he did on October 18), he had the satisfaction of reporting another Indian's death. Some Yakima Indians, seeking to gain advantage with the whites captured Mosheel, the murderer of agent Bolon three years earlier. Soldiers were sent to bring the culprit to justice, but shot him as he attempted to escape.[21]

Just prior to Garnett's departure, he turned Fort Simcoe over to the command of Captain James Archer. Under Archer's direction two more of Bolon's murderers were caught. In the winter of 1856-57, Frederick White had been captured by the Yakima while tending

Fort Simcoe's cattle. In captivity White had identified two more of Bolon's murderers. Hearing that the two suspects were camping at Priest Rapids on the Columbia, on October 15 Archer sent a dozen Indian scouts to capture them. The Indians brought back Woppy and Stuchen, and from gallows erected on the fort's parade ground, these two Indians swung to the beat of the infantry's drummers.

The last Indians to die in the war were captured in November. Hearing that some of the miners' attackers were hiding near the mouth of the Okanogan River, Captain Archer ordered a company under Lieutenant Alexander to march and arrest them. With the assistance of Indians no longer willing to shelter fugitives from the Army, the lieutenant "succeeded in taking five Indians who had murdered white men in times of peace," and returned to Fort Simcoe.[22]

But even as the Indians' days were numbered, so were those of Fort Simcoe. Now that the Yakima were returning to stay on their designated reservation lands, the fort was not needed. The Army abandoned it, turning it over to the Indian Affairs office, on May 25, 1859.

Other events were happening to shape the Pacific Northwest. On September 13, 1858, as Wright was campaigning, the Army split the Pacific division into two Departments. General Clarke was ordered to command the new Department of California. The Northwest was protected by the freshly created Department of Oregon, with a new commander, General William S. Harney. He arrived at his new headquarters, Vancouver Barracks, on October 24, 1858. Harney had hoped for glory in subduing the warring tribes, but on his arrival, found Wright had already achieved peace, if not glory.

One of Harney's first acts was the total refutation of General Wool's restrictions of settling on the lands still thought to be Indian. Whites once more poured into the Walla Walla Valley. And, with the Indian wars settled, more pioneers headed west, particularly as the east seemed threatened by civil war and Bloody Kansas was still fresh. The paradise of Oregon was inviting. With so many people pouring in, with a constitution drafted, and with the contention over slavery in Congress, another free soil state was desired. Thus, on February 14, 1859, Oregon was admitted as a state, with its official motto reflecting the contentious times: "The Union."[23]

Checkmate

With Oregon a state, its new senators voted to ratify the Stevens-Palmer treaties of 1855. On March 8, 1859, the Senate approved the treaties, and they were signed by the Great White Father. Indians resistance to white conquest was over.

Chapter 13 notes

[1] Kip, *Indian War in the Pacific Northwest*, page 67.
[2] Burns, *The Jesuits and the Indian Wars of the Northwest*, page 299.
[3] Kip, pages 67-68.
[4] Burns, page 300.
[5] Schlicke, *General George Wright*, pages 177-178.
[6] Ibid, page 178.
[7] Kip, pages 83-84.
[8] Schlicke, page 179.
[9] Kip, page 93.
[10] Ibid, page 95.
[11] Josephy, *The Nez Perce Indians*, page 383.
[12] From Cliford E. Trafzer's introduction to Mary Moses' Account of the Qualchen's Death, Kip, page 146.
[13] Kip, page 102.
[14] Ibid, pages 103-104.
[15] Ibid, page 104.
[16] Ibid, page 116.
[17] Josephy, page 384.
[18] Schlicke, page 183.
[19] Trafzer and Scheuerman Renegade Tribe, page 91.
[20] Ruby and Brown, *The Cayuse Indians*, page 258.
[21] Guie, *Bugles in the Valley*, page 126.
[22] Ibid, page 136.
[23] The State of Oregon has since changed its motto to return to the Oregon Territory's motto: *She Flies With Her Own Wings*.

Chapter Fourteen

Conclusion

T he white invaders of the Pacific Northwest dealt with the Indians unfairly. That conclusion is easy to demonstrate and prove. What is enigmatic is the thought behind the actions. Did the whites always intend to cheat the Indians? Were American actions always with malice of forethought?

The historian Joseph Ellis, in his excellent work *American Creation*, writes, ". . .virtually every treaty was violated by state governments and white settlers almost immediately upon signing. Even more distressing, the promises the government were making to the tribes were never intended to be kept. They were willful and duplicitous misrepresentations (i.e., lies) designed to establish only temporary borders with Indian Country ....(p. 137)." Was the white action really that malicious? Or were the men a product of their culture and their times, and while their actions tended toward evil, did they think they were acting righteously? Was it evil or self-delusion? What of the men and times of the Oregon Territory?

Certainly, there were men who tried to do the right thing. General John Wool believed the Indians were infamously treated by civilian authority. Many Army officers were sympathetic toward the Indian plight. Still, when ordered, the Army attacked and the Indians lost.

Equally true, there were whites who hated the Indians simply for being different. The 1850s were a time of building pressures throughout the United States. The racial injustices suffered by the Indians were not limited to them, but part of a greater crisis of racial tension that would culminate in the Civil War and whether all men were truly created equal.

The central white treaty figures are representative of the debate. Were Isaac Stevens and Joel Palmer evil men acting to deprive the Indians of what was rightfully theirs, or did they act as honorable men attempting to do the right thing? The historian Alvin Josephy, writing in *The Nez Perce,* makes this observation concerning the two men's efforts at the Walla Walla council: "The transparency of the speeches of Governor Stevens and superintendent Palmer is so obvious that it is a wonder the commissioners could not realize the ease with which the Indians saw through what they were saying. One can only assume either that their ignorance of the Indians' mentality was appalling or that they were so intent on having their way with the tribes that they blinded themselves to the flagrancy of their hypocrisy (p. 318)." I suggest both are true.

It is amazing to read of the 200 years of white dealings with Indians preceding the Walla Walla Council and realize that throughout that time, whites had learned not a scintilla of insight into the peoples they shared a continent with. Stevens and Palmer were part of a tradition of white ignorance about Indian culture.

Equally true, they were intent on having their way. For Stevens firmly believed that his actions, as a father, were in the best interests of the child-like Indians. He had to help these children become fully developed adults. By his benevolence, with his support, given time the Indians could achieve that status.

The crux of the issue was not merely his belief in white supremacy, but in his own personal flaws. His arrogance led him to think of the Indians as being in need of his guidance, but that was true of his attitude toward the whites, also. Stevens believed that no one was as capable as himself, and he was best suited to act as a dictator. He demonstrated that again in his suspension of habeas corpus and martial law.

Palmer often demonstrated that he was aware of his ignorance about Indian culture. He knew he did not know Indians, but he did know whites. Palmer grasped that if the Indians were not removed from direct contact with the whites, then the Indians were destined for destruction. Joel Palmer told the Indians that it was impossible to stop the whites from coming. Palmer warned the Indians by telling the truth: "Can you stop the waters of the Columbia River from flowing on its course? Can you prevent the wind from blowing? Can you prevent the rain from falling? Can you prevent the whites from coming? You are answered no!" If the Indians were to survive, Palmer reasoned that they had to be placed on reservations remote from the whites. Nevertheless, Palmer knew he had been a party to treachery. He would later comment, "It is pretty evident that the signing of the treaty was adverse to the will of the [Indian] nation."

Thus, the answer to Josephy's question is that both of his rhetorical options are true. They were ignorant, and they were intent on having their way.

Edward S. Curtis Collection, Library of Congress
Cayuse woman

And of white promises, less flattering things must be said. While the whites were willing to give the Indians reservations, the promises made to the Indians once they moved to the restricted lands were never intended to be kept. Both of the men, Stevens and Palmer, knew what their superintendency's budgets were, and knew they had nothing in the way of monies to pay for the things they were promising. Given these facts, they knew they were lying.

We are faced with recognizing that the treaties were treacheries, and that our forefathers acted with malice from the beginning toward the Indians. That leaves us with the questions of policy and direction that were stated in the introduction. At the time of the treaties, the Indians asked, "Who can *own* the land? Who can *own* the water?" Today, we ask "Who owns the wind?" and mean it. Should the grandness of the Columbia Gorge be compromised by towering forests of windmills? We must study our history if we are to have any understanding of how it impacts our present, and directs our future.

So, knowing our history, how do we deal with the issues facing us today? It is impossible to undo what has been done. We cannot give back the land to the Indians and simply do things fairly now. We must ask ourselves, do we act as before, or do we renew our efforts to act with justice? Do we engage with all sides in an exchange of honest idea brokerage, or merely let greed dictate actions?

The value of history is not to relive past glories or to lament past injustices. The value of history is in learning from our mistakes. Both sides in this struggle acted at times unfairly and dishonorably. Naturally, the prevailing side always has the opportunity to act most unjustly, having won. So, can we learn from this history, or are we doomed to repeat our mistakes, not merely in the Pacific Northwest, but across the country? Do we act justly, treating others fairly, honoring the rule of law (such as habeas corpus), or do we merely take what we want? These are questions that continue to be debated in our politics.

How will our country act?

Epilogue

For those who wondered of the people mentioned, here is a brief list of what happened to some of the prominent men (and their roles) who took part in Treaties and Treachery.

First and foremost, the greatest of the Indian leaders:

Kamiakin — He was the only great Indian war leader to survive either the battles, or the hangings. After being wounded at the Battle of Spokane Plains, he fled to the Kootenai of British Columbia and then onto the Plains, living with the Crows. He returned to the Pacific Northwest by 1860, and lived with the Palouse. The summer of 1860, he was contacted by an Indian agent (Dr. Richard Landsdale) who offered him gifts and asked him to return to the Yakima Reservation and once more act as the head chief. Kamiakin once more refused, saying he refused to recognize the treaty, and declined the gifts, saying he would not sell his birthright. In April 1877, the great chief died, and was buried. In keeping with the last act of treachery, in April 1878, the body was disinterred and Kamiakin's head was literally twisted from the rotting corpse, and taken. Professor Charles Sternberg removed the head "to make certain measurements."

Archer, James J. — Captain, Ninth U.S. Infantry. Archer became a brigadier general with the Confederate Army, and was captured during Gettysburg. He was exchanged to fight some more, but his year's imprisonment took a toll on his health. He died in 1874.

Augur, Christopher C. — Captain, Fourth U.S. Infantry. In 1861, he was promoted to major in the Thirteenth U.S. Infantry, but made a brigadier general of volunteers the same year. In 1862, he was promoted to major general of volunteers and given a corps to command. He held various general command positions after the Civil War, and retired in 1885.

Buchanan, Robert C. — Major, Fourth U.S. Infantry. Promoted to lieutenant colonel of the Fourth in 1861, brigadier general of volunteers in 1862, made permanent rank of colonel of the First U.S. Infantry in 1864. He retired from the Army in 1870.

Casey, Silas — Lieutenant Colonel, Ninth U.S. Infantry. In 1861, he was made a brigadier general of volunteers. In 1862, he was made a major general of volunteers. His book of instruction for infantry tactics was used by both sides in the Civil War. He retired in 1868.

Cornelius, Thomas R. — Colonel, First Oregon Mounted Volunteers. In addition to his twenty years of service in the Oregon Legislature, Cornelius helped to raise the First Oregon Volunteer Cavalry during the Civil War. He died in 1899.

Crook, George — Lieutenant, Fourth U.S. Infantry. A corps commander during the Civil War, and a major general, he gained his greatest fame after the war as an Indian fighter. Starting as lieutenant colonel of the Twenty-third U.S. Infantry in the Columbia Department in 1866, he would be jumped over more senior members of the service to become a general, eventually returning to his Civil War rank of major general.

Curry, George Law — Territorial Governor of Oregon. After Oregon became a state, Curry gave up politics, and return to his career as a newspaper publisher and editor, for such Portland papers as *The Advertiser* and the *Evening Journal*

Dent, Frederick Tracy — Captain, Ninth U.S. Infantry. Probably Dent's greatest claim to fame was that his sister married, U.S. Grant. He was made a major in the Fourth U.S. Infantry and was twice brevetted for gallantry during the Civil War. In 1870, he was made a lieutenant colonel in the Fifth U.S. Artillery, from which he retired.

Garnett, Robert Shelden — Major, Ninth U.S. Infantry. Garnet would resign from the Army to become a Confederate brigadier general and was an aide to Robert E. Lee. During a July 11, 1861 fight against George McClellan, he was shot and killed leading his troops.

Haller, Granville Owen — Captain, Fourth U.S. Infantry. Promoted to major, he had a short and sad career. Accused of disloyalty for making a drinking toast critical of President Lincoln (which he denied), Haller was dismissed from the service in 1863 for "disloyal conduct." In 1879, a commission found that Haller had been unfairly dismissed, and he was given the colonelcy of the Twenty-third U.S. Infantry. He died in Seattle in 1897.

Keyes, Erasmus Darwin — Captain, Third U.S. Artillery. Promoted to major shortly after the 1858 campaign, and again in 1861 to the colonelcy of the Eleventh U.S. Infantry. With the outbreak of the Civil War, he was made a brigadier general of volunteers, and promoted to major general of volunteers in 1862, commanding a corps. In 1864, he resigned for health reasons, and moved to California.

McClellan, George — Captain, U.S. Engineers. McClellan left before the fighting started, being assigned a Captain of the First U.S. Cavalry in 1855. He was sent to Europe and was an observer in the Crimean War. In 1857, McClellan resigned his commission to become the chief engineer of the Illinois Central Railroad. He advanced within the railroad business until the start of the Civil War, when he was made a major general of volunteers (with his advance into western Virginia causing him to do battle with his old friend Robert Garnett). Because of his success, he was made a major general of the regular army in 1862. Twice commander of the Army of the Potomac, in 1864, he would run for president, on the Democratic ticket. He resigned his commission in 1864. He was elected governor of New Jersey in 1877.

Nesmith, James Willis — Colonel, First Oregon Mounted Volunteers. Appointed Superintendent of Indian Affairs for both Oregon and Washington Territory, he went on to serve as the U.S. Marshal for Oregon, was one of Oregon's U.S. Senators, 1861 to 1867, and was a U.S. Representative for the years 1873 to 1875. He died in 1885.

Olney, Nathan — Indian Agent. Olney largely fades into obscurity after this period of time. In 1866, he falls from his horse and lands on his head, driving an imbedded arrowhead (from an Indian attack in the late 1840s) deeper into his brain, killing him.

Ord, Edward Otho Cresap — Captain, Third U.S. Artillery. He assisted Robert E. Lee in the capture of John Brown in 1859, and after the start of the Civil War, was made a brigadier general of volunteers. He was brevetted for gallantry, and was given a regular commission as a brigadier general in 1866. He retired in 1881, and was made a major general by act of Congress in 1882.

Palmer, Joel — Superintendent of Indian Affairs, Oregon Territory. While he stayed active in local politics, and once ran for governor, Palmer's main activities rested on his farm, near Dayton, and as being president of the Columbia River Road Company. He died in 1881.

Rains, Gabriel James — Major, Fourth U.S. Infantry. In June 1860, he is promoted to lieutenant colonel, but with the start of the Civil War, resigns to accept a brigadier general position with the Confederacy. He died in 1881. Rains' son, Sewer McClean Rains, graduated from West Point in 1876, and was killed in the action against the Nez Perce Indians at Craig's Mountain, Idaho, July 3, 1877.

Reynolds, John — Major Third U.S. Artillery. Reynolds quickly rose to corps command during the Civil War, but was killed during the first day's fighting at Gettysburg.

Sheridan, Philip H. — Lieutenant, First U.S. Dragoons. Sheridan gained glory and fame during the Civil War when he commanded Grant's cavalry, eventually becoming a major general. He would assume command of all the army in 1883.

Smith, Andrew Jackson — Captain, First U.S. Dragoons. During the Civil War, Smith was promoted to Major General and was a corps commander. After the war, he reverted to a permanent rank of colonel, and given command of the newly created Seventh U.S. Cavalry (George Armstrong Custer was Smith's Lieutenant Colonel). It would be Smith who ordered Custer court-martialed after the Civil War, but give up the day-to-day operations of the regiment to assume a district command as a brevet major general.

Steptoe, Edward J. — Major, Ninth U.S. Infantry. Soon after the 1858 campaign, Steptoe was placed on medical leave. In September of 1861, he was given the lieutenant colonelcy of the Tenth U.S. Infantry, but was forced to resign for health reasons November 1 of the same year. He died shortly thereafter at Lynchburg, Virginia.

Stevens, Isaac I. — Washington Territorial Governor. After being elected territorial representative to the Congress, Stevens resigned to become first the colonel of the Seventy-ninth Regiment of New York Volunteers and then became a brigadier general of volunteers at the commencement of the Civil War. He was killed in 1862 at the front of his troops at the Battle of Chantilly (Virginia).

Wool, John Ellis — Brigadier General, Department of the Pacific. Made a Major General in 1862, he was given the command of the Department of Virginia and was based at Fort Monroe, Virginia. He retired from active service in 1863, and died in Troy, New York 1869.

Wright, George — Colonel, Ninth U.S. Infantry. During the Civil War, Wright was made a brigadier general and given command of the Department of the Pacific. With the end of the Civil War, he was given command of the Department of the Columbia and was en route on a ship when it sank near Crescent City, California on July 30, 1865, drowning Wright and his wife.

Bibliography

Aderkas, Elizabeth von. *American Indians of the Pacific Northwest*. University Park: Osprey Publishing, 2005.

Alfred, B. et al, editors. *Great Western Indian Fights*. Lincoln: University of Nebraska Press, 1960.

Beckham, Stephen Dow. *Oregon Indians, Voices from Two Centuries*. Corvallis: Oregon State University Press, 2006.

———. *Requiem for a People*. Corvallis: Oregon State University Press, 1998.

Beeson, John. *A Plea for the Indians*. Fairfield: Ye Galleon Press, 1998.

Berg, Laura, editor. *The First Oregonians*. Portland: Oregon Council for the Humanities, 2007.

Bischoff, William Norbert. "The Yakima Indian War, 1855-1856." Unpublished doctoral dissertation, Loyola University, Chicago, 1950.

Bonney, William P. "The Death of Lieutenant Slaughter," *History of Pierce County*, Volume 1.

Braly, David. *Juniper Empire: Early Days in Eastern and Central Oregon*. Prineville: American Media, 1976.

Brown, William Compton. *The Indian Side of the Story*. Spokane: C.W. Hill Printing, 1961.

Burns, Robert I. *The Jesuits and the Indian Wars of the Northwest*. New Haven: Yale University Press, 1966.

Butruille, Susan G. *Women's Voices from the Oregon Trail*. Boise: Tamarack Books, 1993.

Calloway, Colin G. *One Vast Winter Count. The Native American West before Lewis and Clark*. Lincoln: University of Nebraska Press, 2003.

Carey, Charles H. *General History of Oregon*. Portland: Binfords and Mort, 1971.

Carpenter, Cecelia Svinth. *The Nisqually, My People.* Tacoma: Tahoma Research Publications, 2002.

Clark, Robert Carlton. "Military History of Oregon," *Oregon Historical Quarterly.* March 1935.

Converse, George L. *A Military History of the Columbia Valley.* Walla Walla: Pioneer Press, 1988.

Coward, John M. *The Newspaper Indian. Native American Identity in the Press, 1820-90.* Urbana: University of Illinois Press, 1999.

Cresap, Bernarr. "Captain Edward O.C. Ord in the Rogue River Indian War," *Oregon Historical Quarterly.* June 1953.

Crook, George., Martin F. Schmitt, editor. *General George Crook, his autobiography.* Norman: University of Oklahoma Press, 1960.

Dary, David. *The Oregon Trail. An American Saga.* New York: Alfred A. Knopf, 2004.

Douthit, Nathan. "Between Indian and White Worlds on the Oregon-California Border, 1851-1857." *Oregon Historical Quarterly.* Winter, 1999.

——. *Uncertain Encounters. Indians and Whites at Peace and War in Southern Oregon, 1820s-1860s.* Corvallis: Oregon State University Press, 2002.

Drew, Charles S. *An Account of the Origin and Early Prosecution of the Indian War in Oregon.* Fairfield: Ye Galleon Press, 1973 (reprint of the 1860 report).

Eckrom, J.A. *Remembered Drums. A History of the Puget Sound Indian War.* Walla Walla: Pioneer Press Books, 1989.

Elliott, T. C. "The Murder of Peu-Peu-Mox-Mox," *Oregon Historical Quarterly.* June 1934.

Glassley, Ray H. *Indian Wars of the Pacific Northwest.* Portland: Binsford and Mort, 1972.

Guie, H. Dean. *Bugles in the Valley. Garnett's Fort Simcoe.* Portland: Oregon Historical Society Press, 1977.

Haines, Francis. *The Nez Perces: Tribesmen of the Columbia Plateau.* Norman: University of Oklahoma Press, 1955.

Bibliography

Hicks, Urban. "Battle of Connell's Prairie." Lewis and Clark College, Portland, Oregon, microfilm collection, dated February 10, 1886.

Holmes, Kenneth L. *Covered Wagon Women*. Lincoln: Bison Books, 1983.

Jackson, John C. *A Little War of Destiny. The First Regiment of Oregon Mounted Volunteers and the Yakima Indian War of 1855-56*. Olympia: Ye Galleon Press, 1996.

Josephy Alvin M., Jr. *The Nez Perce Indians and the Opening of the Northwest*. Boston: Houghton Mifflin Company, 1997.

Karson, Jennifer, editor. *As Days Go By. Our History, Our Land, and Our People. The Cayuse, Umatilla and Walla Walla*. Pendleton: Tamastslikt Cultural Institute, 2006.

Knuth, Priscilla. *"Picturesque" Frontier. The Army's Fort Dalles*. Portland: Oregon Historical Society Press, 1987.

Kip, Lawrence. *Army Life on the Pacific*. Fairfield: Ye Galleon Press, 1986.

——. *Indian War in the Pacific Northwest*. Lincoln: University of Nebraska Press, 1999.

Kowrach, Edward J. *Mie Charles Pandosy, OMI., a Missionary of the Northwest*. Fairfield: Ye Galleon Press, 1992.

Lockett, Jim and Reita. *Tales from the Past*. McMinnville: Oregon Lithoprint, 2005.

Madsen, Brigham D. *The Bannock of Idaho*. Moscow: University of Idaho Press, 1996.

Madsen, John A. "An Analysis of the Nez Perce Communications Strategies in the Council of Walla Walla—1855." Unpublished doctoral thesis, University of Kansas, 1982.

McWhorter, L. V. *Hear Me, My Chiefs! Nez Perce Legend and History*. Caldwell: Caxton Press, 2001.

——. *Tragedy of the Whk-shum: The Death of Andrew J. Bolon, Yakima Indian Agent, as told by Su-el-lil, Eyewitness*. Issaquah: Great Eagle Publishing, 1994.

Morgan, Murray C. *Skid Road*. Seattle: University of Washington Press, 1982.

Murray, Keith A. *The Modocs and Their War*. Norman: University of Oklahoma Press, 1959.

Neils, Selma. *The Klickitat Indians*. Portland: Binford and Mort, 1985.

Newell, Gordon. *Totem Tales of Old Seattle*. Seattle: Superior Press, 1956.

O'Donnell, Terence. *An Arrow in the Earth*. Portland: Oregon Historical Society Press, 1991.

Pambrun, Andrew Dominique. *Sixty Years on the Frontier in the Pacific Northwest*. Fairfield: Ye Galleon Press, 1978.

Prosch, Thomas W. "The Indian War in Washington Territory," *The Oregon Historical Society Quarterly*, March 1915.

Rau, Weldon Willis. *Surviving the Oregon Trail 1852*. Pullman: Washington State University Press, 2001.

Reese, J. W. "OMV's Fort Henrietta: On Winter Duty, 1855-56," *Oregon Historical Quarterly*. June 1965.

Relander, Click, editor. *The Yakimas*. Yakima: The Republic Press, 1955.

Richards, Kent D. *Isaac I. Stevens: Young Man in a Hurry*. Pullman: Washington State University Press, 1993.

Richardson, David. "The Old Ship's Log Reveals the Story Behind the Port Gamble Incident," *Seattle Times*, April 2, 1967.

Ruby, Robert H., and John A. Brown. *The Cayuse Indians, Imperial Tribesmen of Old Oregon*. Norman: University of Oklahoma Press, 1972.

——. *A Guide to the Indian Tribes of the Pacific Northwest*. Norman: University of Oklahoma Press, 1986

——. *Indians of the Pacific Northwest*. Norman: University of Oklahoma Press, 1988.

Scheuerman, Richard D., and Michael O. Finley. *Finding Chief Kamiakin. The Life and Legacy of a Northwest Patriot*. Pullman: Washington State University Press, 2008.

Schlicke, Carl P. *General George Wright, Guardian of the Pacific Coast*. Norman: University of Oklahoma Press, 1988.

Bibliography

Schlissel, Lillian, Byrd Gibbens, and Elizabeth Hampsten. *Far from Home.* New York: Schocken Books, 1989.

Schwartz, E.A. *The Rogue River Indian War and its Aftermath, 1850-1980.* Norman: University of Oklahoma Press, 1997.

Sheridan, Philip H. *Indian Fighting in the Fifties in Oregon and Washington Territories.* Fairfield: Ye Galleon Press, 1987.

Slickpoo, Allen P., Sr, and Deward E. Walker. *Noon Nee-Me-Poo.* Idaho: Nez Perce Tribe, 1973.

Splawn, A. J. *Ka-Mi-Akin: The Last Hero of the Yakimas.* Portland: Binfords and Mort, 1944.

Stevens, Isaac Stevens. *A True Copy of the Record of the Official Proceedings at the Council in the Walla Walla Valley 1855.* Fairfield: Ye Galleon Press, 1996.

Trafzer, Clifford E., and Richard D. Scheuerman. *Renegade Tribe: The Palouse Indians and the Invasion of the Inland Pacific Northwest.* Pullman: Washington State University Press, 1986.

Trenholm, Virginia Cole, and Maurine Carley. *The Shoshonis: Sentinels of the Rockies.* Norman: University of Oklahoma Press, 1964.

Underwood, Amos. "Reminiscences of the Cayuse War," *Skamania County Heritage*, June 1986.

Utley, Robert M. *Frontiersmen in Blue.* Lincoln: University of Nebraska Press, 1967.

——, and Washburn, W. *American Heritage Library of Indian Battles.* Boston: Houghton Mifflin, 1977.

Victor, Frances Fuller. *The Early Indian Wars of Oregon.* Salem: State Printer, 1894.

Walsh, Frank K. *Indian Battles Along the Rogue River, 1855-56.* North Bend: Te-Cum-Tom Publications, 1986.

The Author

Kurt Nelson attended George Washington University and graduated from Portland State University with majors in Political Science and History. Kurt has also earned a Master of Public Administration degree from Lewis and Clark College as well as a Certificate in Crime and Intelligence Analysis from the California State University at Sacramento.

With nearly three decades of criminal justice experience, Kurt has certification in crime analysis, corrections, and law enforcement. He has taught criminal justice subjects at the college level, as well for local criminal justice agencies. He is currently a supervisor of park rangers.

In addition, Kurt Nelson has served in the Peace Corps (Afghanistan), and has honorable discharges from the Marine Corps and Coast Guard. He earned a Master's License from the Merchant Marine, and was a mountain climbing leader for organizations such as the Mazamas and Outward Bound. He also has done volunteer work with the National Oceanic and Atmospheric Administration (NOAA) and the National Park Service.

Kurt and his wife, Sandi, live in Milwaukie, Oregon.

Acknowledgements

As with every endeavor, there are many who contribute to the effort who deserve to be mentioned. To those I forget, I apologize and attribute it to my failure, not the effort you made.

I would like to thank Lisa Gleed Palmer of Clackamas Community College's library. Lisa searched diligently for my many requests for unpublished sources and produced a surprising number of documents, manuscripts, and books. Thank you!

Once the research was completed, my sounding board and first editor was my wife, Sandi Nelson. Her support, critical review, and editing made this book, and my life, better.

Larry LaBeck was the professional editor I have used before and again on this book to bring it to the point of submission to Caxton Press. Larry is a meticulous reviewer who added to the readability of the book.

Bruce Coorpender lent support and his camera. A friend in need, indeed!

I am grateful to Lloyd Johnson for his production of the excellent maps used in this book.

And for Caxton, my thanks to Wayne Cornell. Not only did he edit the book, he helped with the indexing. Not a bad effort for a man who had retired from the business.

Index

Index

Index

Other titles about
the West
from

Caxton Press

The Pony Express Trail
Yesterday and Today
by William Hill
ISBN 978-0-87004-476-2, 302 pages, paper, $18.95

The Lewis and Clark Trail
Yesterday and Today
by William Hill
ISBN 978-0-87004-439-7, 300 pages, paper, $16.95

A Fate Worse Than Death
Indian Captivities in the West
by William Hill
ISBN 978-0-87004-473-1, 552 pages, paper, $19.95

The Deadliest Indian War in the West
The Snake Conflict 1864-1868
by Gregory Michno
ISBN 978-0-87004-460-1, 450 pages, paper, $18.95

Massacre Along the Medicine Road
The Indian War of 1864 in Nebraska
by Ronald Becher
ISBN 0-87004-289-7, 500 pages, cloth, $32.95
ISBN 0-87004-387-0, 500 pages, paper, $22.95

For a free catalog of Caxton titles write to:

Caxton Press
312 Main Street
Caldwell, Idaho 83605-3299

or

Visit our Internet web site:

www.caxtonpress.com

Caxton Press is a division of The Caxton Printers, Ltd.